EQ8

LESSONS FOR BEGINNERS

Step-by-Step Exercises for Learning EQ8 Software

The Electric Quilt® Company
Bowling Green, OH 43402
www.ElectricQuilt.com

EQ8 Lessons for Beginners

Copyright © 2017
By The Electric Quilt Company
All rights reserved.

Sixth printing.

The Electric Quilt Company
500 Lehman Avenue
Bowling Green, OH 43402 USA

1-419-352-1134 (Technical support)
1-800-356-4219 (Sales)

FIND US ONLINE AT: ElectricQuilt.com
On our website you will find product add-ons, books, free project downloads, and a full support website with videos, lessons, and articles.

No part of this book may be reproduced in any form except by the original purchaser for personal use. The written instructions and designs are intended for the personal use of the retail purchaser and are protected under copyright laws. They are not to be photocopied, duplicated or reproduced by any means for commercial use.

We do encourage the use of this book for teaching purposes. Teachers may use the information from the chapters of this book as lessons to teach EQ8 if they give credit to The Electric Quilt Company and *EQ8 Lessons for Beginners*. Copyright law forbids teachers from reproducing any part of the printed material for distribution to students. Students wanting a copy of the lesson will need to purchase the book.

CREDITS:
Author and Editor: Ann Rutter
Copy Editor: Diane McEwen-Martin
Designer: Sara Seuberling

Attention!

EQ8 has been updated since the original printing of this book. If you notice any visual differences between the book steps and your EQ8, it's because of the improvements we have made to EQ8 since its release.

It's very important that you make sure your EQ8 is up to date. To check if you are running the most current version, please go to our website (ElectricQuilt.com) and use the main navigation to find **Product Updates**. Follow the instructions to update your EQ8.

TABLE OF CONTENTS

Introduction
Getting Started with EQ8.. 6

Chapter 1
Learning the EQ8 Basics
Lesson 1: Basics of the Quilt Worktable 10
Lesson 2: Basics of the Block Worktable 33
Lesson 3: Basics of the Image Worktable 55

Chapter 2
Quilt Worktable: After the Basics
Lesson 1: Understanding Layers in EQ.............................. 76
Lesson 2: Creating a Custom Quilt Layout from Scratch.... 81
Lesson 3: Creating a Custom Quilt from a Block............... 85
Lesson 4: Making A Quilt Label 87
Lesson 5: Using Pre-designed Quilt Labels 90
Lesson 6: Making a T-Shirt Quilt 92

Chapter 3
Block Worktable: After the Basics
Lesson 1: PolyDraw Basics for Pieced Blocks..................... 96
Lesson 2: Eight Point Star Grid and the PolyLine Tool 100
Lesson 3: Drawing Arcs with the PolyArc Tool................. 103
Lesson 4: Drawing Basics for Applique Blocks 106
Lesson 5: Applique Motif vs. Applique Block.................... 110

Chapter 4
Important to Know — Yet Just for Fun
Lesson 1: Creating Blocks with Serendipity 116
Lesson 2: Searching for Blocks by Category..................... 119
Lesson 3: Searching for Fabrics by Color 120
Lesson 4: Understanding Rotary Cutting Charts in EQ..... 121
Lesson 5: Creating Your Own Default Project 124
Homework.. 125

Index
Index... 126

INTRODUCTION

Getting Started with EQ8

Do you find yourself wondering if you can use a computer to help with your quilting? Then this book is for you! We have spent over 25 years developing quilt design software, and we are the best teachers of our software. We know EQ8, inside and out. We want to share our knowledge with you. Congratulations on choosing EQ8 and the best book to go with it!

~ Your friends at The Electric Quilt Company

Who this Book is For..6
How to Use this Book 6
When You're Done with this Book..7
Before We Get Started—Restore Default Settings 7

EQ8 Lessons for Beginners

GETTING STARTED WITH EQ8

EQ8 has a whole new face! And we are delighted that you've chosen EQ to help with your quilt designing, pattern printing and craft making! After 25 years of development, we decided it was time to give EQ a fresh new look. We've made the tools larger and better labeled. We have incorporated new tabs and a ribbon across the top of the screen to help steer you in a logical and guided way to create new designs. If you have used previous versions of EQ, we think you'll be surprised at the number of new features—some may have existed before, but you didn't know it. Our new interface helps make old features new and hidden features found!

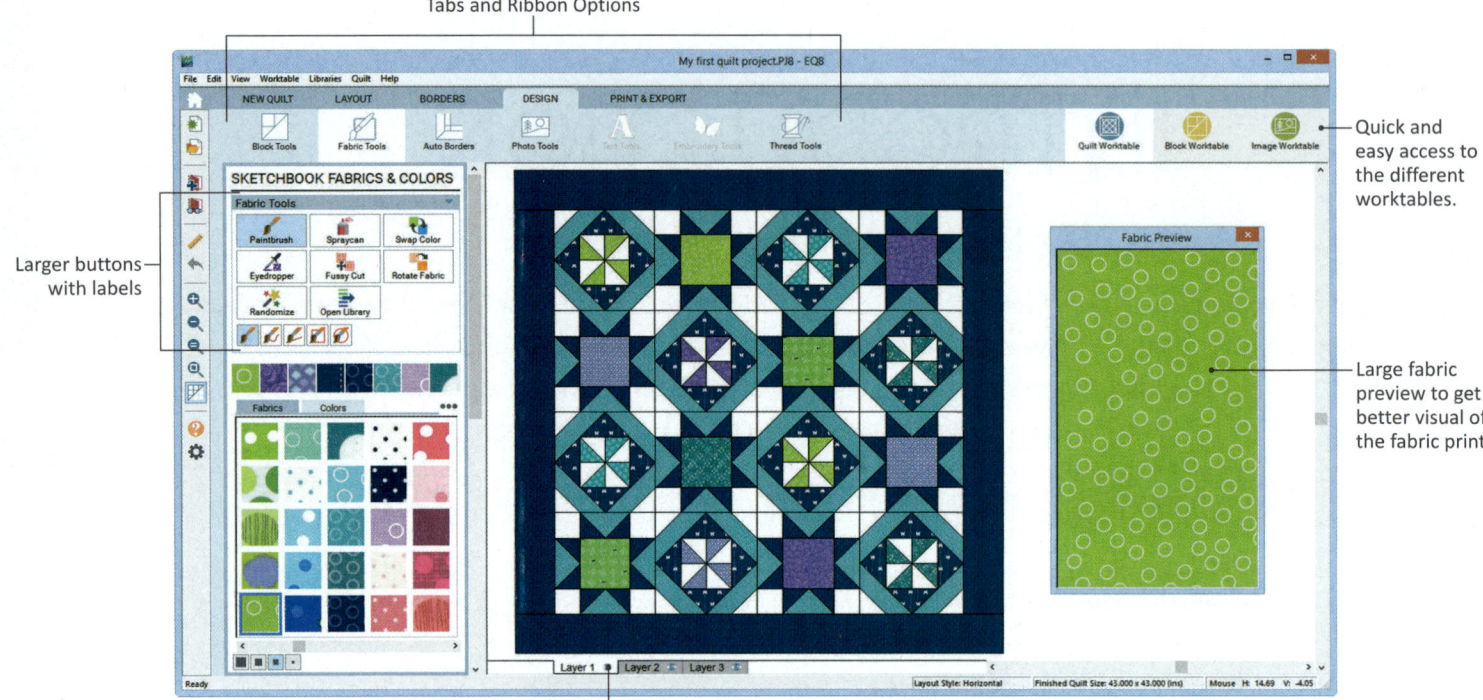

Who this Book is For

This book exists for one purpose: to help you get started using EQ8 and equip you with the knowledge you need to complete basic tasks, like drawing blocks and designing quilts. Plus, we'll teach you how to find the help you need for more complicated designs. This book is suitable for anyone wishing to gain a good fundamental understanding of the key features of the three main worktables in the program. You will learn to print patterns and yardage charts. You will make your own quilt label. You will draw blocks and build libraries. You will complete many projects along the way, and most of all, you will have fun and be amazed at the depth of sophistication EQ8 has for you.

How to Use this Book

Chapter 1 is made up of three powerful lessons that cover the basics of each of the three worktables. At the end of each lesson is a bulleted list of the tasks learned in the lesson. **We strongly urge you to complete the first three lessons of Chapter 1 in order.** Chapters 2, 3 and 4 offer a variety of shorter lessons that can be done in any order. If you want to skip around or skip over lessons, you can. If you want to repeat lessons, do it. Simply completing these step-by-step lessons is not the same as learning it and retaining it, at least not for all of us. Everyone learns differently so don't worry if you need to repeat some of the lessons. The more you repeat, the more you will retain.

When You're Done with this Book

When you're done with this book – what then? That's a good question! Our goal is to provide you with enough knowledge to make you an independent EQ user. You will be ready to start creating designs on your own. Of course you'll continue to have questions, and we will help you find the answers. There are many features in the program that are not covered in this book, so you will have plenty of room to continue to explore and learn about the program. After completing these lessons, you will be able to navigate your way through the software to design your own quilts. When you are done with this book, all you will need are ideas for the quilts you want to make!

Before We Get Started—Restore Default Settings

As you use the program, settings get saved and restored each time you start EQ8. To ensure that we all see the same thing, we recommend that you take your program to the factory settings—the way it was when you first installed it. This will guarantee that the steps provided in this book will flow the way we intended.

Step 1

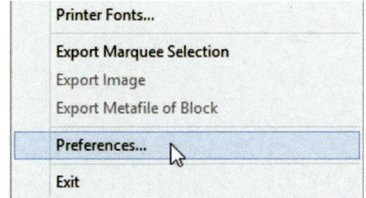
Step 2

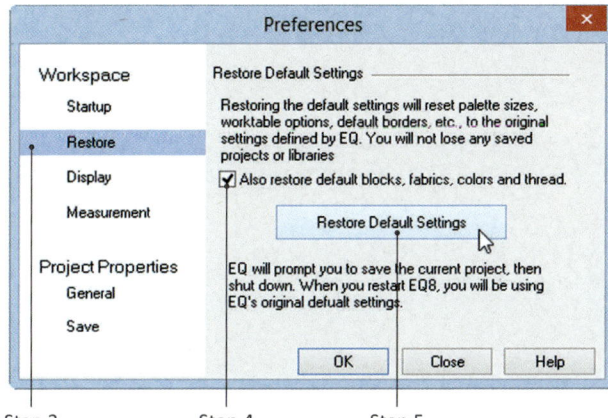
Step 3   Step 4   Step 5

1. Start **EQ8**.

2. Click **File > Preferences**.

3. Click **Restore** on the left of the Preferences dialog box.

4. Make sure there is a check in **Also restore default blocks, fabrics, colors and thread**.

5. Click the **Restore Default Settings** button.

6. You will see a message that EQ8 will need to restart. Click **OK**.

7. Start EQ8 again to begin Chapter 1.

Step 6

Step 7

CHAPTER 1
Learning the EQ8 Basics

These first three lessons are the most important lessons in this book. Work through each one at your own pace. Complete them in order. When you've finished this chapter, you will have learned the basics of the three different worktables in EQ8.

Lesson 1: Basics of the Quilt Worktable 10

Lesson 2: Basics of the Block Worktable 33

Lesson 3: Basics of the Image Worktable 55

LESSON 1: BASICS OF THE QUILT WORKTABLE

The Home screen will display when you start EQ. If you don't see the Home screen, click the Home button in the upper-left corner of the EQ window. This screen helps you navigate to the different worktables depending on what you want to do with the program.

You can also change to the different worktables by clicking on the circular worktable buttons found on the ribbon along the upper-right of the EQ window.

1. Click **Design a quilt from scratch** on the Home screen under DESIGN QUILTS.

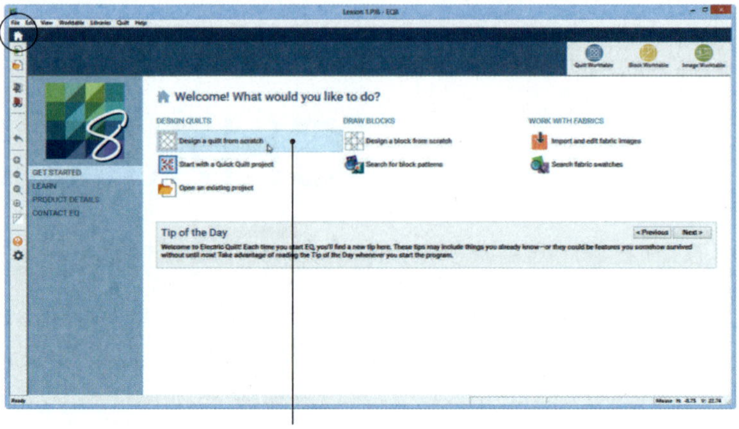

This changes to the Quilt Worktable. Notice the circular Quilt Worktable button on the ribbon looks pressed indicating that it's the active worktable.

Each worktable has tabs and ribbons to help you navigate your options.

Starting a New Quilt

2. The **NEW QUILT** tab gives several different layout styles on the ribbon. Take a minute to read the description of the Horizontal Layout style.

3. Click on a couple other layout styles on the ribbon and read their descriptions.

4. Click on **Horizontal**. We'll make a horizontal style quilt for our first quilt design.

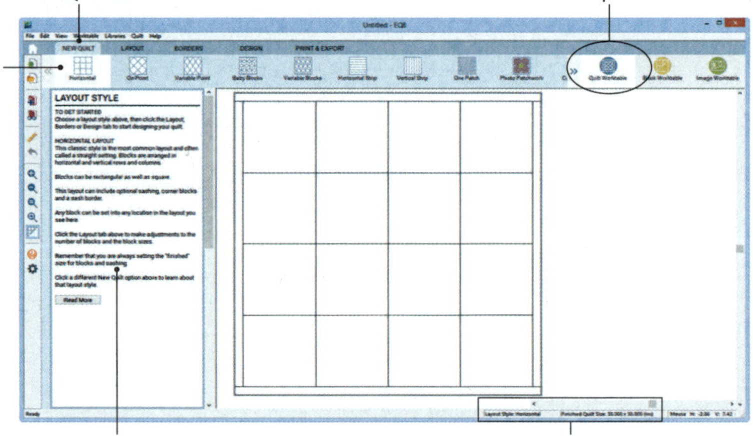

5. Click the **LAYOUT** tab. Here we can make changes to the number of blocks and the size of the blocks. You can also choose to add sashing and borders. For this quilt, we will leave the default sizes. Our blocks are nine inches with 4 horizontally and 4 vertically.

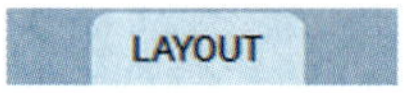

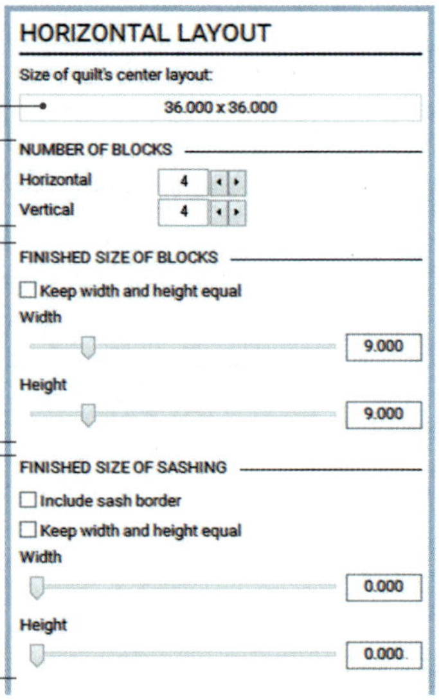

> **Note:** The top of the palette gives you the size of the quilt's center layout without any borders. Now look on the status bar in the lower-right corner of the EQ window. Here you will see the overall size of your quilt including the borders.
>
>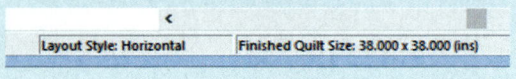

Chapter 1: Learning the EQ8 Basics

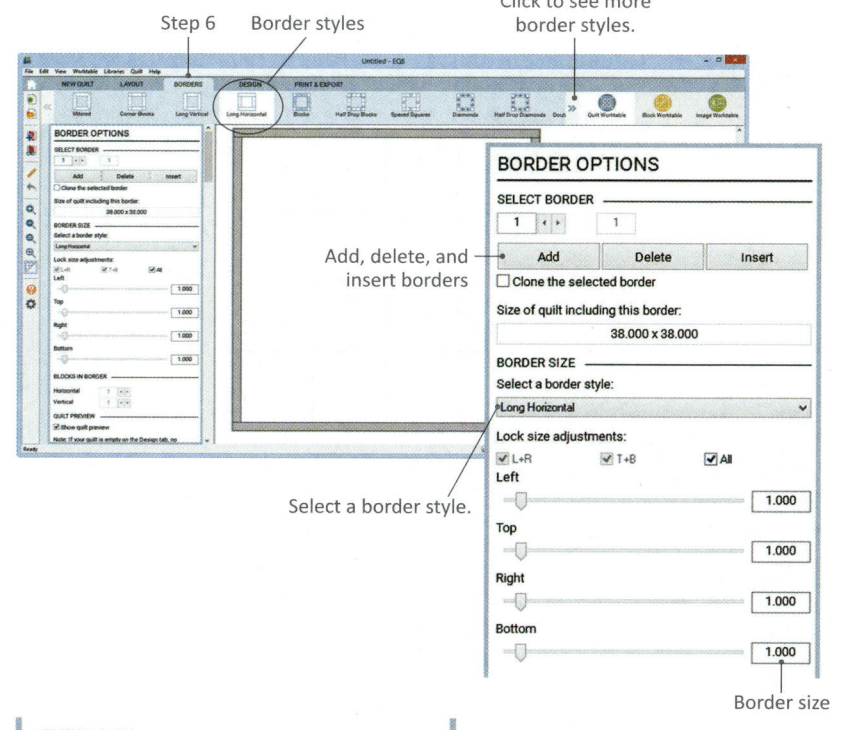

Adjusting the Borders

6. Click the **BORDERS** tab. Here we can add, remove, resize and select styles for the borders of your quilt. You can remove all borders or add several different borders. Each border can have its own style and each side of a border can have its own width.

The default border style is Long Horizontal. Notice Long Horizontal is selected on the ribbon. Click the right-pointing arrow button to see more border styles.

You can also change styles using the drop-down box in the palette. Click the down arrow in the drop-down box to see the list of border styles. Click the arrow again to close the list.

The default size for the border is 1 inch. This looks too small next to nine inch blocks. Let's make the border wider.

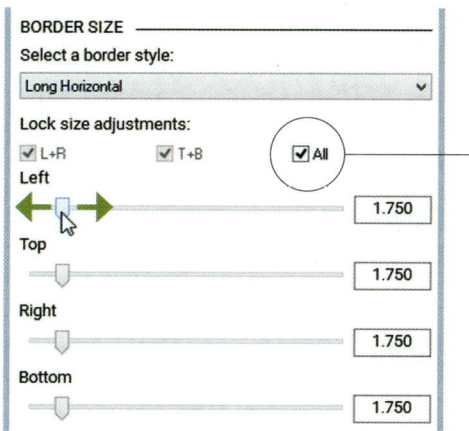

Drag the border slider bar left or right to adjust the border size.

With All checked, all four sides of the selected border will adjust at the same time.

7. **Drag one of the border sliders to adjust the size.** To drag, position the cursor over the small bar on the slider and press and hold the left mouse button as you drag the bar to the right or left. You will see the size change in the entries. You will also notice that all four sliders move at once.

The checkboxes above the sliders give you flexibility over each side of the border. By default, **All** is checked so that all four sides of the selected border will resize at the same time as you adjust the slider bar.

8. Let's make the border wider. Adjust the sliders to **3.500** inches. Clicking directly on the slider to the right or left of the bar will jump the sliders by quarter-inch increments. Try clicking directly on the slider to adjust the size to 3.500 inches.

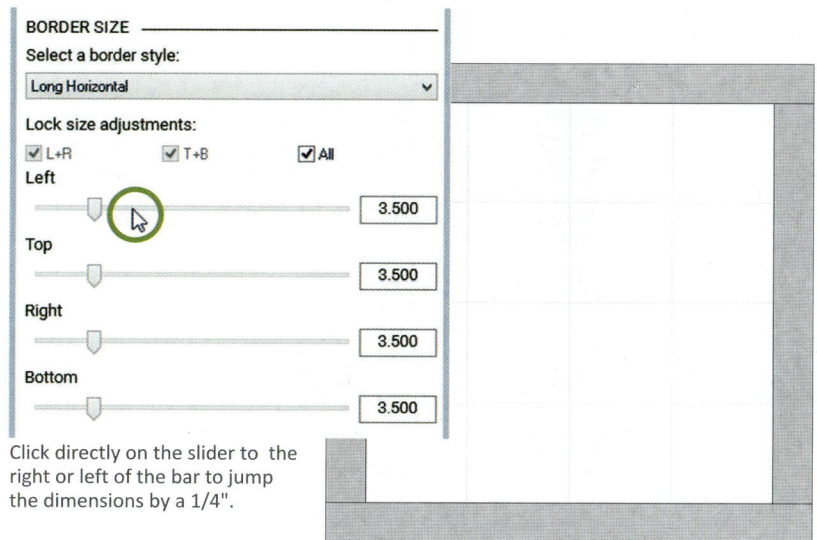

Click directly on the slider to the right or left of the bar to jump the dimensions by a 1/4".

11

9. Click the **DESIGN** tab.

10. Click **Block Tools** on the ribbon.

11. Click the **Set Block** tool in the palette.

Every new project that you start in EQ comes with default blocks, fabrics, colors and thread. These items, along with all the new items that you create or gather from the libraries make up the Project Sketchbook.

12. **Float your cursor over a block in the palette**. A tooltip will appear and display the block name.

13. Find the down-pointing arrow on the blue bar labeled Block Tools in the palette. **Click the arrow**. This will close the toolbox and create more room for the blocks.

14. Find the display buttons in the lower-left of the palette. **Click on the various display buttons** to observe how the blocks change in the display. If you float the cursor over these buttons, you will see, from left to right, Large, Medium, Small and Tiny.

15. Click on the display button for **Small** sized blocks.

16. Click the down-pointing arrow on the blue bar to display the toolbox again.

17. Click **Fabric Tools** on the ribbon. Here you'll see the default fabrics for every project you start.

18. Just above the fabrics, you'll find two tabs labeled Fabrics and Colors. Click the **Colors tab** to see the default colors.

19. Click the **Fabrics tab** to see the fabrics.

The ribbon has several other sets of tools that you'll be able to use when designing. We'll explore those in future lessons.

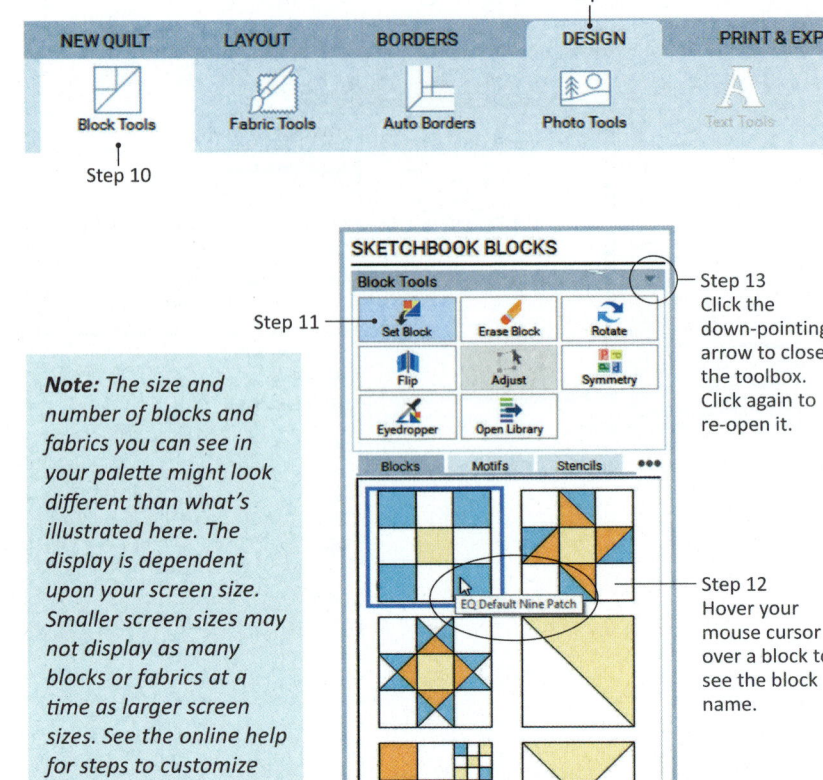

Note: The size and number of blocks and fabrics you can see in your palette might look different than what's illustrated here. The display is dependent upon your screen size. Smaller screen sizes may not display as many blocks or fabrics at a time as larger screen sizes. See the online help for steps to customize your workspace.

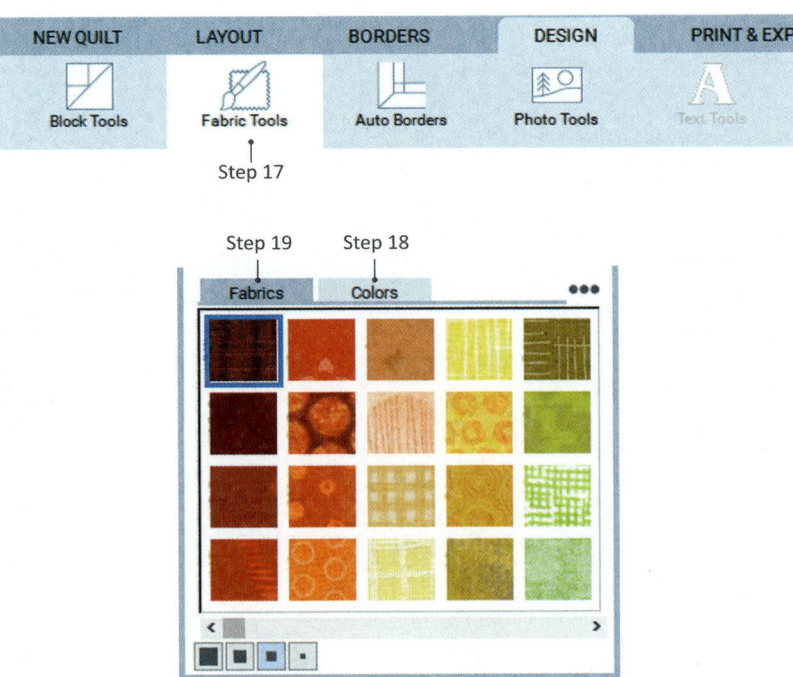

Chapter 1: Learning the EQ8 Basics

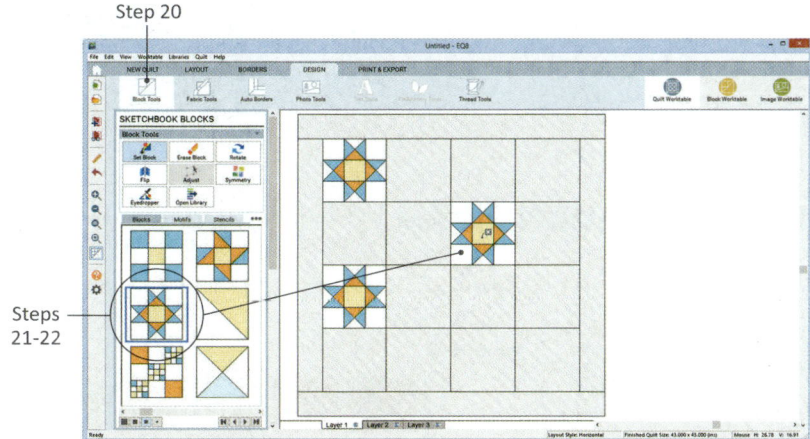

Step 20

Steps 21-22

Setting Blocks in the Quilt

20. Click **Block Tools** on the ribbon. Let's set some blocks into our first quilt.

21. **Click on any block in the palette**. This will select the block. You'll see a frame appear around the block when you click on it.

22. **Click anywhere on the quilt to set the block**. Continue to click on the quilt to set the block in several locations.

23. **Click on a different block** in the palette.

24. **Click on top of an existing block in the quilt**. The new block will replace the previous block. You can use the **Erase Block** tool if you want, or simply replace any block with a new block.

25. **Click on a different block** in the palette.

26. Press and hold the **CTRL key** (Command on Mac) and **click anywhere on the quilt**. This will set the same block in *all locations* with a single click.

27. **Click on a different block** in the palette.

28. Press and hold the **ALT** key (Option on Mac) and **click on any block on the quilt**. This will set the block in *alternating locations* in the quilt.

29. You can also drag blocks from the palette and drop them into the quilt. **Drag several blocks from the palette to the quilt**.

30. The speed keys, CTRL and ALT (Command and Option) work with drag and drop as well. **Try using any of the speed keys with drag and drop**.

31. **Continue to set blocks to create the quilt shown here** with Mosaic, No. 2(2) and Variable Star blocks in alternating positions.

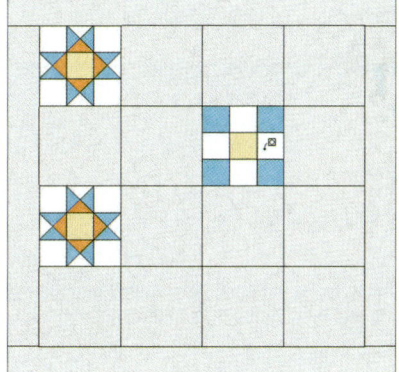
Step 24
Click on top of a block to replace it.

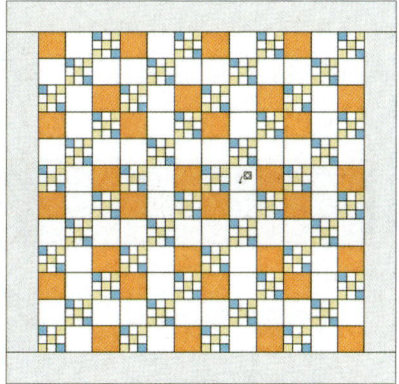
Step 26
CTRL+ click (or Command+click)

Step 28
ALT+ click (or Option+click)

Steps 30-31
Use the speed keys with the drag and drop method to create this quilt.

13

EQ8 Lessons for Beginners

Using the Fabric Tools

32. Click **Fabric Tools** on the ribbon.

The Fabric Tools palette can be adjusted in the same way as the block palette.

33. Click the **down-pointing arrow** on the blue bar at the top to close the toolbox. Click it again to re-display the Fabric tools.

34. Click the **display buttons** in the lower-left corner of the palette to observe the change in the swatches.

The fabric preview appears above the fabric swatches.

35. Click the small **Detach** button in the lower-right corner of the fabric preview. This will pop the preview off the palette and into a new window.

36. **Drag the corner** of the Fabric Preview window to resize it.

37. **Drag the title bar** of the Fabric Preview window to reposition it anywhere on the screen. For this quilt, there is room on the screen to the right of the quilt.

38. **Click on other fabric swatches in the palette** to see them load automatically into the Fabric Preview window.

39. **Drag the scrollbar** beneath the fabric swatches all the way to the right. Then drag it back to the left so that you get a chance to view all the default fabrics.

The **Paintbrush** tool will color a single patch with a click of the mouse. The CTRL and ALT (Command and Option) speed keys work with this tool.

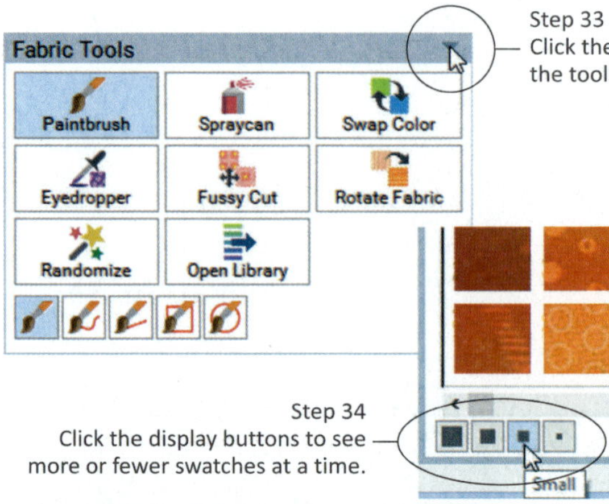

The **Spraycan** tool recolors all matching fabrics within a block with a click of the mouse. With this tool, the speed keys recolor the entire quilt.

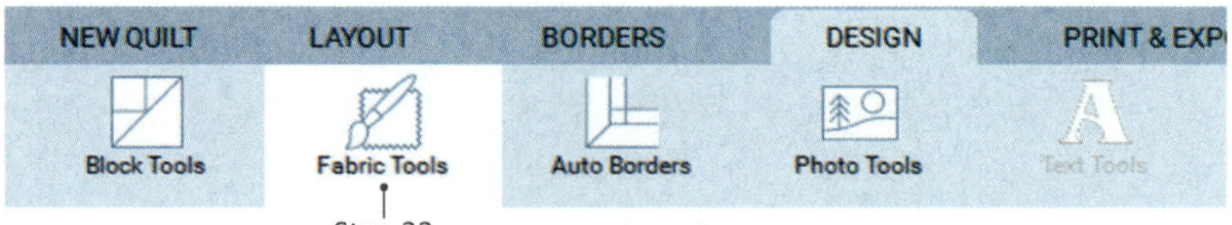

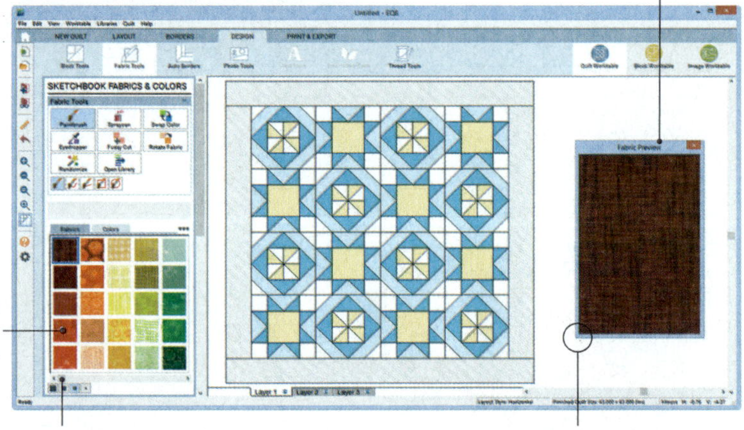

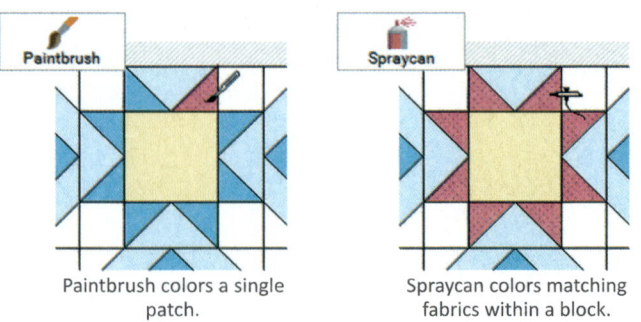

Paintbrush colors a single patch.

Spraycan colors matching fabrics within a block.

14

Chapter 1: Learning the EQ8 Basics

Step 40
Step 42

Step 44

Step 46

Step 48

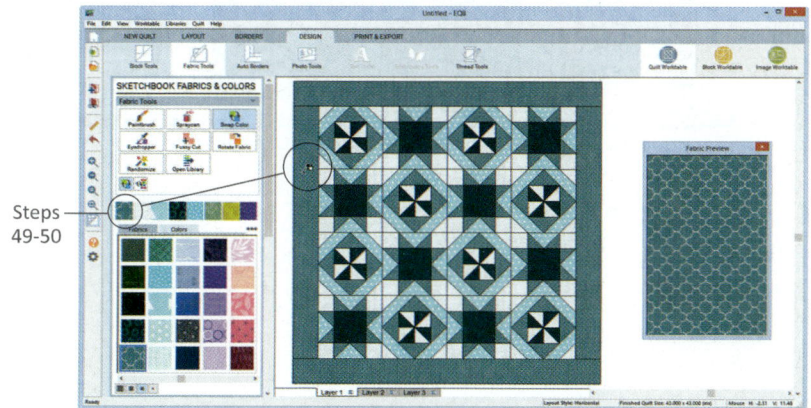
Steps 49-50

To recolor all matching fabrics in the quilt at once use the **Swap Color** tool.

40. Click the **Swap Color** tool.

41. **Find a fabric** in the palette and click on it to select it.

42. **Click on one of the points of the Variable Star block**. All the matching fabrics in the quilt will recolor.

43. **Find another fabric swatch** in the palette and click on it to select it.

44. **Click on the center of the Variable Star block** to recolor all matching fabrics in the quilt.

45. **Find a third fabric** in the palette and click on it to select it.

46. **Click on one of the diagonal patches in the Mosaic, No. 2(2) block**. This will replace the three solid colors in these two blocks with fabrics.

47. Scroll to the end of the fabric swatches and **select a light fabric**.

48. **Click on one of the white patches in the quilt** to recolor all the white to the new fabric.

Each time you use a fabric in the quilt, a most recently used fabric list of swatches will appear above the fabric swatches.

49. **Click on one of the fabrics from the most recently used list**. That fabric will be automatically selected for you. This is a great way to find a fabric that you've used.

50. **Click on the border** to recolor the entire border at once.

Our quilt is complete. We want to make sure that we save it.

15

EQ8 Lessons for Beginners

Naming the Project

As mentioned earlier, blocks, fabrics, colors and thread are part of any new project that you start. Now we want to add a quilt to the Project Sketchbook.

51. Look at the title bar at the very top of the EQ window and notice that our project is **Untitled**.

52. Click the **Add to Project Sketchbook** button to add the current quilt on the worktable to your project.

Whenever you click Add to Project Sketchbook the first time on a new project that is Untitled, you will see this Save As box. This allows you to name the project. All projects are given **PJ8** as the extension to the name. Projects should be saved in the **My EQ8\Projects** location on your computer.

53. Type **Chapter 1 Quilts** in the *File name* box.

54. Click **Save**. The project has been named, and you may hear a sound indicating the quilt has been added to the Project Sketchbook.

Notice the new project name appears on the top title bar of the window. Now that your project is named, every time that you click Add to Project Sketchbook, the **Chapter 1 Quilts** project automatically updates and saves. Let's look at the current contents of the Sketchbook.

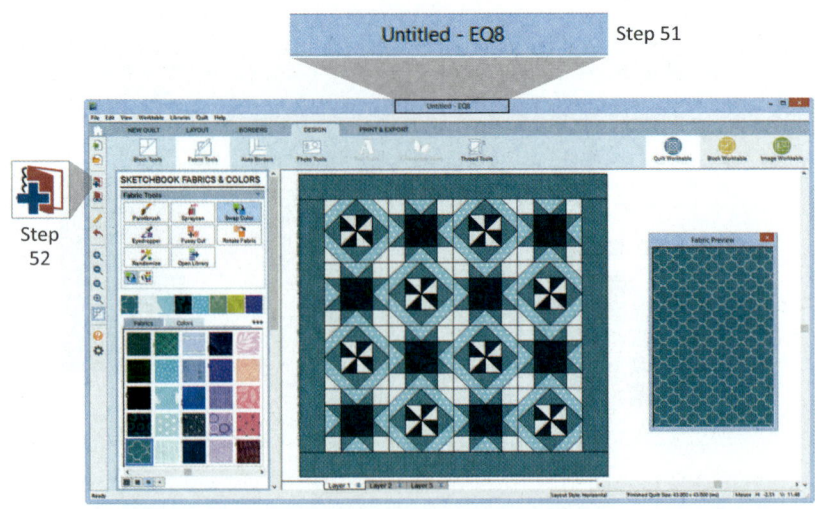

Step 51

Step 52

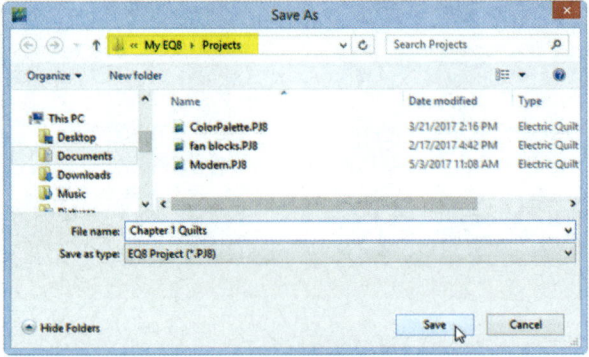

Steps 53-54

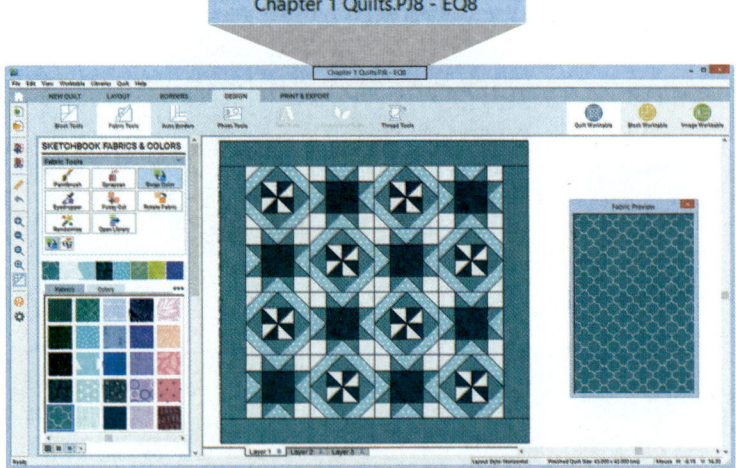

Project is named Chapter 1 Quilts.PJ8

Chapter 1: Learning the EQ8 Basics

Step 55

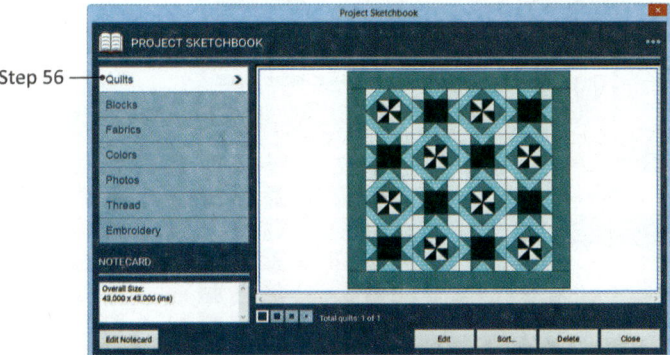
Step 56

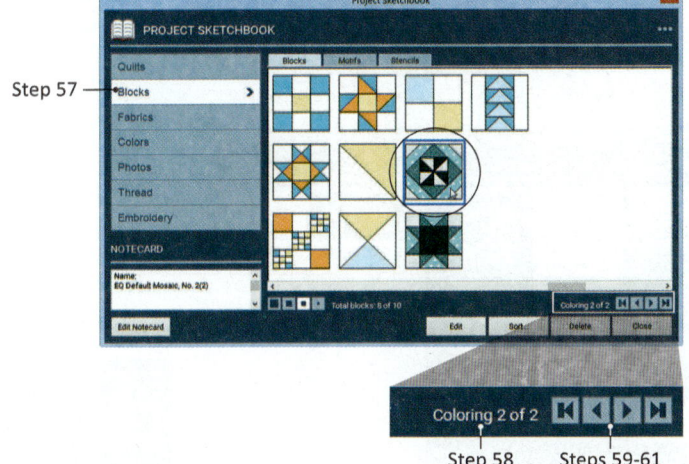
Step 57

Coloring 2 of 2 — Step 58   Steps 59-61

Coloring 2 of 2

Coloring 1 of 2

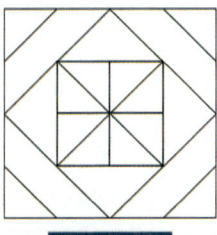
Coloring 0 of 2

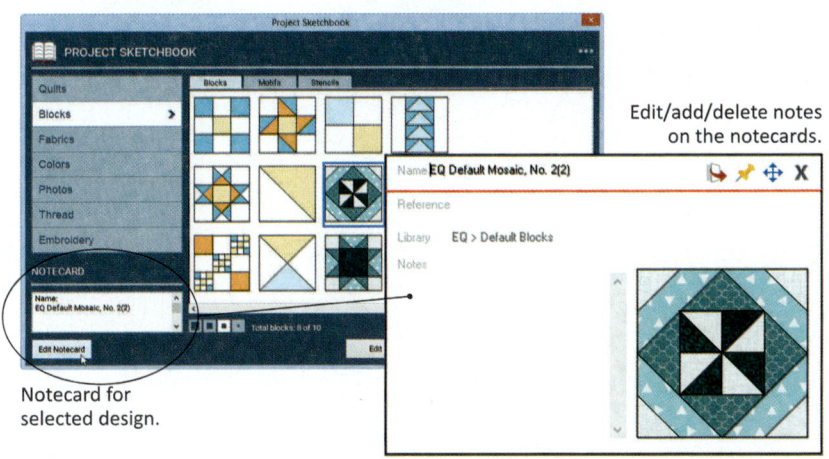
Notecard for selected design.

Edit/add/delete notes on the notecards.

Exploring the Project Sketchbook

55. Click the **View Project Sketchbook** button.

The large buttons on the left display the different designs in the Project Sketchbook.

56. Click **Quilts** to see the quilt you just designed and added to the Sketchbook.

57. Click **Blocks** to see the default blocks and the newly colored blocks.

We no longer see the default coloring for two of the blocks.

58. **Click on one of the newly colored blocks**. Note that the Sketchbook tells us this is **Coloring 2 of 2**.

59. **Click the left-pointing arrow one time**. Now you'll see the default coloring and the Sketchbook tells us this is **Coloring 1 of 2**.

60. **Click the left-pointing arrow again**. Now you will see the drawing of the block and the Sketchbook tells us this is **Coloring 0 of 2**.

61. **Click the right-pointing arrow twice** to return to **Coloring 2 of 2**.

Each block can have two colorings. If a third coloring gets made and saved, then a new block will appear and colorings will pile on it until it has two colorings. This process will continue as you continue to add block colorings. You can use **File > Preferences** to adjust the number of colorings per block. The default is 2.

The Notecard information for each design in the Sketchbook appears in the lower-left. The Notecard allows you to put your own notes about the block, quilt or fabrics. You can edit the Notecard whenever you like by clicking the **Edit Notecard** button.

62. Click **Fabrics** in the Sketchbook window.

63. Click **Colors**. Colors can be used just like fabrics in EQ.

64. Click **Photos**. No photos are in the default project.

65. Click **Thread** to see the default thread colors.

66. Click **Embroidery**. No embroidery designs are in the default project. Embroidery designs in EQ serve as a visual element on a quilt. The files cannot be exported for your machine from EQ.

67. Click **Quilts** again. Let's name our quilt.

68. Click the **Edit Notecard** button in the lower-left.

69. Type **My First Quilt** in the name line.

70. Click the **X** to close the Notecard.

71. Click **Close** to close the Project Sketchbook.

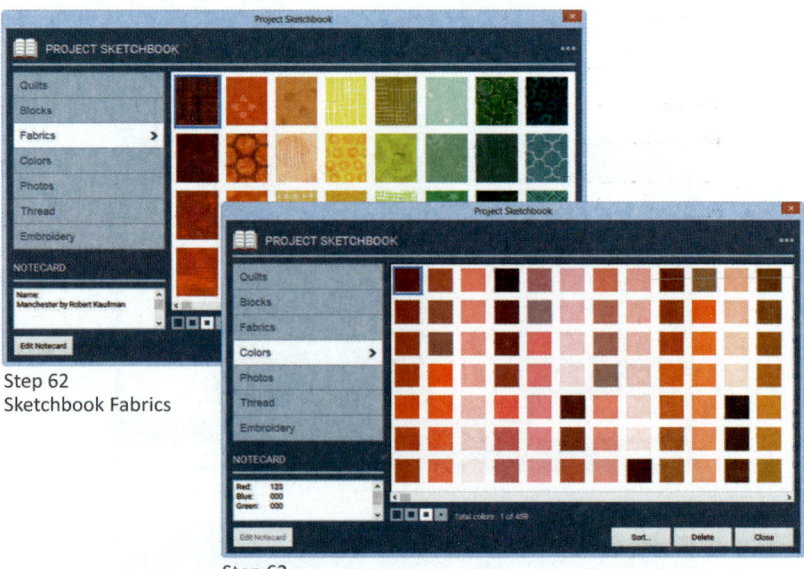

Step 62
Sketchbook Fabrics

Step 63
Sketchbook Colors

Step 68

Step 69

Step 70

Coffee Break!

This would be a great point to take a break. You have learned so much about the Quilt Worktable and some of the tools. But there's so much more to show you!

If you want to continue on, perfect. Jump to step 1 on page 19.

If you need to put EQ8 away, simply choose File > Exit. Your project was saved in step 54 and can be opened up again later to continue the lesson.

Chapter 1: Learning the EQ8 Basics

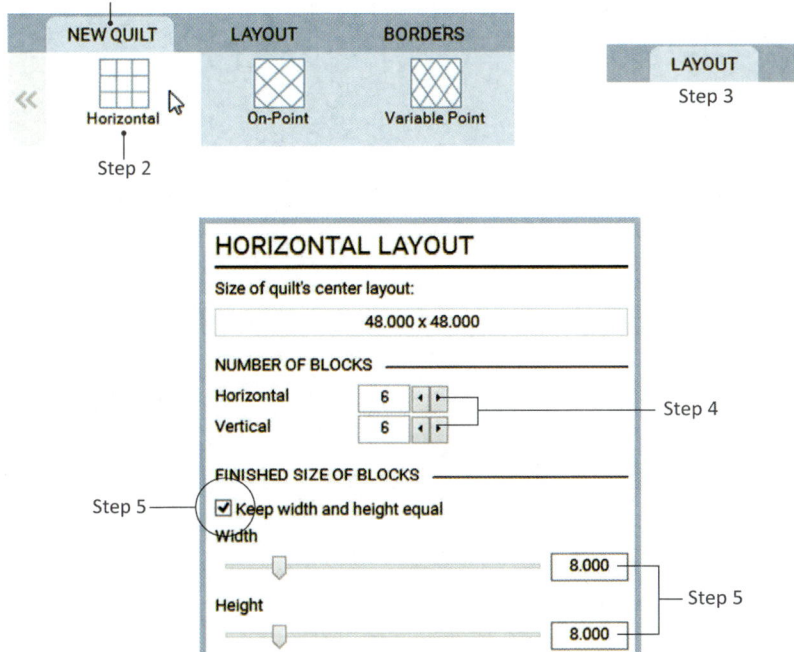

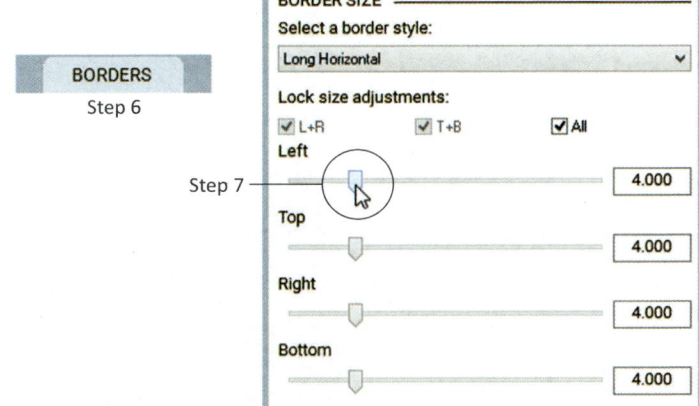

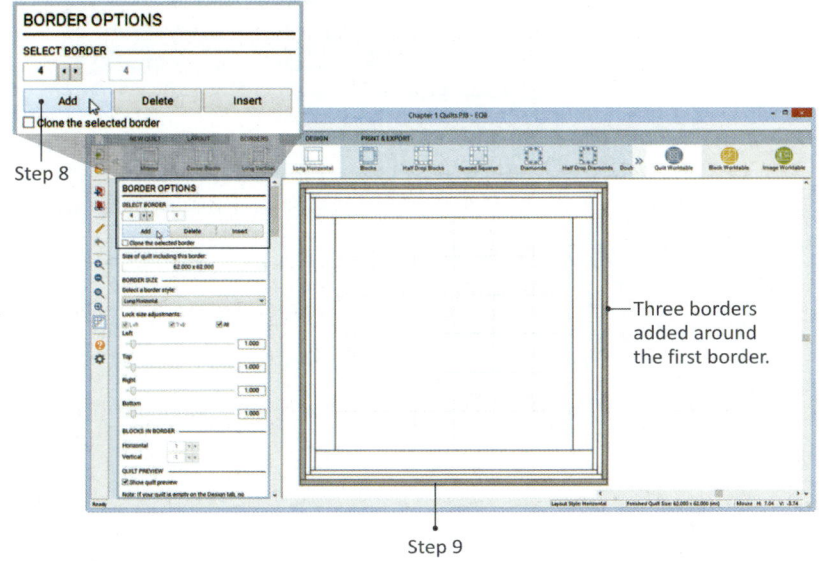

NEW QUILT, DIFFERENT TOOLS, SAME PROJECT

If you closed EQ8 after the last section, you'll need to open it again to get started. We want to continue using the same Chapter 1 project from the first section.

*On the Home screen, click **Open an existing project**, choose **Chapter 1 Quilts** from the list, then click **OK**. Click the **Close** button to close the Project Sketchbook. The title bar at the top will say Chapter 1 Quilts.PJ8. Click the **Quilt Worktable** button on the right of the top ribbon.*

1. Click the **NEW QUILT** tab.

2. Click **Horizontal**.

3. Click the **LAYOUT** tab.

4. **Change the number of blocks horizontal and vertical to 6** by clicking the arrows to change the numbers.

5. With **Keep width and height equal** checked, drag the sliders to change the **block width and height to 8 inches**.

Adding Multiple Borders

6. Click the **BORDERS** tab.

7. Drag the slider to **change the size of the border to 4 inches**.

8. Click **Add three times** to add three more borders.

Notice that the selected border appears in gray. To change the selected border, click directly on a different border of the quilt. Another way to change the selected border is in the palette. Click the arrows in the palette to change borders. Remember the size that appears in the palette is the size of the quilt's center including the selected border.

9. **Click on the outer border** so that the palette says Border 4 of 4.

EQ8 Lessons for Beginners

10. Click the **Delete** button in the palette. Now the palette should say Border 3 of 3.

11. Click the **Delete** button again. Now the palette should say Border 2 of 2 and this border should be 1 inch. Let's keep that.

12. Click the **DESIGN** tab. Let's add some new blocks to the Sketchbook from the Block Library.

Getting Blocks from the Block Library

13. Click **Block Tools** on the ribbon.

14. Click the **Open Library** tool. The Block Library will display.

Every library is broken into sections. The **EQ Block Library** contains all the pre-drawn blocks that come with the program.

15. Click **My Favorite Blocks**. This section is where you can build your own library of blocks for quick and easy access.

16. Click **Current Sketchbook** to see the blocks in your project.

17. Click **Search Results**. When you use the Search button to find blocks, the results will appear in this window. From here you can decide which ones you want to add to your project.

18. Click **Import Results**. The Import button will allow you to import blocks from other EQ projects.

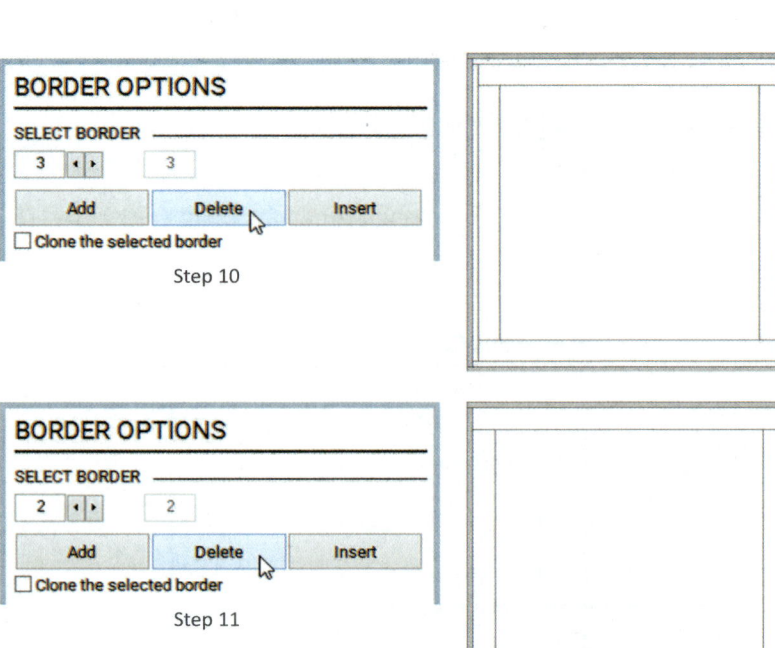

Step 10

Step 11

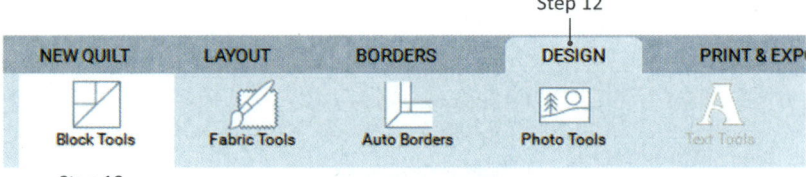

Step 12

Step 13

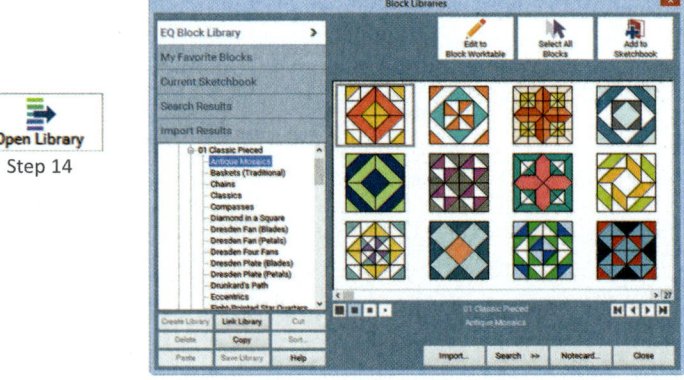

Step 14

Block Library

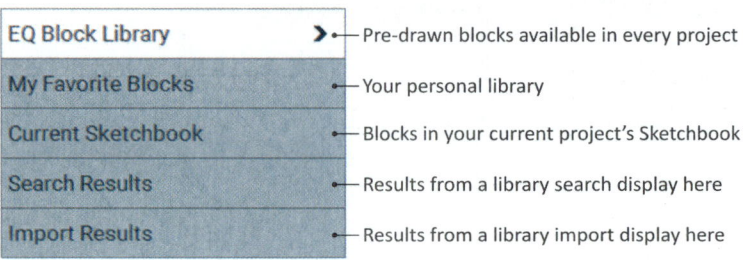

Chapter 1: Learning the EQ8 Basics

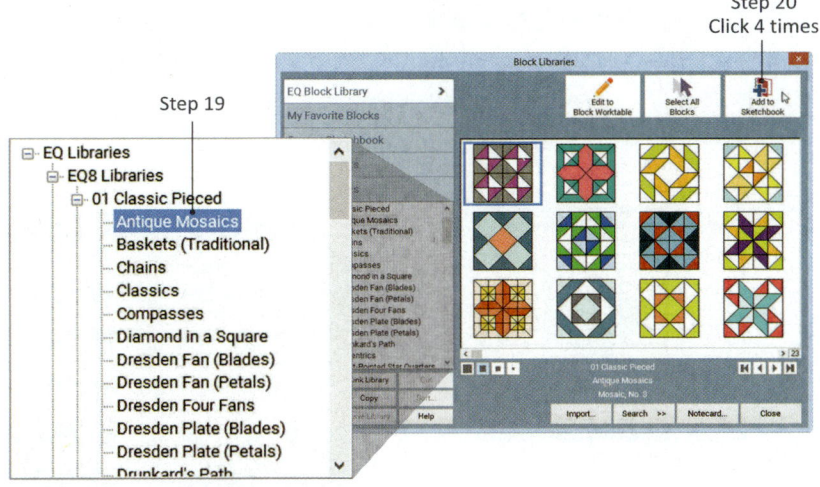

Step 20 Click 4 times
Step 19

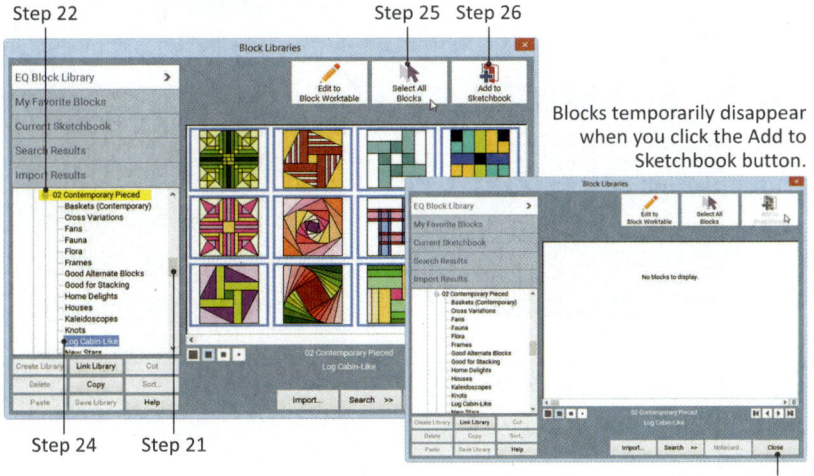

Step 22 Step 25 Step 26

Blocks temporarily disappear when you click the Add to Sketchbook button.

Step 27
Step 24 Step 21

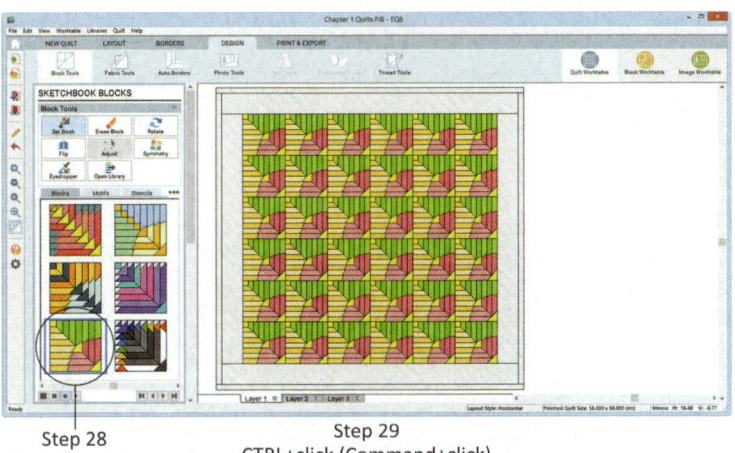

Step 28
Fan Rails Block

Step 29
CTRL+click (Command+click)

19. Click **EQ Block Library**. The blocks are organized into 10 different libraries. **01 Classic Pieced** will be open. If it is not open, click the + sign to open it and click the first style, **Antique Mosaics**.

20. Click the **Add to Sketchbook** button at top of the library window *four times*. Each time you click the button, the selected block will be added to the Project Sketchbook. You will see the block temporarily disappear from the library. Don't worry. The blocks in the library can never be lost or deleted. The blocks that have temporarily disappeared will be there the next time you open the library.

21. Drag the scrollbar down until you see **02 Contemporary Pieced**.

22. Click the **+ sign** in front of **02 Contemporary Pieced** to open that library.

23. Click on any style to see the blocks.

24. Click on **Log Cabin-Like**.

25. Click the **Select All Blocks** button to select all the blocks in the style.

26. Click the **Add to Sketchbook** button. All the blocks temporarily disappear.

27. Click **Close** on the Block Library.

28. In the palette, find the **Fan Rails** block and click directly on it to select it. You may have to scroll to find it.

29. Press and hold the **CTRL** key (Command on Mac) and click on the quilt. This will set the same block in all locations on the quilt.

EQ8 Lessons for Beginners

Using the Eyedropper tool

30. Click **Fabric Tools** on the ribbon.

31. Click the **Eyedropper** tool.

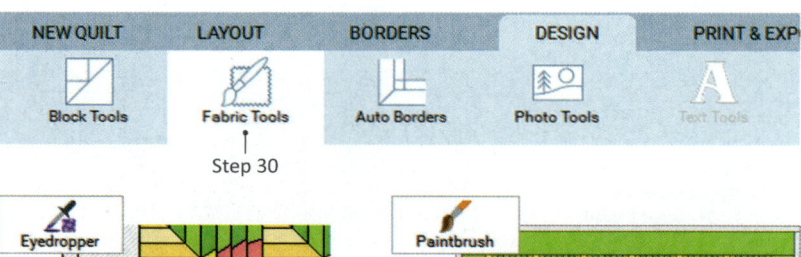
Step 30

The Eyedropper tool is used to pick up a fabric or color from the quilt and select it for you in the palette. It's a great way to find a fabric or color that has been used.

32. **Click on any patch in the quilt** to find the matching color.

33. Click the **Paintbrush** tool.

34. **Click on all fours sides** of the *wide border* to color it.

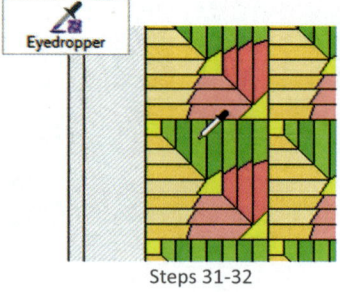
Steps 31-32

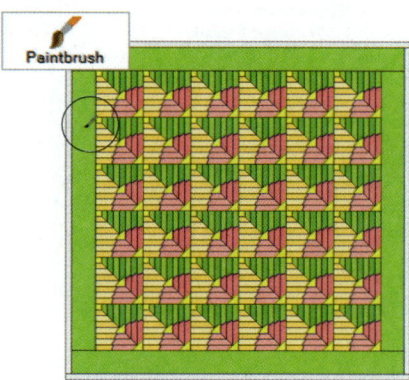
Steps 33-34

35. Click the **Eyedropper** tool.

36. **Click on a different patch in the quilt** to find a different color.

37. Click the **Paintbrush** tool.

38. **Click on all fours sides** of the *narrow border*.

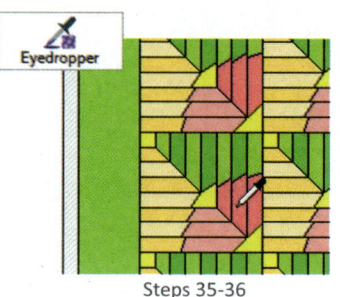
Steps 35-36

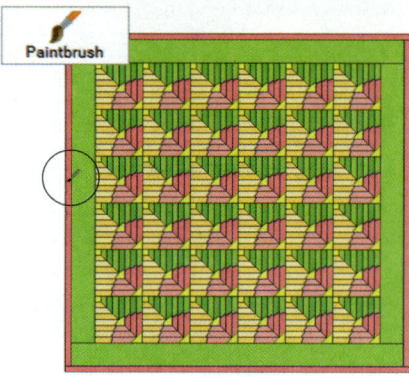
Steps 37-38

Remember that if you make a mistake you can click the **Undo** button.

Using the Symmetry Tool

39. Click **Block Tools** in the ribbon.

40. Click the **Symmetry** button. Read the tip in the palette about the Symmetry tool. The Fan Rail block works great with this tool because of its asymmetric design.

41. **Click on the quilt** to see the first symmetry applied.

42. Click **Add to Project Sketchbook**.

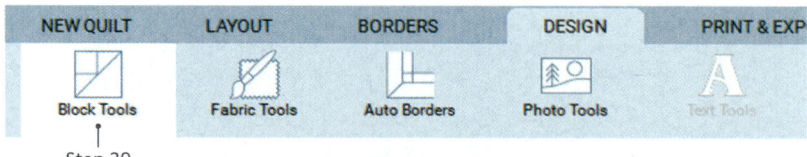
Step 39

Step 40

Step 41

Step 42

Chapter 1: Learning the EQ8 Basics

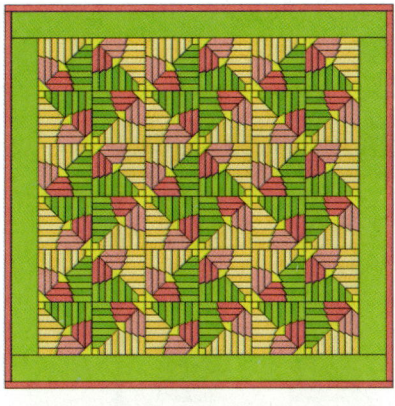
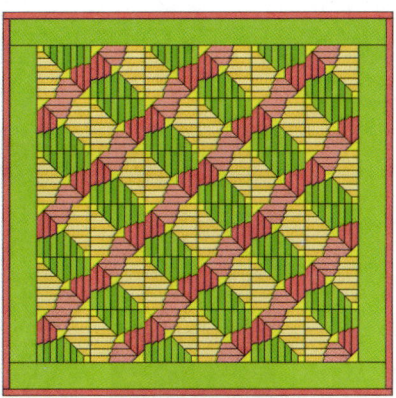
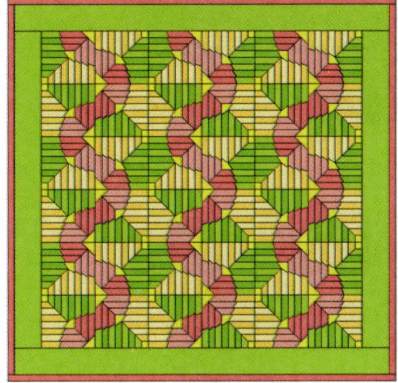
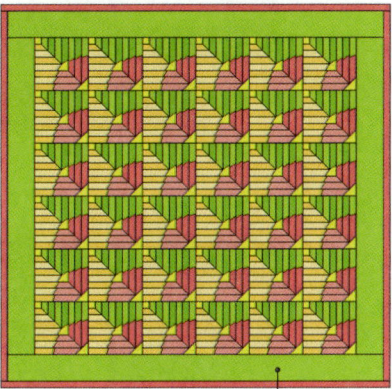

Step 43
Continue to click on the quilt to see more variations.
The 17th click will bring you back to the original setting, as shown above.

Step 44

43. **Continue to click on the quilt** to observe the variations.

44. Click **Add to Project Sketchbook** for as many variations as you like.

If you continue to click 16 times, you will see 16 variations of this quilt. The 17th click will end up back at the original orientation for all the blocks. In the next section, you'll get to see all the variations you saved in your Sketchbook.

Coffee Break!
Are you ready for another break? No problem. Next we'll learn how to print patterns for your quilt!

If you want to continue on, jump to step 1 on the next page.

If you need to put EQ8 away for now, simply choose File > Exit. Your project is already saved and can be opened up again later to continue the lesson.

Homework!
Try other asymmetrical blocks with the Symmetry tool to see what you get. Use the blocks you gathered from the Library, or go back to the Block Library to find some more. Use the Symmetry tool and add as many of your favorite quilt versions to the Sketchbook as you want.

Did you know that symmetrical blocks will work with the Symmetry tool if the block is *colored* asymmetrically? Try it! Go to Fabric Tools and with the Paintbrush, hold the CTRL key (or Command key on a Mac) and click in a block to color it asymmetrically. Holding CTRL (Command) will color all blocks at once.

23

PRINTING & EXPORTING

If you closed EQ8 after the last section, you'll need to open it again to get started with this last section of Chapter 1.

On the Home screen, click **Open an existing project**, choose **Chapter 1 Quilts** from the list, then click **OK**. The Sketchbook will display. Continue to step 2 below.

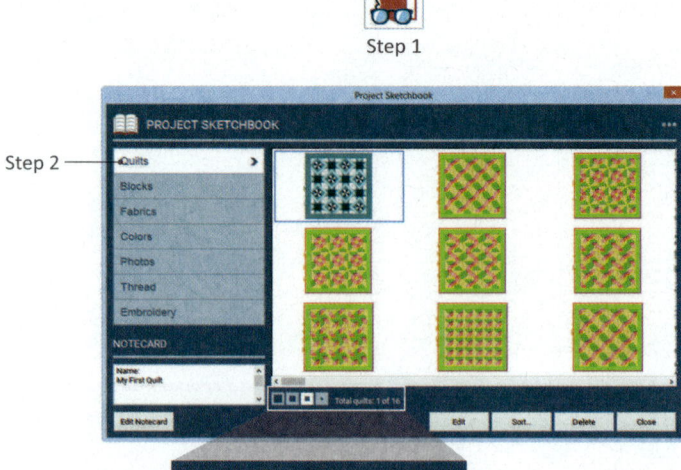

Step 1

Step 2

Step 3

Editing a Quilt from the Project Sketchbook

1. Click **View Project Sketchbook**.

2. Click **Quilts** in the Sketchbook window.

3. Click the **display button** so that you can see more than one quilt at a time.

4. To get any quilt from a project back on the worktable for printing or editing, you'll need to find it in the Sketchbook and edit it.

5. **Click directly on the first quilt** in the Sketchbook to select it.

6. Click the **Edit** button.

If you see a message saying that the quilt on the worktable has not been saved, then you can choose to save it if you like. Once you've answered the message, your original quilt will be back on the worktable. Let's do some printing.

Steps 5-6

Step 7 Step 8

Printing a Quilt

7. Click the **PRINT & EXPORT** tab.

8. Click **Print** on the ribbon.

9. Click the **Quilt** tool in the palette to open the Print Quilt dialog.

The name of the quilt appears at the top. If you decide you want to edit the name, you can do so by clicking the **Edit Name** button. The quilt appears with a special note underneath that reminds us that the printout will look better than the preview on the screen.

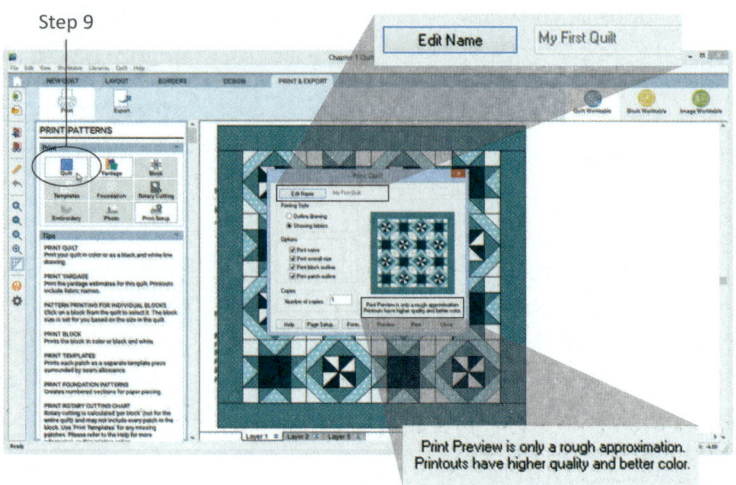

Step 9

Chapter 1: Learning the EQ8 Basics

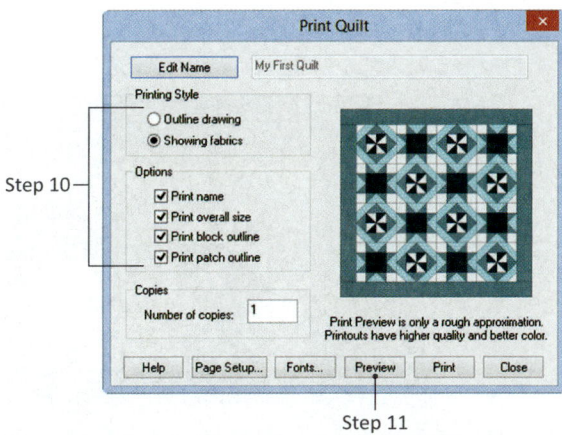

Step 10
Step 11
Step 12

10. Make sure the printing style is **Showing fabrics** and that **all checkboxes are checked under Options**.

11. Click **Preview**.

It is always a good idea to preview any printout before actually printing.

12. Click **Print**.

Printing Yardage Estimates

13. Click the **Yardage** tool in the palette. The Print Yardage Estimates dialog box appears.

This dialog lets you select from various fabric widths. Notice the buttons along the bottom. Most of the dialog boxes that appear in EQ include a Help button. When you click on one of these buttons, EQ will open your internet browser and take you directly to more information on The Electric Quilt Company website about this specific dialog.

If you like, click the Help button and read how EQ estimates yardage. If you don't click the Help button now, please do this first when you have a question about the estimates.

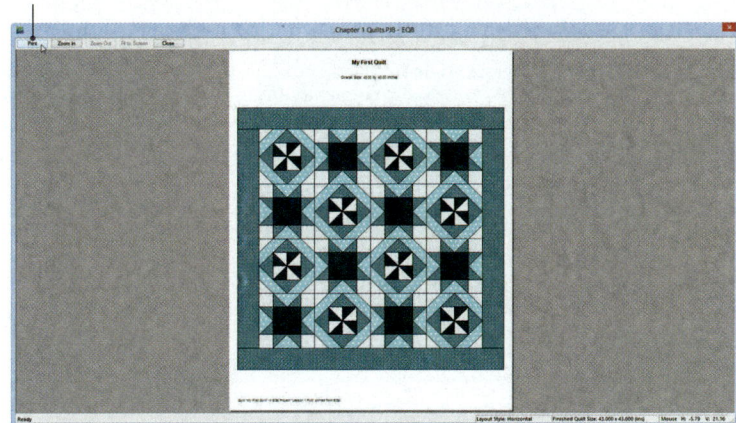

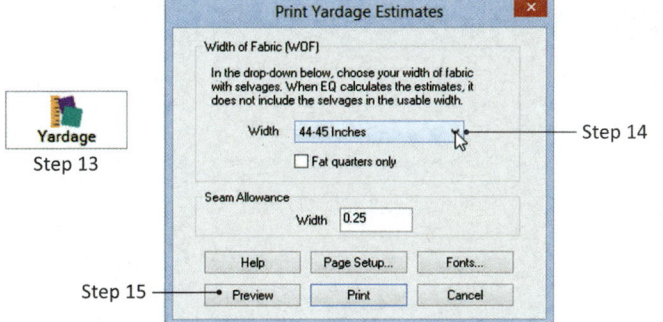

Step 13
Step 14
Step 15

14. Click the down arrow next to **Width** and choose **44-45**.

15. Click the **Preview** button.

Let's zoom in on this printout so that we can read it more easily.

16. Click the **Zoom In** button. The cursor will change to a magnifying glass.

17. **Drag diagonally across the top half of the page.** A marquee box will appear as you drag to indicate the area that you want to zoom. Drag to create a box around the text. When you release the mouse button, the screen will refresh in a zoomed view.

18. Click **Print** to print the yardage chart.

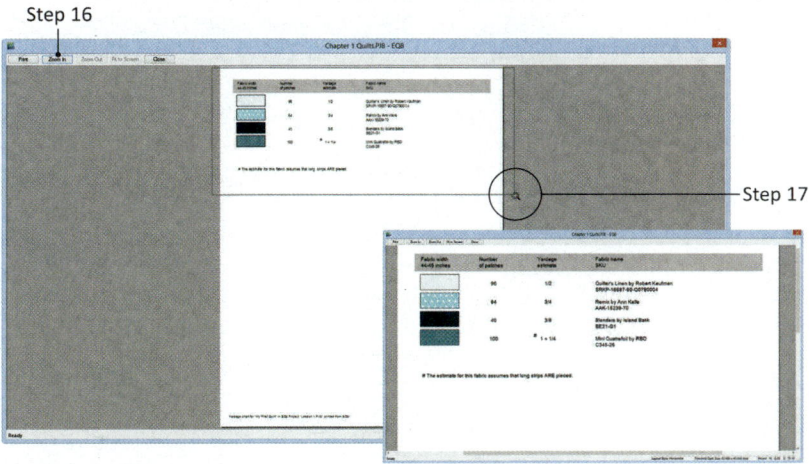

Step 16
Step 17

Print Preview zoomed in

25

Printing Foundation Patterns

Now let's print some patterns. First we need to select a block. We don't need any special tool. Simply click on a block in the quilt to select it. You'll see a frame around the block, and the pattern printing tools in the palette will enable.

19. **Click on any Mosaic, No. 2(2) block** in the quilt.

Foundation patterns, also referred to as paper piecing patterns, are a great method for sewing quilt blocks. Because you are sewing to a paper pattern and stitching straight lines, this method makes it easy to achieve perfection on any block. It is especially useful for blocks with fine points. Using a foundation pattern to sew long thin points is much easier with this method than with individual templates. You will love EQ's ability to create a foundation pattern for you.

20. Click **Foundation** in the palette.

21. Click the **Options** tab at the top of the dialog.

We can see in the Print Foundation Pattern dialog that EQ automatically sets the size of the pattern to be the size of the block in the quilt. The Style is **Color fill** which is very helpful when you're at the sewing machine constructing the block. You will see the color of the next fabric you need to sew by looking at the pattern. Several options are checked, including **Mirror**. Foundation patterns always need to be the reverse image of the finished block. If the design is symmetrical, it won't matter if Mirror is checked. If the design is asymmetrical, then you need to make sure Mirror is checked so that when you sew the block, it appears as you see it in your quilt design.

22. Click the **Numbering** tab. Again, EQ numbers each section for you. You can change the numbers or keep what you see. Let's keep EQ's numbering.

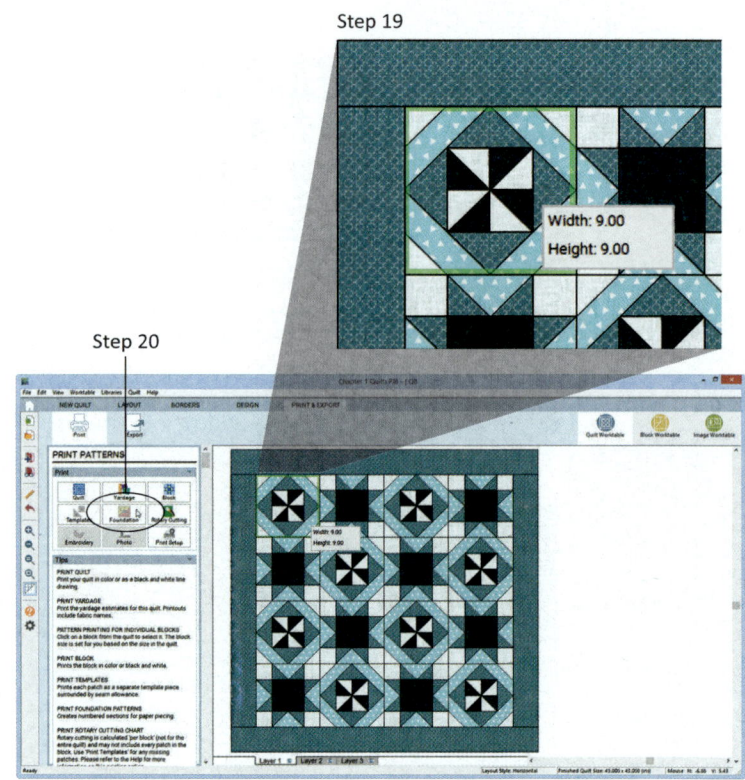

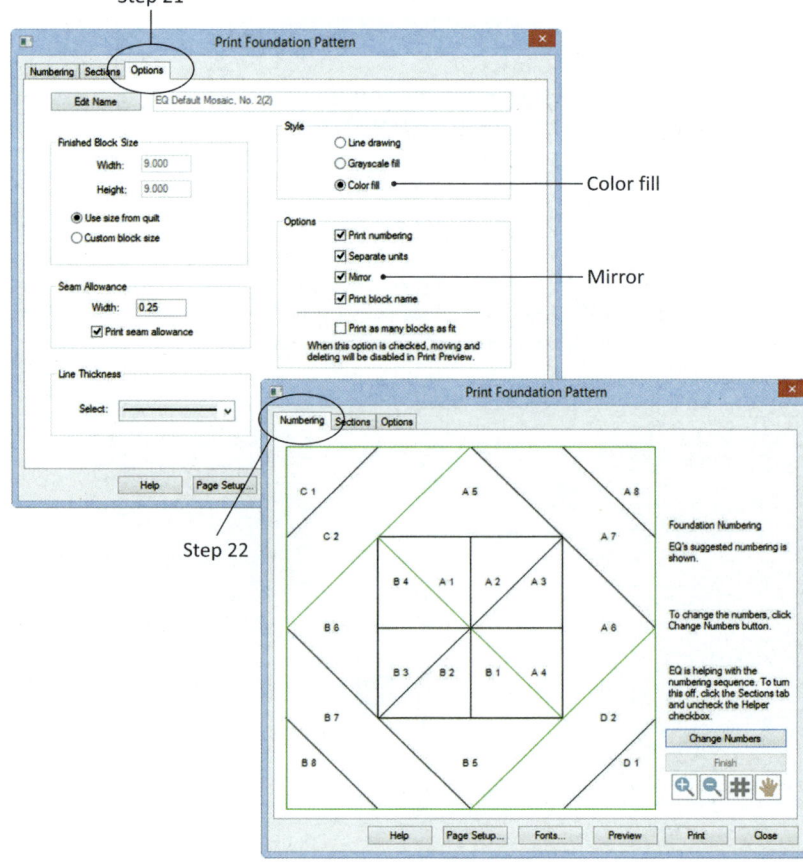

Chapter 1: Learning the EQ8 Basics

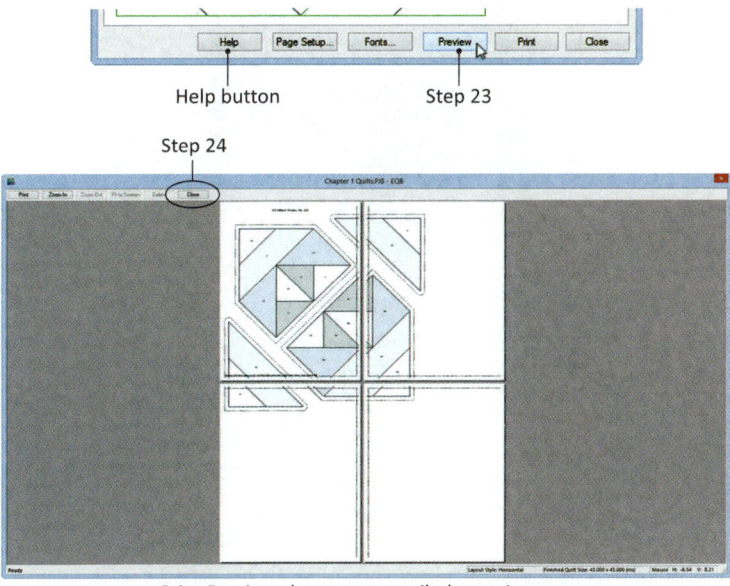

Help button   Step 23

Step 24

Print Preview shows pattern tiled over 4 pages.

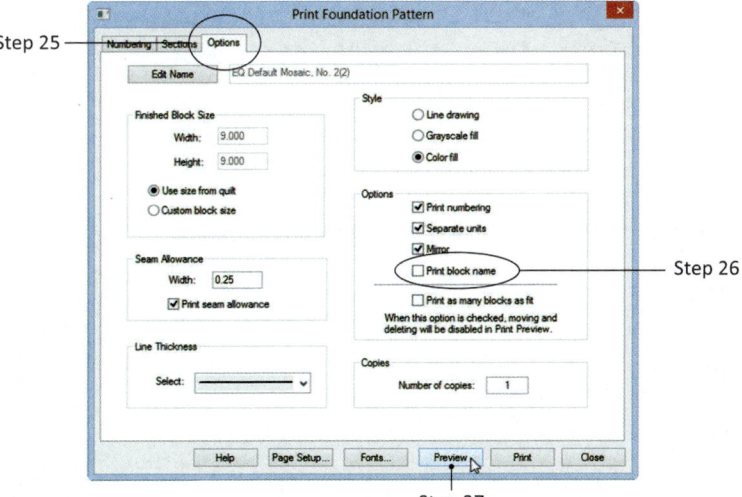

Step 25

Step 26

Step 27

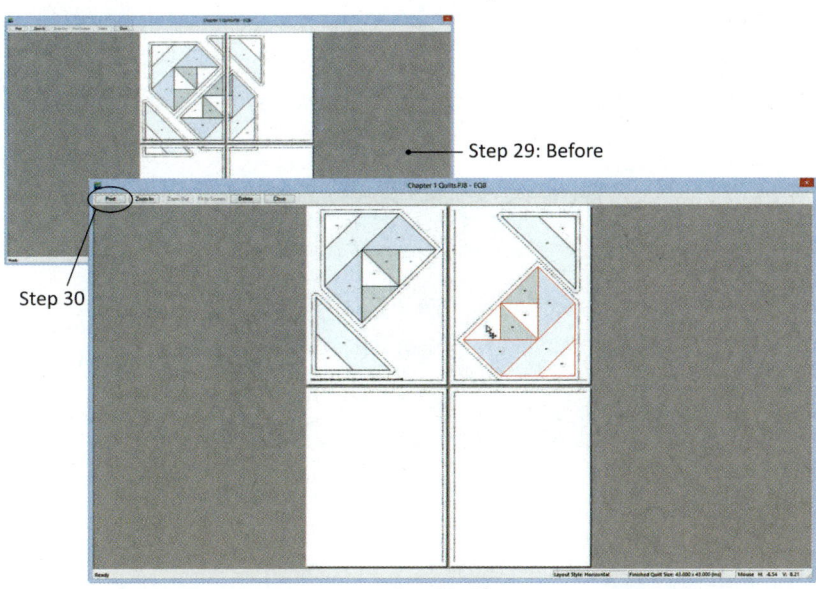

Step 29: Before

Step 30

Step 29: After
Click to move patches. Blank pages do not print.

Remember that you can click the Help button to get much more information about using all the features of the Print Foundation dialog.

23. Click **Preview**.

If your block is large it may require tiling the pattern over several pages since most printers only print on 8½ by 11 inch paper. Since our block is 9 inches and has four sections, it tiles over four pages. You may be able to avoid the tiling by moving templates or changing some settings in the dialog. We don't really need the name of this pattern printed at the top since we will be cutting these sections apart anyway. Let's turn that off.

24. Click **Close**.

25. Click the **Options** tab at the top of the dialog.

26. Click to **uncheck Print block name**.

27. Click **Preview**. Now let's move the sections so each fits on a page without tiling over two pages.

28. **Click on a section**. It will turn red. **Drag it to a new location** on the page.

29. **Move all four sections** so that you have two sections on a page. It's a tight squeeze, but they should fit.

30. Click **Print**. The blank pages do not print, and we are back looking at our quilt.

31. **Click the Variable Star block** in the quilt.

32. Click **Foundation** in the palette.

33. Click the **Options** tab.

34. Let's leave **Print block name unchecked**.

35. Click the **Sections** tab. This block also has four sections.

36. Click the **Numbering** tab.

37. Click **Preview**.

38. **Move the sections** further apart on the two pages.

39. Click **Print**.

Printing Templates

Now let's print the template for these two blocks.

40. **Click on any Mosaic, No. 2(2) block** in the quilt.

41. Click **Templates** in the palette. The Print Template dialog box will display.

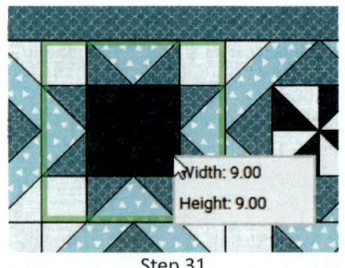
Step 31

Step 32

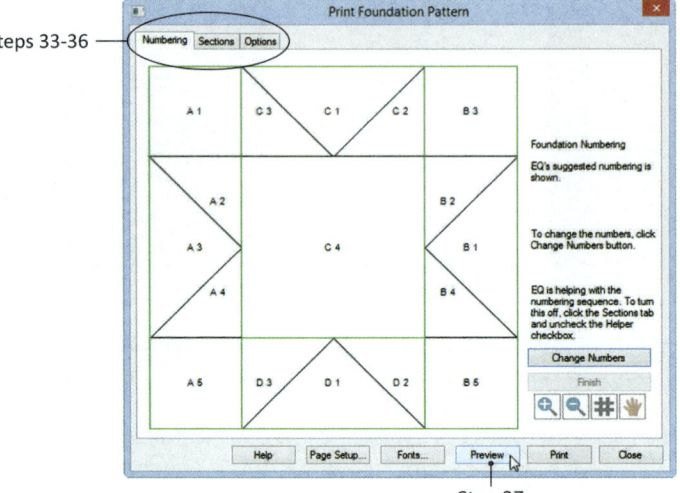
Steps 33-36

Step 37

Step 39

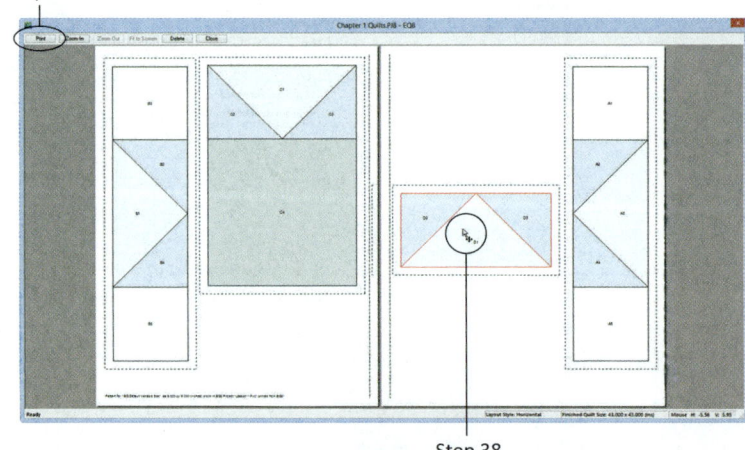
Step 38

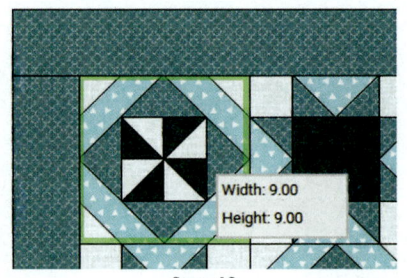
Step 40

Step 41

Chapter 1: Learning the EQ8 Basics

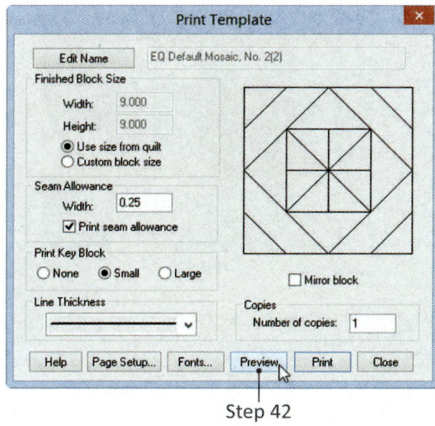

Step 42

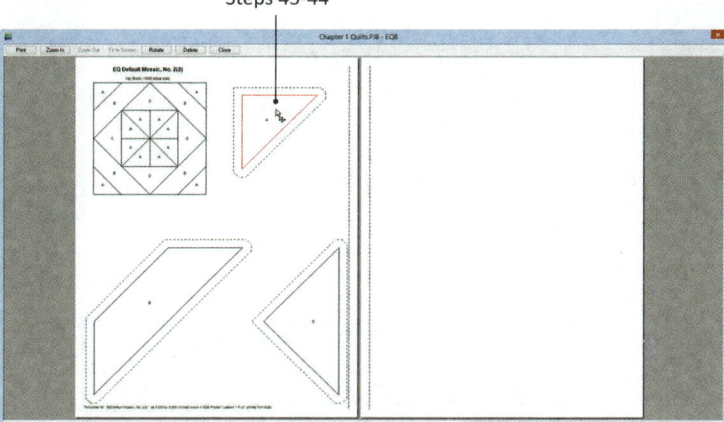

Steps 43-44

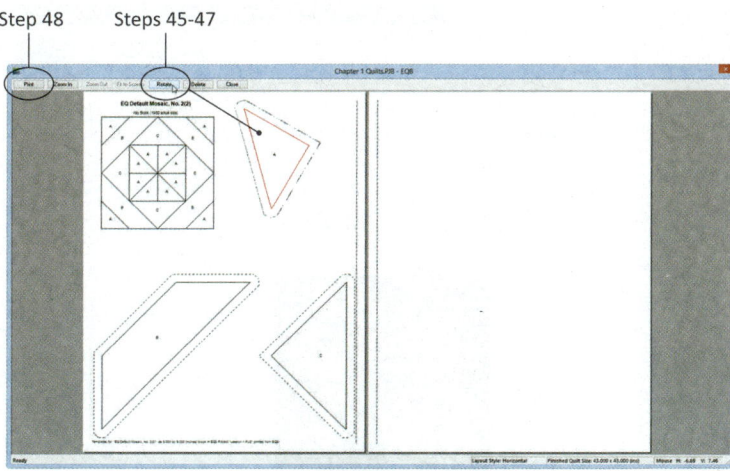

Step 48   Steps 45-47

EQ automatically sets the size of the pattern to be the size of the block in the quilt. The printout will include a small key block. Note that **Mirror** is an option. We don't need to mirror the templates for a pieced block. You will want to mirror the templates if you're printing applique designs and applying fusible to the back of the fabric.

42. Click **Preview**.

The first page will show the key block if it has been included. EQ leaves the space to the right of the key block empty so you can easily move the template that's on page two into that space so the printout will be one page. Blank pages will still appear in the preview, but will not print.

43. **Click on the template on the second page**. It will turn red to indicate it is selected.

44. **Drag it to the first page** to the right of the key block.

Rotating Templates Before Printing

Notice that when you have a template selected, the Rotate and Delete buttons at the top of the window are enabled. These features will help you conserve paper and make the most of the printable area. Let's look at how rotate works.

45. Click the **Rotate** button. The patch rotates clockwise 30 degrees.

46. **Click Rotate again**. The patch continues to rotate another 30 degrees.

47. If you like, you can continue to click 10 more times to return the patch to the original position or leave it in any rotated position that fits.

48. Click **Print**.

49. **Click one of the Variable Star blocks** in the quilt.

50. Click **Templates** in the palette.

We will keep the same settings in the Print Template dialog.

51. Click **Preview**.

52. **Drag the templates** from the second page to the first page.

53. Click **Print**.

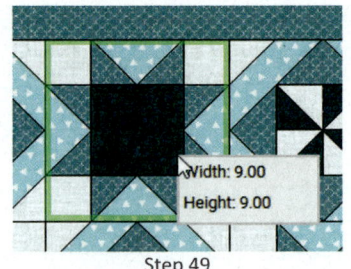
Step 49

Step 50

Sharing to Facebook

54. Click **Export** on the ribbon.

55. Take a minute to read the exporting options in the palette.

If you have a Facebook account, we would love to have you share your designs so all of your Facebook friends can see your latest designs!

56. Click **Facebook** in the palette.

57. Click **Continue** to give EQ permission to start the upload.

58. When the upload is complete, click **Continue to Facebook**.

59. Follow the prompts to **log into** your Facebook account, if you are not already logged in.

60. **Type a message** to go along with your post.

61. Click **Post to Facebook** at the bottom of the box.

62. Go to your Facebook page to view your post!

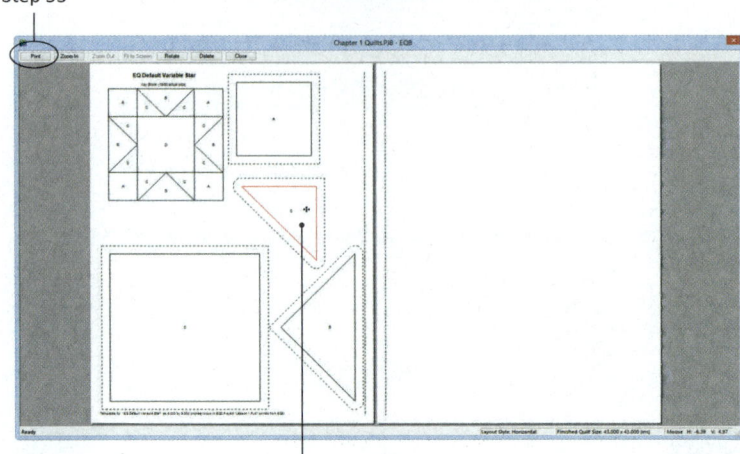
Step 53

Step 52

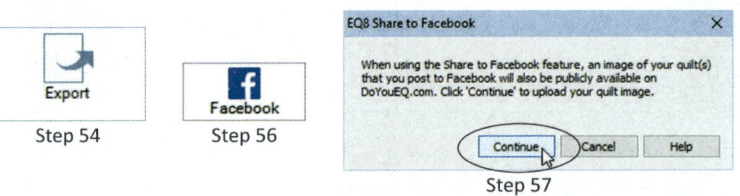
Step 54 Step 56 Step 57

Step 58

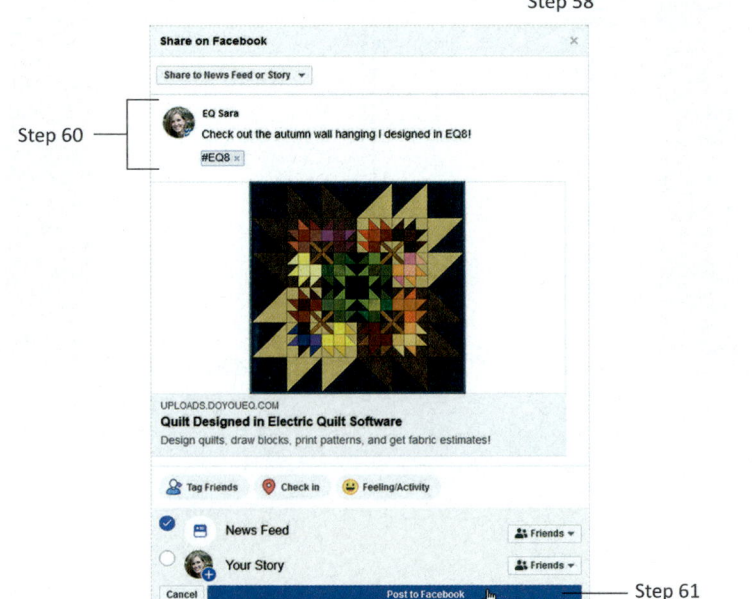
Step 60

Step 61

Chapter 1: Learning the EQ8 Basics

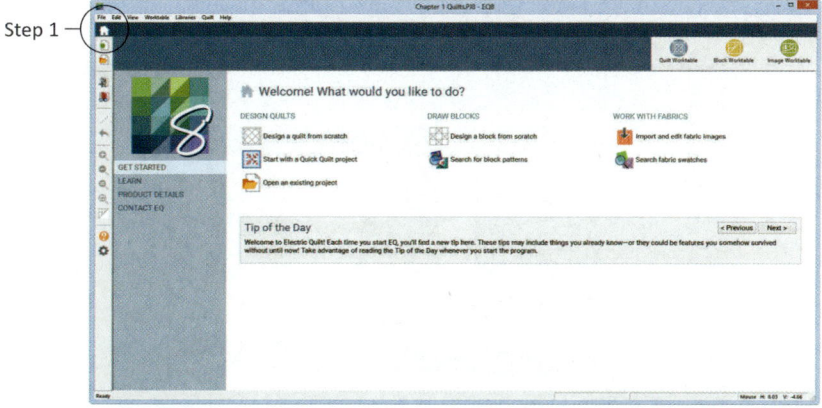

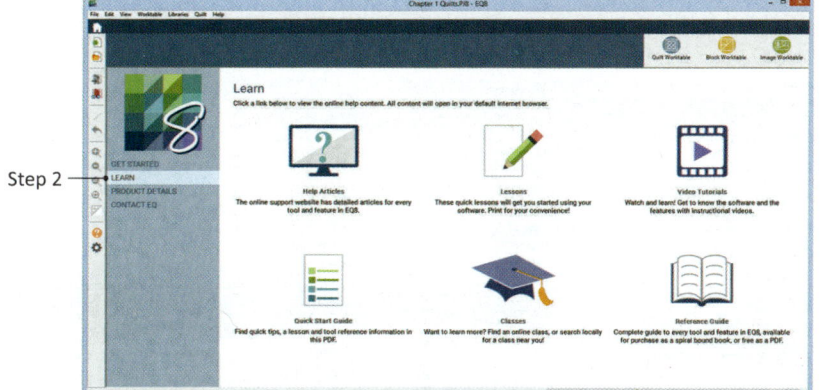

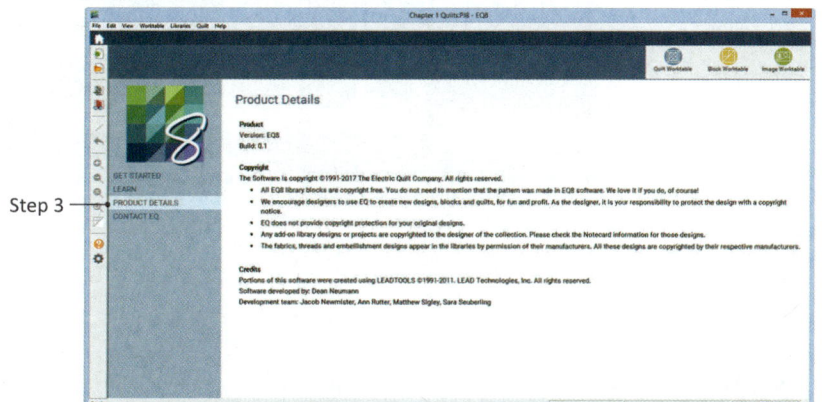

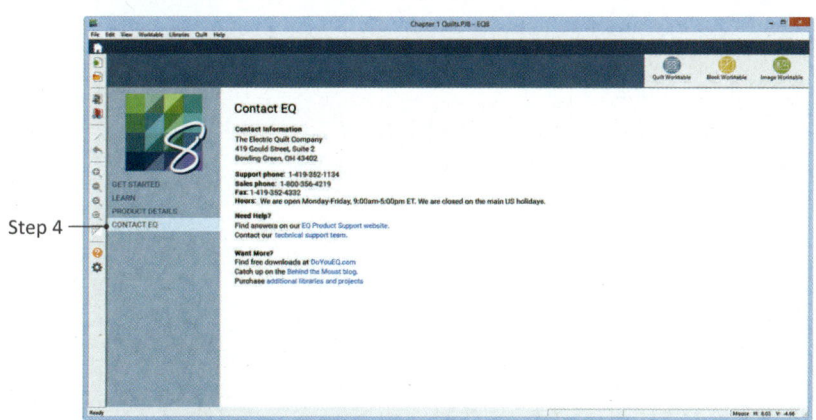

Congratulations!

You've completed Lesson 1! Before we take off on Lesson 2, let's go back to the Home screen and see the other options available there.

1. Click the **Home** button in the upper-left.

This is the opening screen that you see when you start the program. Notice the **Tip of the Day** notes at the bottom. You will find many useful tips here. We suggest that you read one or two of them each time you open the program.

2. Click **Learn** under the EQ logo.

This is your main resource for help using EQ8. Each link takes you to pages on the EQ website. You will find lessons, videos, and many helpful ideas for getting the most out of your software. Please check these links often, as we update and add new articles frequently.

3. Click **Product Details** under the EQ logo.

This page lists details about EQ and our copyright statement. The fabrics, threads and embroidery designs appear in the EQ Libraries by permission of their manufacturers.

4. Click **Contact EQ**.

We take great pride in our support team. And we love to hear from you. This page is your source for contacting us for whatever you need.

Let's take a quick review of our project and what we've learned in our first lesson.

5. Click **View Project Sketchbook**.

The name of this project is **Chapter 1 Quilts**. We see that name on the title bar. The contents of this project will be saved with that project name the next time that you want to open this project and continue adding to it.

6. Click on **Quilts**. Change the display to view all of your quilts. All of these quilts were created in this lesson.

7. Click on **Blocks**. We see the blocks that we recolored and new ones we added from the Block Library.

8. We didn't add any other new elements to this project. Click **Close**.

9. Click **File > Exit** to close EQ.

You've completed Lesson 1 on the basics of the Quilt Worktable. We wanted you to become familiar with starting a new quilt, finding blocks in the library and learning to recolor the quilt. Plus we touched on some of the printing possibilities. We'll explore the other layout styles and creating custom quilts in later lessons.

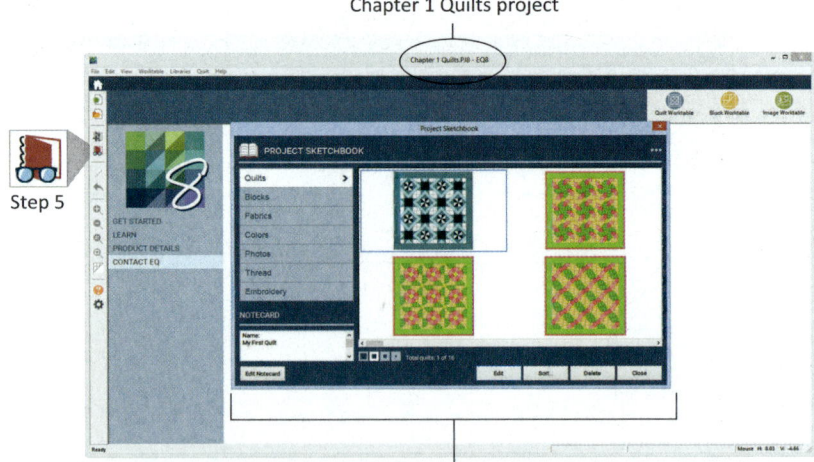

The contents of your project (everything that's included in your Project Sketchbook) is saved within the *Chapter 1 Quilts* project file.

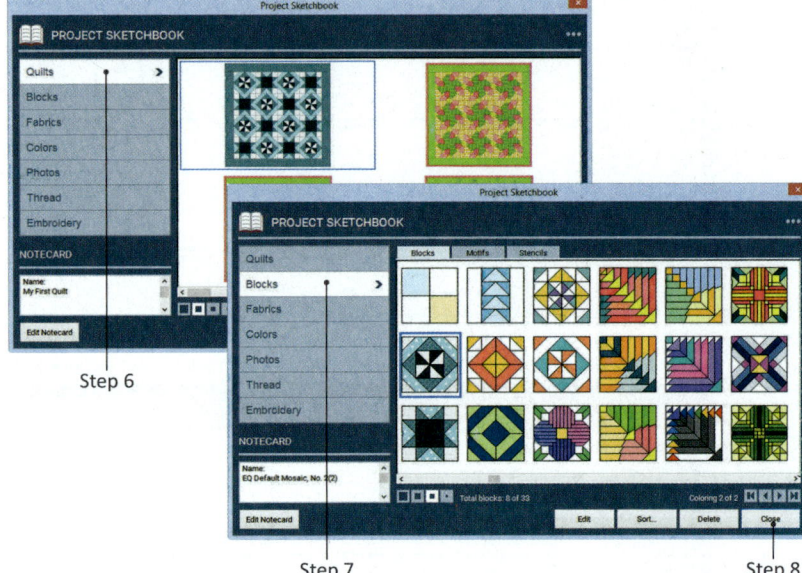

Here's what we learned in this lesson:

- Restoring default settings
- Using the Home screen
- Changing worktables
- Naming a project
- Viewing the Project Sketchbook
- Selecting a quilt layout
- Making changes to a layout
- Adding, removing and resizing borders
- Setting blocks
- Speed keys for setting blocks
- Hide/show tools in the palette
- Adjusting the display of blocks and fabrics in the palette
- Floating the Fabric Preview window
- Using the Swap tool
- Using the Paintbrush tool
- Using the Eyedropper tool
- Adding a quilt to the Project Sketchbook
- Naming a quilt
- Seeing the block colorings in the Sketchbook
- Adding blocks from the Block Library
- Printing Quilts, Yardage, Foundations and Templates
- Zooming in Print Preview
- Moving templates and foundation sections
- Rotating templates
- Finding help

Chapter 1: Learning the EQ8 Basics

LESSON 2: BASICS OF THE BLOCK WORKTABLE

In this lesson, we will learn the basics of the Block Worktable.

At the beginning of the book we suggest that you restore the default settings of the program before completing the first three lessons. If you are continuing on from Lesson 1, you don't need to Restore Defaults. If you've been using the program for a time, you may want to Restore Defaults before starting this lesson. See page 7 for details.

The Home screen will display when you start EQ8. If you don't see the Home screen, click the Home button in the upper-left corner of the EQ window.

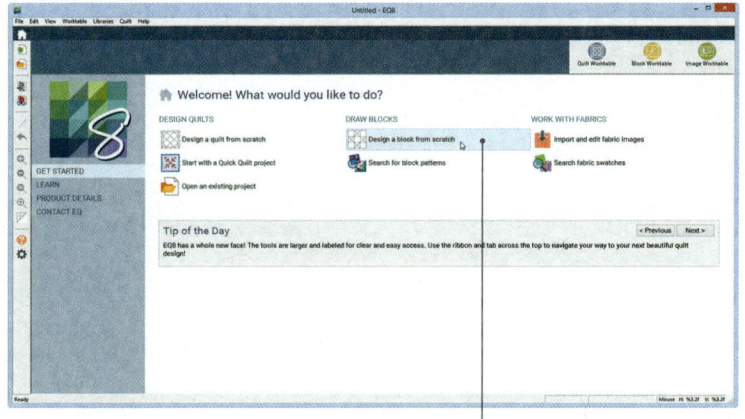
Step 1

1. Click **Design a block from scratch** on the Home screen under DRAW BLOCKS.

   Now we are looking at the Block Worktable. Notice the circular Block Worktable button on the ribbon looks pressed indicating that it's the active worktable. This worktable has a gold color scheme, and its own set of tabs and ribbon options.

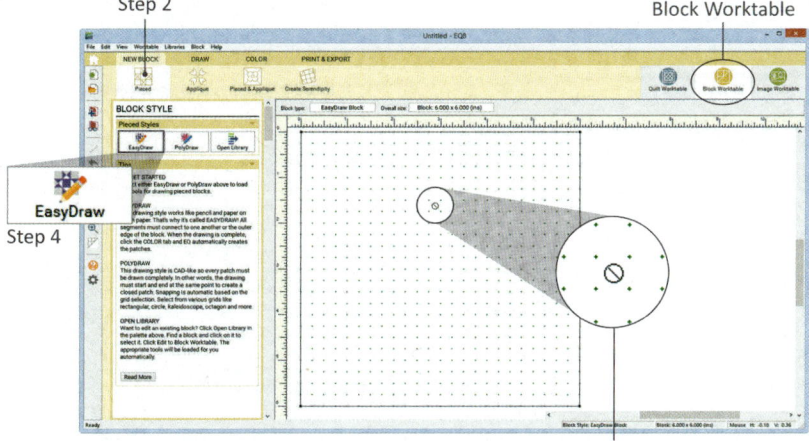
Step 2 — Block Worktable — Step 3 — Step 4

DRAWING BASIC PIECED BLOCKS

2. Click **Pieced** on the ribbon. The palette tells us we can choose from two different drawing styles, EasyDraw or PolyDraw. Take a minute to read the descriptions in the palette.

3. Float the cursor over the main worktable. We have not chosen a drawing style yet so the 'no' cursor displays.

4. Click **EasyDraw** in the palette. The EasyDraw drawing style is the most popular set of tools for drawing pieced blocks in EQ. This drawing style is like drawing with paper and pencil.

Notice that we've changed to the DRAW tab with Drawing Tools selected on the ribbon. The palette has changed to the EasyDraw tools.

5. Float the cursor over the worktable to see a pencil cursor indicating that we can draw.

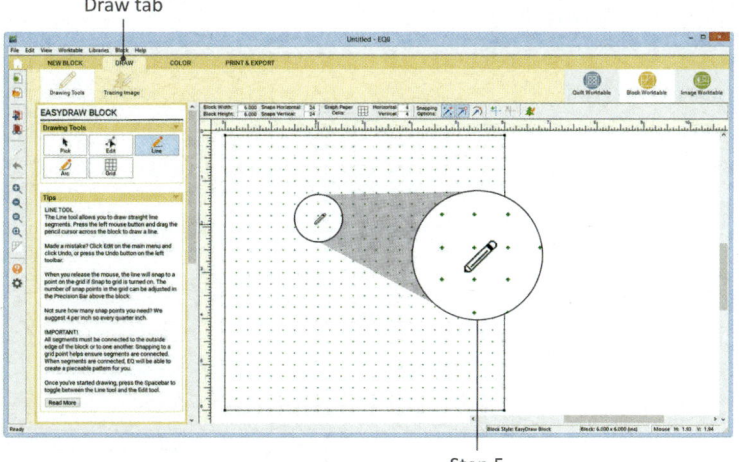
Draw tab — Step 5

33

EQ8 Lessons for Beginners

1

Discovering the Tools and Rules of EasyDraw

Before we begin drawing, let's make some observations. The Precision Bar appears just below the ribbon along the top of the block. This bar is a great way to change settings. The default block is 6 inches and Snaps Points are set to 24.

When you want to change any of the numbers, double-click inside a number box to highlight the current number. Type a new number. Press the keyboard Enter key to make the change to the drawing board. Or press the keyboard Tab key to move to the next box in the Precision Bar.

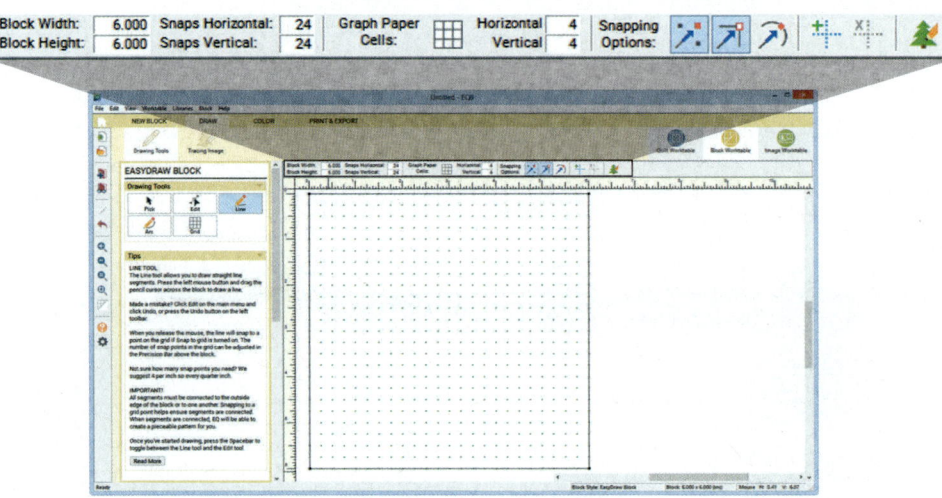

Default EasyDraw precision bar

6. Click the **Graph Paper Cells** button to turn on the graph paper lines on the block. These lines are nice guides when drawing, they are not part of the design.

Let's change the Graph Paper Cells to 2 by 2.

7. Double-click in the *Horizontal* box to **highlight the 4**.

8. **Type 2 and press the keyboard Enter key.** Notice the change in the graph paper.

9. Double-click in the *Vertical* box to **highlight the 4**.

10. **Type 2 and press the keyboard Enter key.** Notice the change in the graph paper.

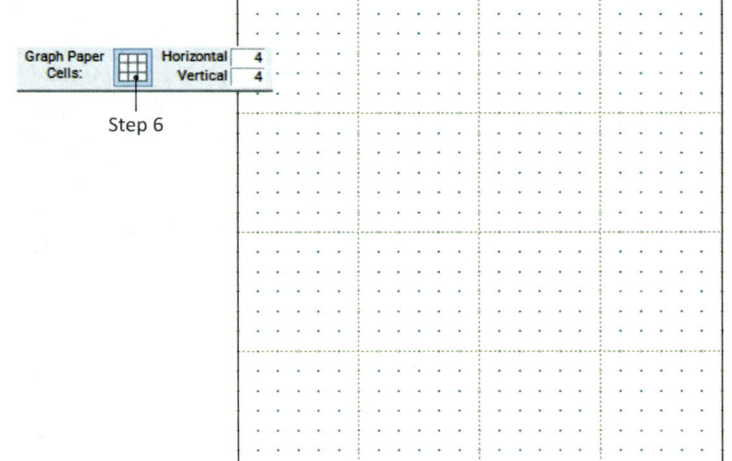

Step 6

Graph paper with default 4 x 4 grid.

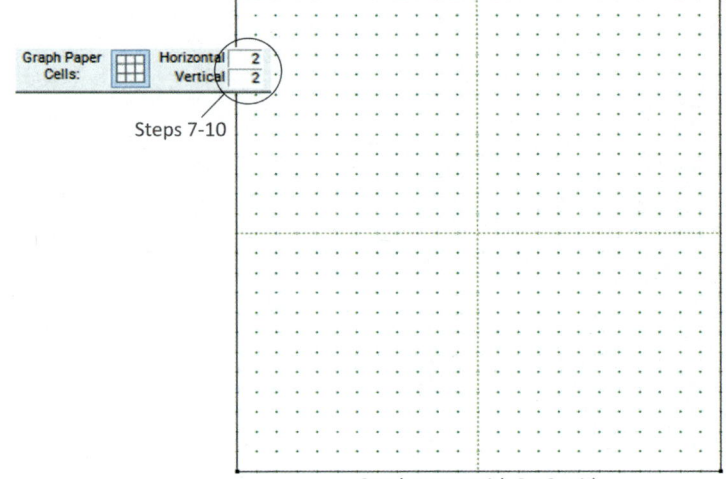

Steps 7-10

Graph paper with 2 x 2 grid.

34

Chapter 1: Learning the EQ8 Basics

There are three Snapping Options buttons. The first two buttons should be pressed to indicate they are turned on. **You will want to keep these two turned on when drawing.**

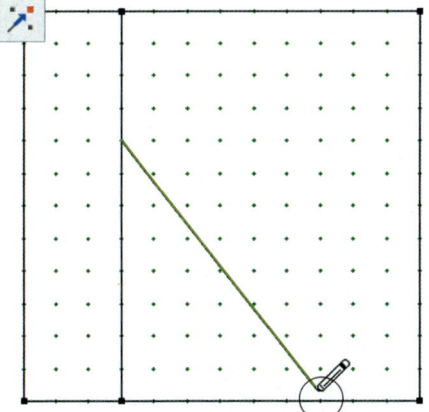

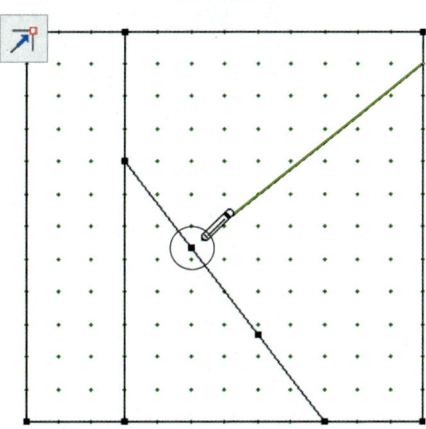

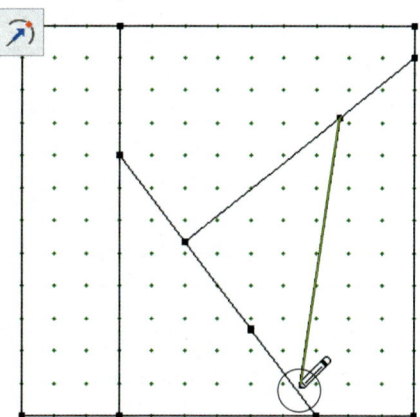

The first button is **Snap to grid points on worktable** and will snap the segment to one of the grid points on the worktable when you release the mouse.

The second button is **Snap to nodes of drawing** and will snap the segment to another node. A node is indicated by a small black square. Every segment (line or arc) that you draw will have a node at each end. Other nodes get created when segments cross over one another, or when they get added using the Edit tool.

The third button is **Snap to lines and arcs of drawing** and can be kept turned off for most any block you draw with EasyDraw. The line will snap to a line or arc already on the worktable. Only the more advanced block designs require changing these snapping options.

A good rule to follow when drawing your own blocks is to **make sure that the number of Snap Points is a multiple of the block size**. We also suggest setting the **Snap Points to every ¼ inch**. This rule works well for most blocks and gives you enough snap points to achieve the design that you want. Since our block is 6 inches, Snap Points are set to 24 (6 x 4 = 24). You can increase or decrease the snap points as long as you keep the number a multiple of the block size. Six snap points would snap every inch, 12 would snap every ½ inch, 24 would snap every ¼ inch, 48 every 1/8 inch and so on.

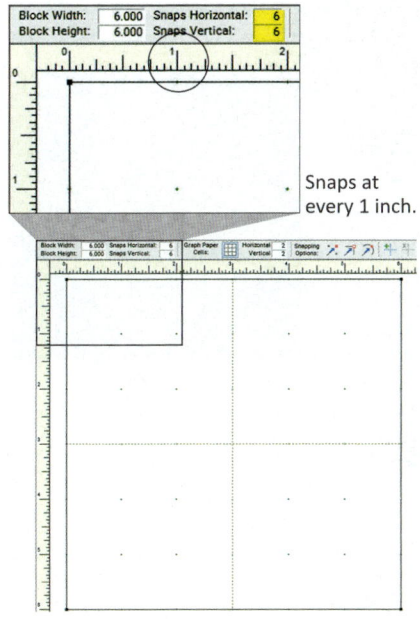

Snaps at every 1 inch.

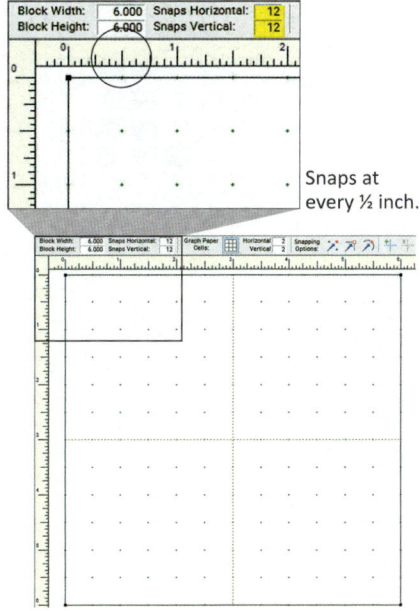

Snaps at every ½ inch.

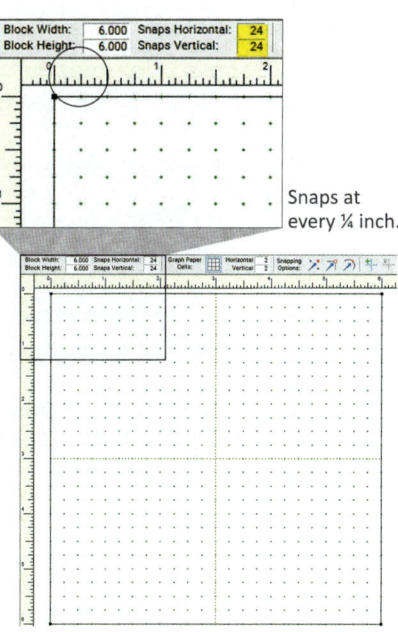

Snaps at every ¼ inch.

35

11. Click the **Line** tool and read the information in the palette.

EasyDraw Rule – All lines must connect with each other or to the edges of the block.

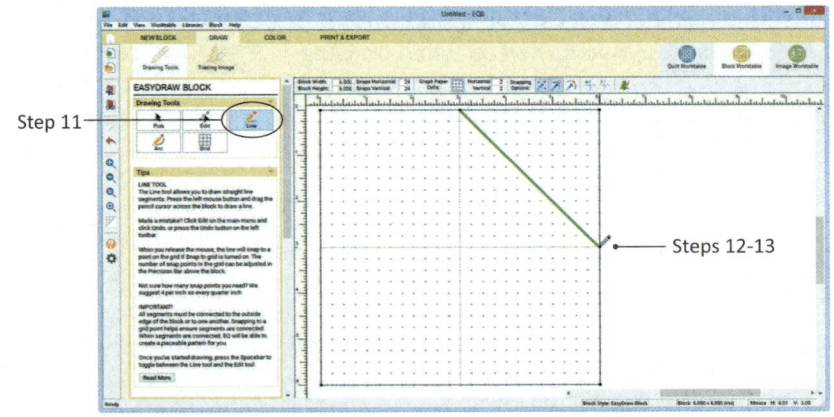
Step 11
Steps 12-13

12. To draw, position the cursor at the 3 inch mark at the center top of the block. Press and hold the left mouse button as you **drag diagonally to the middle of the right edge**. The graph paper lines help you find the middle.

13. Release the mouse button. The line will snap to the outer edge.

14. Starting at the same location, press, hold and **drag to the center bottom and release the mouse**.

15. Draw **two more lines** to create the Square in a Square.

If you make a mistake, click the Undo button. This will undo your most recent action.

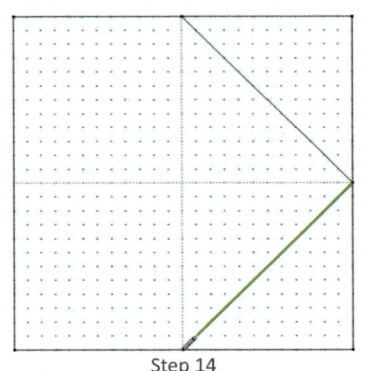
Step 14

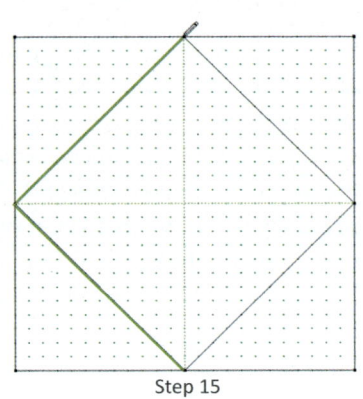
Step 15

16. Click the **COLOR** tab on the ribbon. Several of the Fabric Tools that you see here are the same as the Quilt Worktable's Fabric Tools.

17. Click the **Paintbrush** tool.

18. Click the **Colors** tab in the palette to change from fabrics to colors.

19. **Select a solid color** from the palette by clicking directly on the color swatch.

20. Click on the **center square** to fill it with the color.

21. Click on a **different color** in the palette.

22. Click on **each of the four corners** of the block to paint them with color.

23. Click **Add to Project Sketchbook** to add the current block on the worktable to your project.

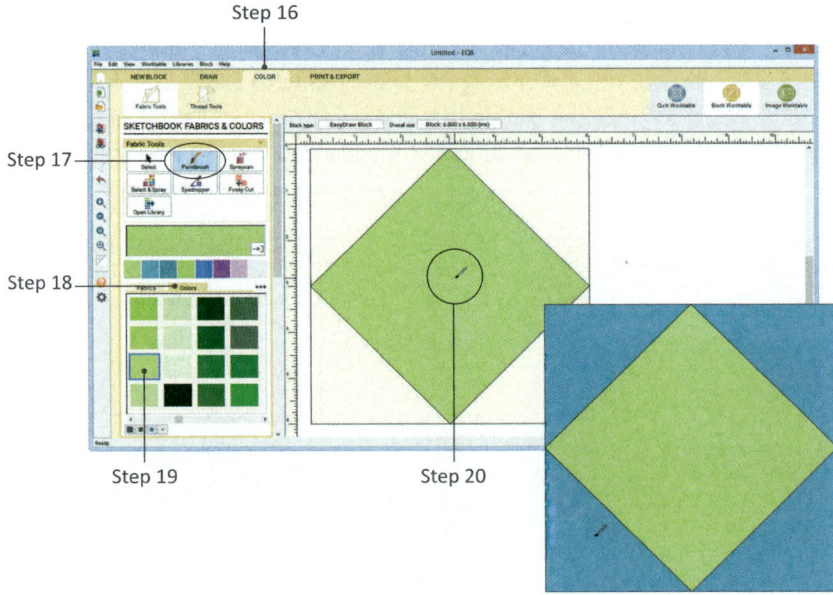
Step 16
Step 17
Step 18
Step 19
Step 20
Step 22

Step 23

Chapter 1: Learning the EQ8 Basics

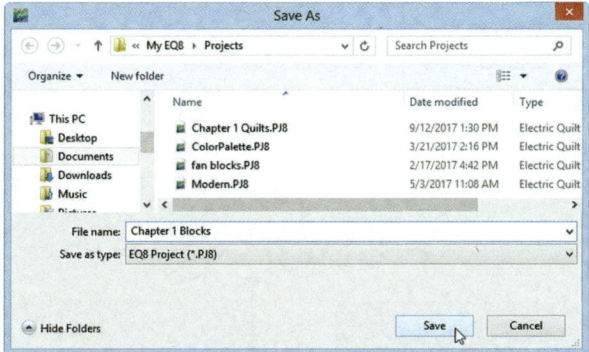

Steps 24-25

Step 26

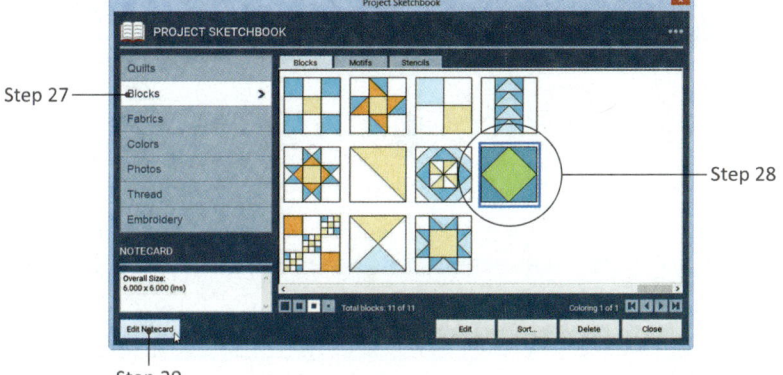

Step 27
Step 28
Step 29

Step 30   Step 31

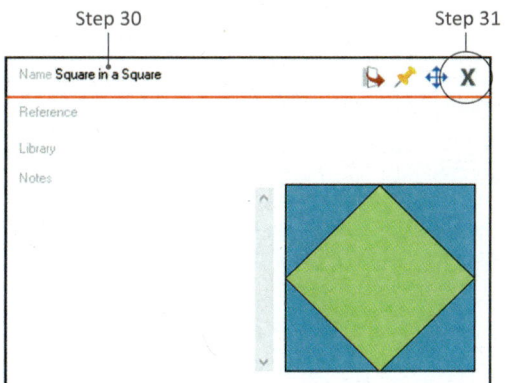

Naming the Project

Remember that whenever you click Add to Project Sketchbook the first time on a new project that is Untitled, you will see the Save As box. This allows you to name the project. The Save As box should be saving to **My EQ8\ Projects** location.

24. Type **Chapter 1 Blocks** in the File name box.

25. Click **Save**. The project has been named, and you may hear a sound indicating the block has been added to the Sketchbook.

Notice the project name now appears on the top title bar of the Window. Now that our project is named, every time that you click Add to Project Sketchbook, the Chapter 1 Blocks project automatically updates and saves. Let's look for the block in the Sketchbook.

26. Click **View Project Sketchbook**.

Naming a Block

27. Click **Blocks** to see the default blocks and the newly drawn block. Let's name the block.

28. Click directly on the block to select it.

29. Click the **Edit Notecard** button.

30. Type **Square in a Square** in the Name line.

31. Click the **X** to close the Notecard.

32. Click **Close** to close the Project Sketchbook.

37

EQ8 Lessons for Beginners

Let's continue to edit the drawing of this block instead of starting a new block.

33. Click the **DRAW** tab.

34. First, let's turn off the visibility of the Graph Paper Cells. We don't really need those now. Click the button on the Precision bar to **turn them off**.

35. With the Line tool, draw **two long diagonal lines** across the block like a large X.

36. Click the **COLOR** tab. The Paintbrush tool should still be selected.

37. Click on a **new color in the palette** and **recolor two squares** in the center.

38. Click a **different color** and **recolor 4 triangles in the outer corners** of the block. Keep using solid colors in the same family.

39. Click **Add to Project Sketchbook**.

Deleting Segments in a Drawing

40. Let's continue to edit. Click the **DRAW** tab.

41. Instead of drawing more lines, let's delete some lines. Click the **Pick** tool.

42. Click on one of the **diagonal lines** in the center of the large square of the block. Small squares will appear around the selected line to indicate that it's selected.

43. Click **Delete** in the palette. (You can also press the Delete key on the keyboard to delete.) The line will disappear.

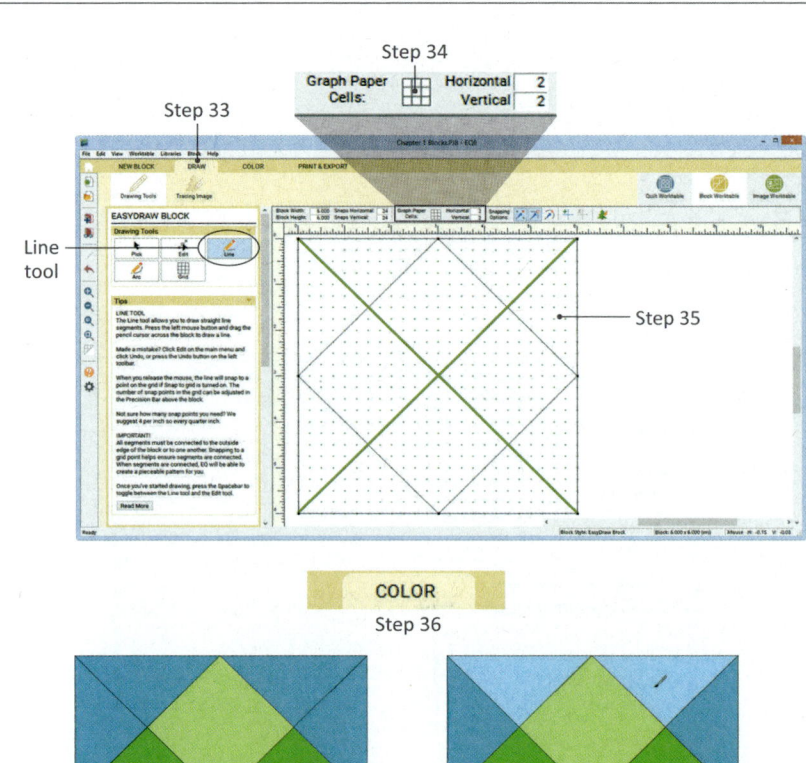

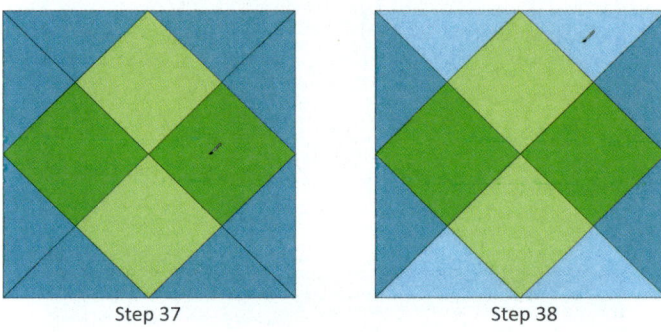

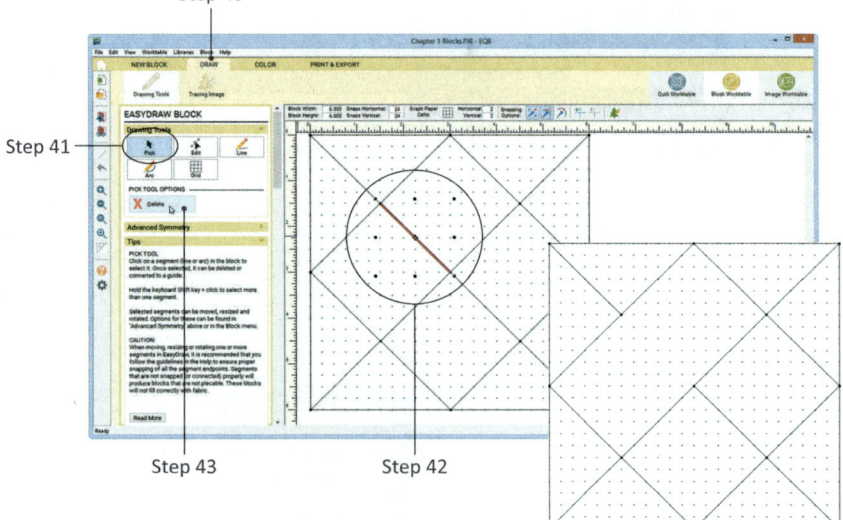

38

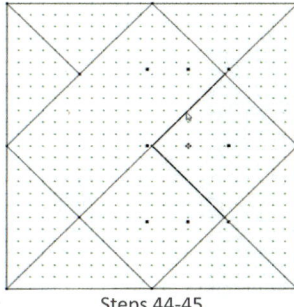
Steps 44-45
Hold SHIFT and click to select.

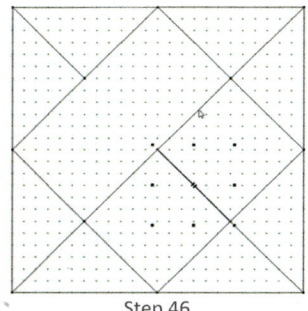
Step 46
Hold SHIFT and click to deselect.

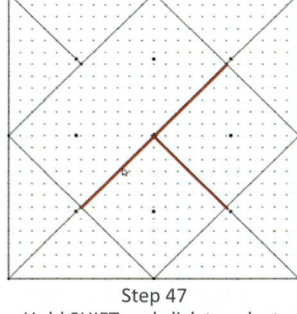
Step 47
Hold SHIFT and click to select.

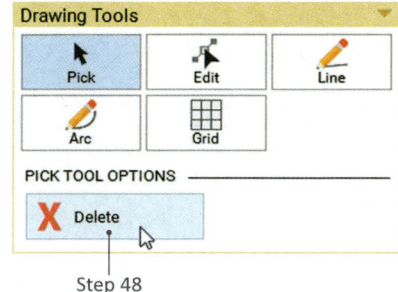
Step 48

44. Click on **another line** in the center square to select it.

45. Press and hold the **SHIFT** key and click on another line in the center square. The small squares will now surround both segments. This is how you multiple-select segments.

46. Without moving the cursor, **click the line again, still holding the SHIFT key**, to deselect it.

47. Again, without moving the cursor and continuing to hold the **SHIFT** key, click on the line and then on the final line in the center square.

48. Click **Delete** in the palette. Our center square is solid again. We have another new drawing. Let's go color it.

49. Click the **COLOR** tab.

50. If you want to recolor the block, you can. If you make a mistake in your coloring, click the Undo button. If you're happy with the coloring, click **Add to Project Sketchbook**.

51. Click the **DRAW** tab.

52. Click the **Line** tool.

53. Draw a **small square inside the larger square** snapping to the nodes of the diagonal lines.

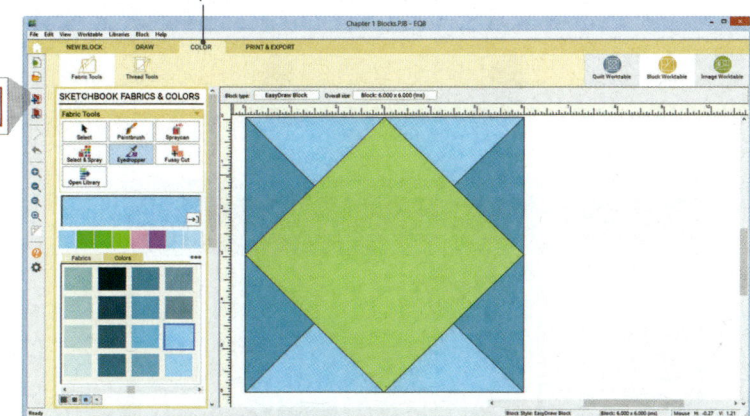
Step 49 / Step 50

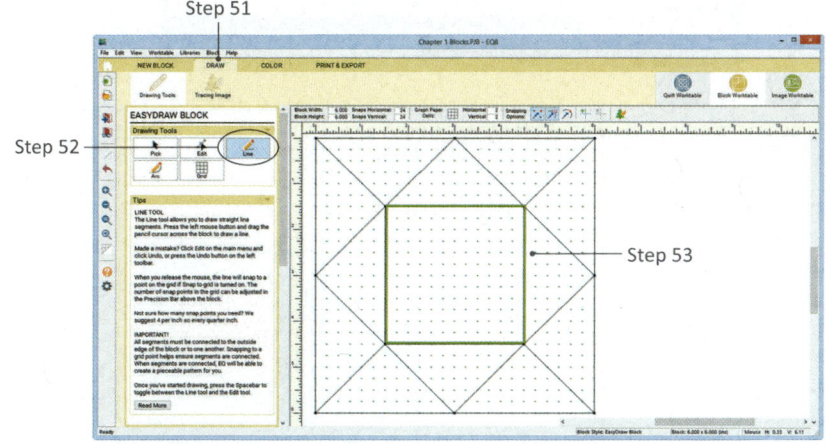
Step 51 / Step 52 / Step 53

54. Click the **COLOR** tab.

55. With the **Paintbrush** tool, recolor the small square in the center and any other patches that you want.

56. Click **Add to Project Sketchbook**.

57. Let's do one more edit of this drawing. Click the **DRAW** tab.

58. Click the **Pick** tool.

59. **Delete the lines that connect the large square with the four corners of the block**. You can delete them one at a time or multiple-select and delete them all at once.

60. Click the **COLOR** tab.

61. Recolor as desired using the **Paintbrush** tool. You will find the most recently used colors just above the swatches in the palette. You can click directly on one of those to find a color.

62. When you are happy with your coloring, click **Add to Project Sketchbook**.

63. Click **View Project Sketchbook**.

64. Click **Blocks**. You may need to scroll or change the display to see all the newly drawn blocks. Each one will have one coloring. Only the first block is named with the Notecard.

65. If you like, use the **Edit Notecard** button on each block and name them Square in a Square Variation 1, 2 and so on.

66. Click **Close** to close the Project Sketchbook.

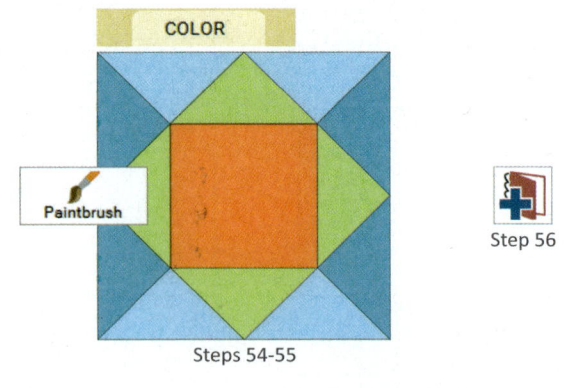

Steps 54-55

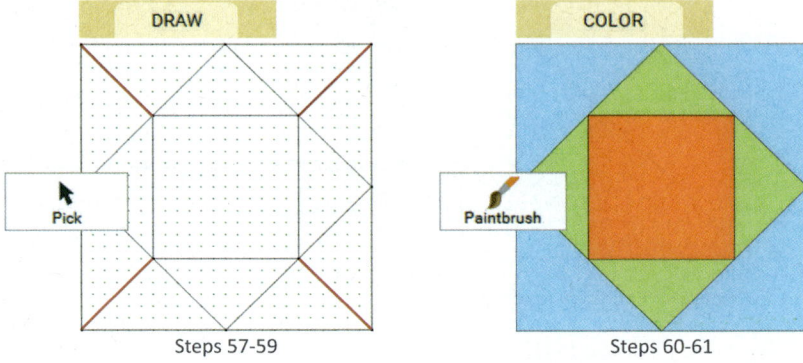

Steps 57-59   Steps 60-61

Step 62   Step 63

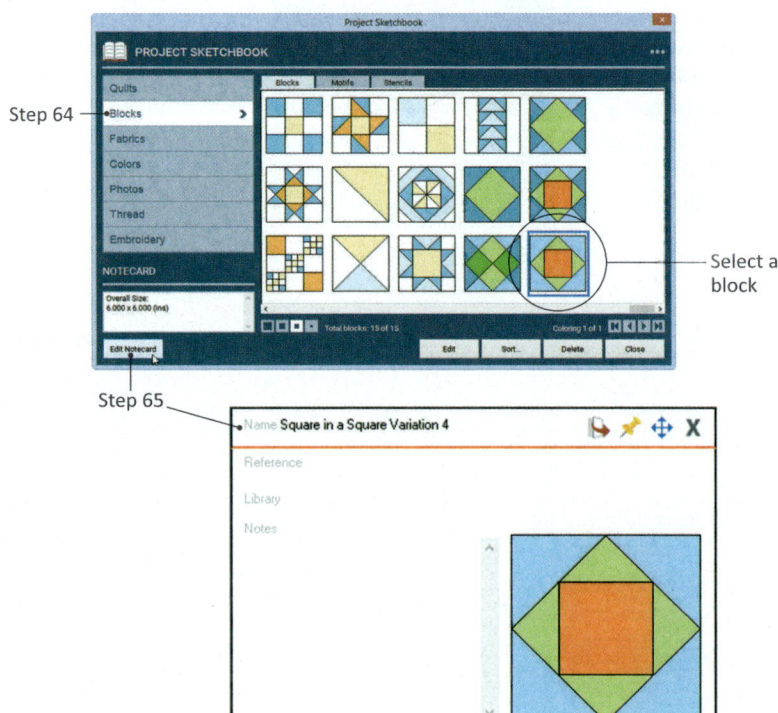

Chapter 1: Learning the EQ8 Basics

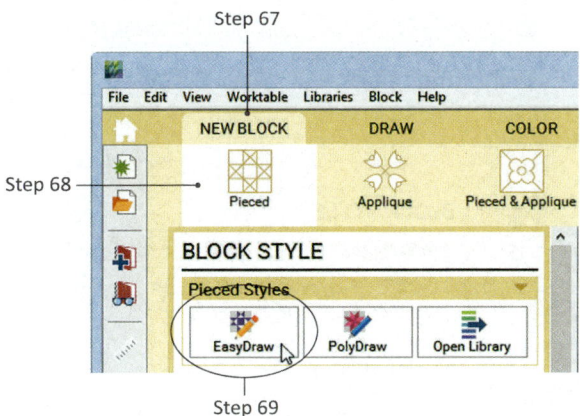

Step 67
Step 68
Step 69

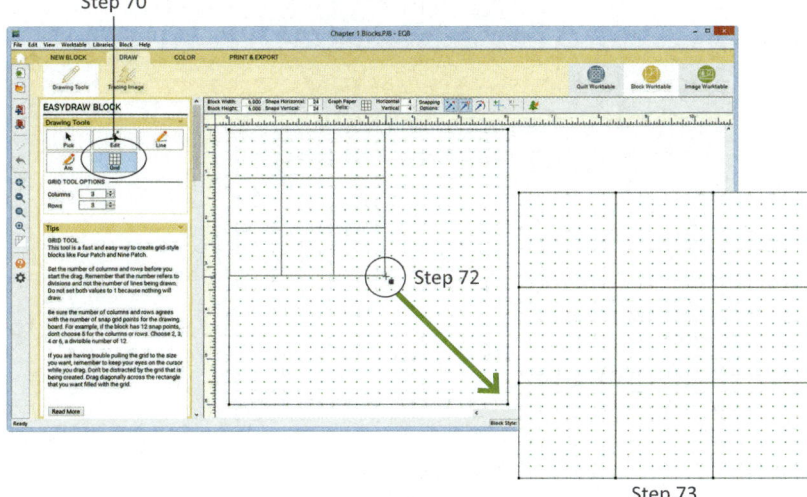

Step 70
Step 72
Step 73

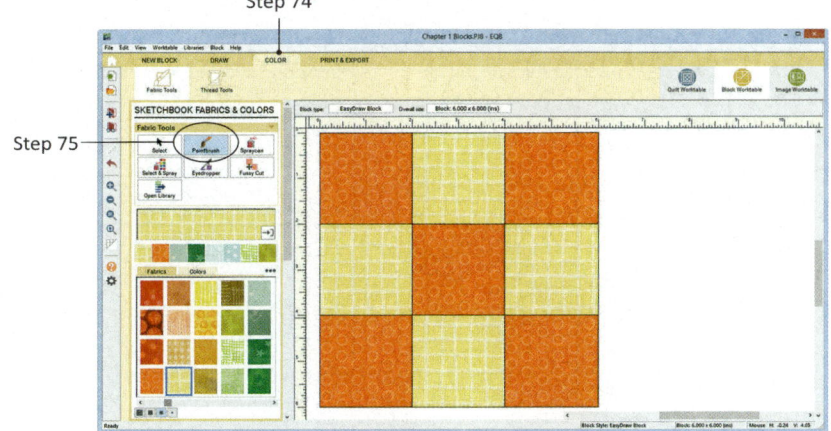

Step 74
Step 75

Step 76

Drawing a Nine Patch

Let's start a new block.

67. Click the **NEW BLOCK** tab.

68. Click **Pieced** on the ribbon.

69. Click **EasyDraw**. Now we are back on the drawing board with an empty block.

70. Click the **Grid** tool in the palette. The Columns and Rows should be set to 3. If they are not, click the arrows to adjust the entries.

71. Position the crosshair of the cursor at the upper-left corner of the block.

72. Press and hold the left mouse button as you **drag the cursor to the lower-right corner** of the block. A grid will draw as you drag. Be sure to keep your eyes on the cursor so you don't get too distracted by the drawing grid.

73. Make sure the crosshair of the cursor is over the lower-right corner of the block and release the mouse button. The lines will snap into place. If you released the mouse button too soon, click the Undo button and try again. That's a fast way to create a nine patch block!

The Grid tool draws multiple lines at once. Don't confuse Grid tool lines and Graph Paper lines. Graph paper lines are guides for tracing over. The Grid tool draws lines that become part of the block drawing.

74. Click the **COLOR** tab.

75. Use the **Paintbrush** to color the nine squares in any way you like.

76. Click **Add to Project Sketchbook**.

41

Drawing A Drunkard's Path Block

Now let's use the Arc tool to draw a Drunkard's Path block.

77. Click the **NEW BLOCK** tab.

78. Click **Pieced** on the ribbon and **EasyDraw** in the palette.

79. Click the **Graph Paper Cells** button to turn on the graph paper.

80. Double-click in the Horizontal box to **highlight the number**.

81. Type **6**.

82. Press the **Tab** key on your keyboard. This will highlight the number in the Vertical box.

83. Type **6** and press the **Enter** key on your keyboard. The graph paper shows 36 small squares in our block.

84. Click the **Line** tool.

85. Find the 3-inch mark on the horizontal ruler and **draw a line from the top to the bottom** of the block.

86. Find the 3-inch mark on the vertical ruler and **draw a line across the middle** of the block.

We've created a four patch block. When you look at each of the four squares, you see the graph paper creates a nine patch inside each patch. To create a Drunkard's Path block, we want to draw an arc inside of each of the four patches using the graph paper to guide us.

87. Click the **Arc** tool in the palette.

The Arc tool will draw a perfect quarter-circle as you drag. While you are dragging the arc, you can press the keyboard's **Spacebar** to flip the arc to the opposite direction.

88. Position the cursor at the one-inch mark of the top ruler. Press, hold and **drag downward** to the 3-inch mark horizontally and the 2-inch mark vertically.

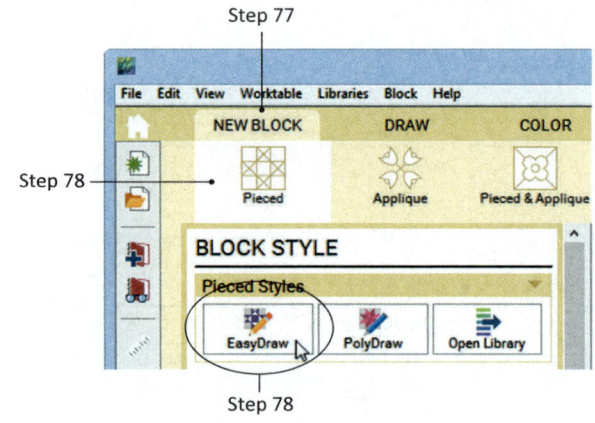
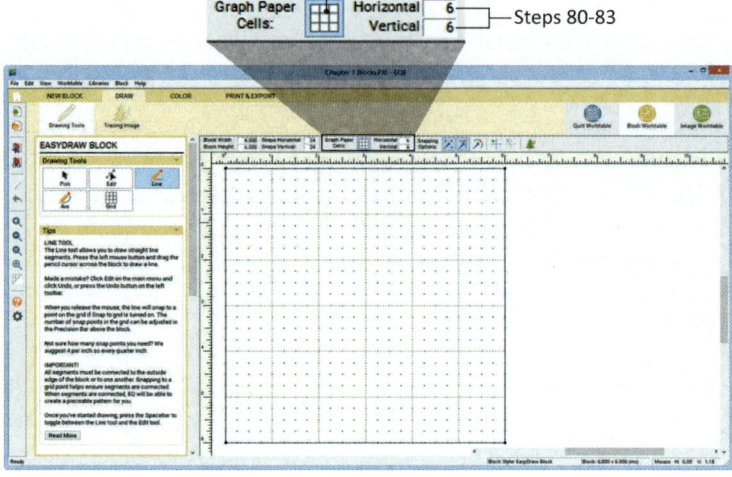
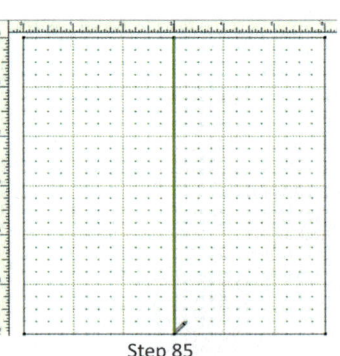
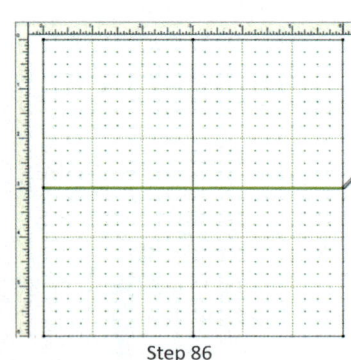
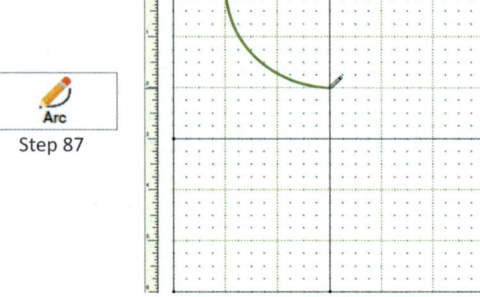

42

Chapter 1: Learning the EQ8 Basics

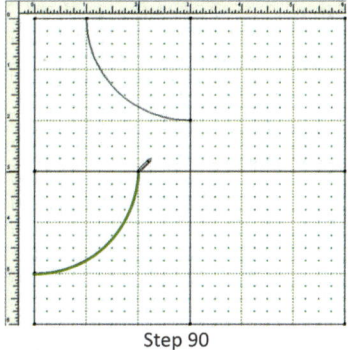
Step 90

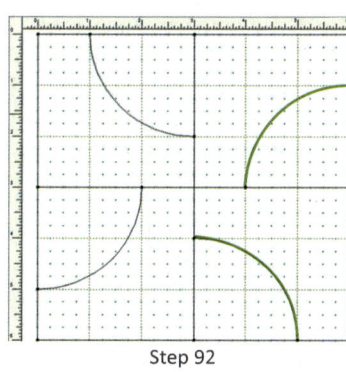
Step 92

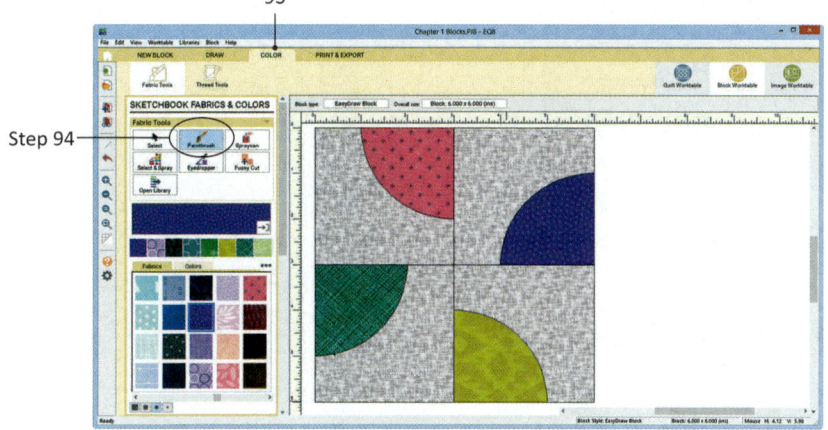

Step 95

A few of the EasyDraw blocks drawn in this lesson.

89. Release the mouse to snap the arc to the node.

90. Position the cursor at the 5-inch mark along the left edge of the block. Press, hold and **drag upward** to the 3-inch vertical and 2-inch horizontal mark.

91. Release the mouse button to snap the end of the arc to the node.

92. Continue to **draw arcs** in the other two sections of the block as illustrated. Remember to press the **Spacebar** if you need to flip the direction of the arc.

93. Click the **COLOR** tab.

94. Use the **Paintbrush** tool to color the block.

95. Click **Add to Project Sketchbook**.

You now have the background for drawing EasyDraw blocks. The most important thing to remember about EasyDraw is that you must **make your lines and arcs touch one another AND the outside edge of the block**. The best way to achieve this is to keep the snapping turned on.

Coffee Break!

Whew! It's definitely time for a break. We packed a lot of information into this first part about pieced blocks. Next we'll learn how to draw applique.

If you want to continue on, jump to step 1 on the next page.

If you need to put EQ8 away for now, simply choose File > Exit. Your project is already saved and can be opened up again later to continue the lesson.

DRAWING AN APPLIQUE BLOCK

If you closed EQ8 after the last section, you'll need to open it again to get started with this next section of Chapter 1.

On the Home screen, click **Open an existing project**, choose **Chapter 1 Blocks**, then click **OK**. Click the **Close** button to close the Sketchbook. The title bar at the top will say Chapter 1 Blocks.PJ8. Click the **Block Worktable** button on the top-right.

Let's make a very simple applique block next.

1. Click the **NEW BLOCK** tab.

2. Click **Applique** on the ribbon. Take a minute to read the information in the palette about the difference between an applique block and an applique motif.

3. Click **Motif** in the palette.

4. Click the **Shapes** tool.

5. Under PATCHMAKER SHAPES, click **PosieMaker**. The PosieMaker dialog appears.

6. There are many options to play with here, but for now, click the **first Auto Shape** button in the lower-left.

7. Click **OK**.

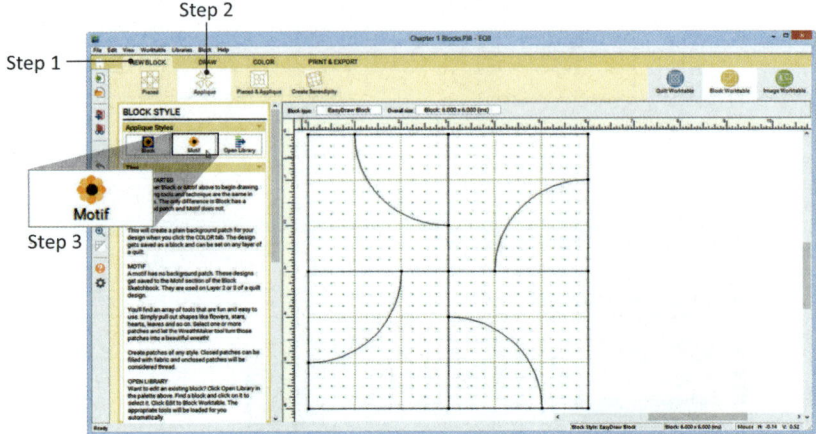

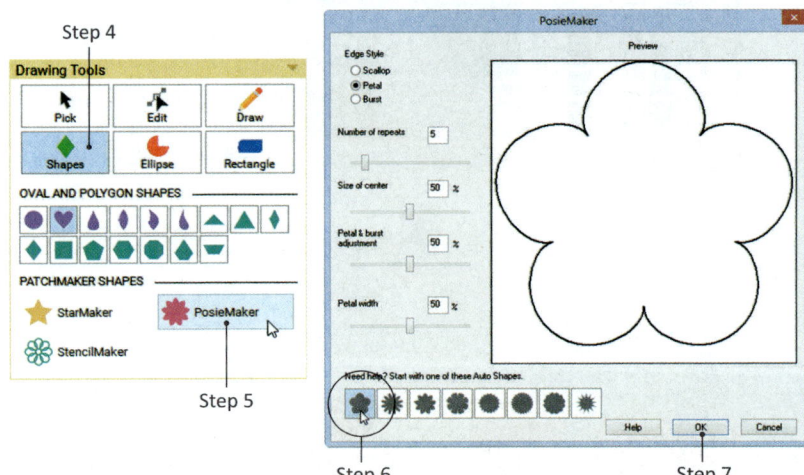

The patch is created automatically for us and appears in the upper-left corner of the block.

8. Click the **Pick** tool.

9. Click **Center in Block** in the palette.

10. Click **Resize** in the palette.

> **Note:** You may need to use the palette's scrollbar to see the Resize button.

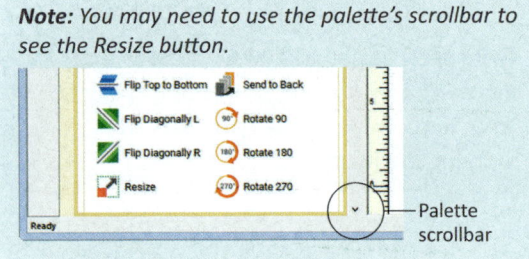

11. Drag the sliders to **300** for both Horizontal and Vertical.

12. Click **OK**. Now our patch fills the block.

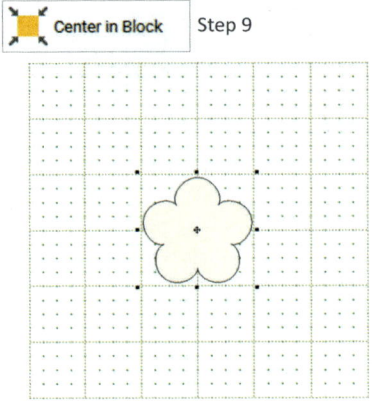

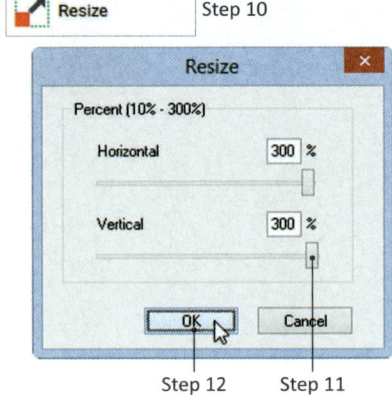

44

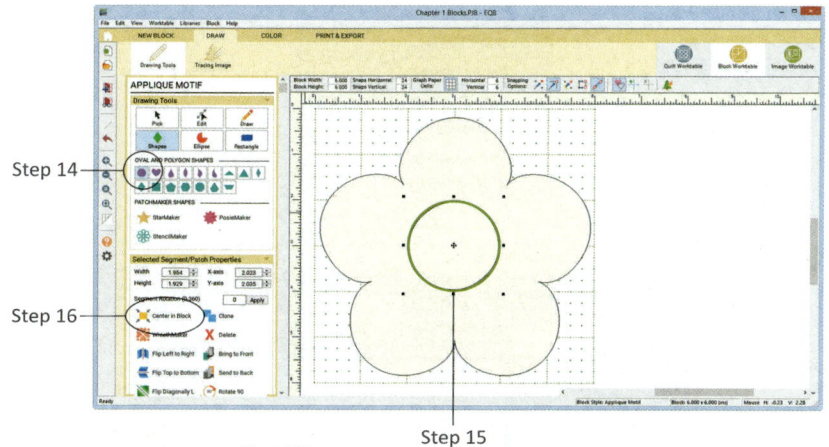

Step 14
Step 16
Step 17
Step 15

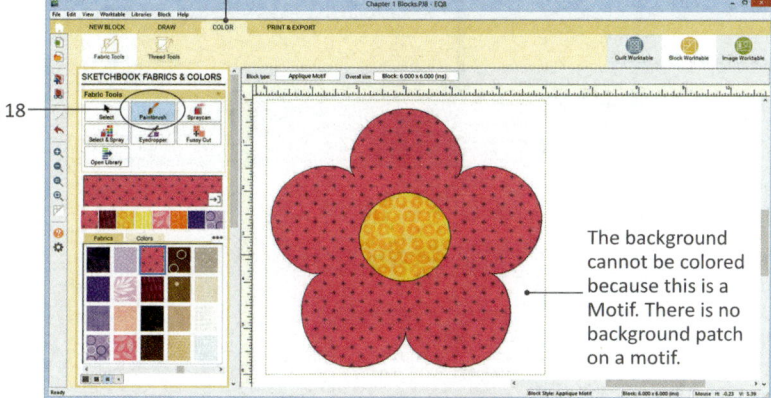

Step 18

The background cannot be colored because this is a Motif. There is no background patch on a motif.

Step 19   Step 20

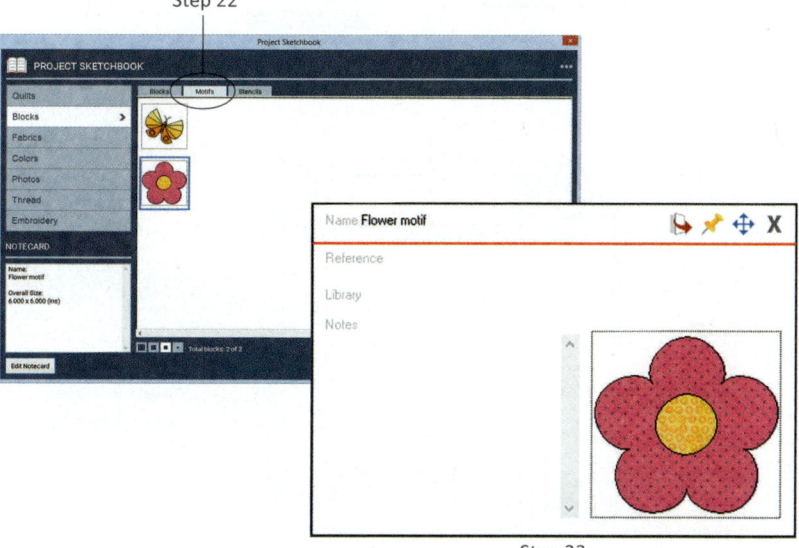

Step 22

Step 23

13. Click the **Shapes** tool in the palette.

14. Click the **small purple circle** in the palette under OVAL AND POLYGON SHAPES.

15. Position the mouse cursor over the posie-shaped patch on the worktable. **Press the left mouse button and drag in any direction**. As you drag the mouse, a circle will display and be drawn for you. The size and position of the circle will be determined by the length and direction that you drag the cursor. If you don't like the size or position, click the Undo button and try again.

16. While the patch is still selected, click **Center in Block** in the palette.

17. Click the **COLOR** tab.

18. Use the **Paintbrush** tool to color the applique flower. Be aware that you cannot color the background of this motif.

19. Click **Add to Project Sketchbook**.

Let's look at our new collection of blocks.

20. Click **View Project Sketchbook**. We should still be on the Blocks section of the Sketchbook.

21. Scroll to the end to see the blocks. We don't see our applique motif.

22. Click the **Motifs** tab. Motifs will automatically save to this tab.

23. If you want to name the motif, click on the motif and then click **Edit Notecard**.

24. Click **Close**.

USING THE BLOCK LIBRARY

Creating a Custom Block Library

These blocks are in our project. Our project name is **Chapter 1 Blocks**. But what if you want to start a new project and use these blocks? A good way to make the blocks available for any project is to create your own library of blocks. Let's do it.

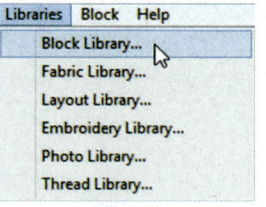

Step 25

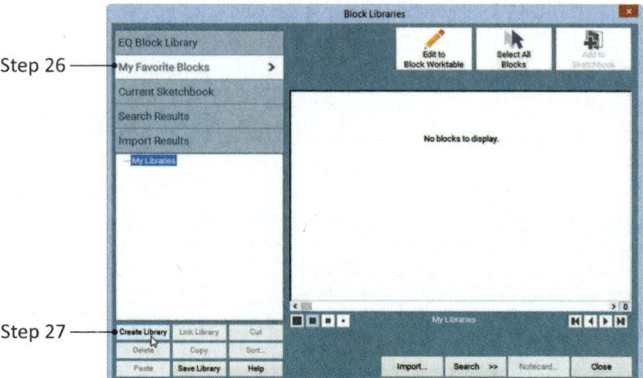

25. Click **Libraries > Block Library** on the main menu. This is the same library that we used during Lesson 1. It's available from any worktable.

26. Click **My Favorite Blocks**.

27. Click **Create Library**. The Add New Library dialog box will display.

28. Type **Lesson Blocks**. We'll leave the number of styles set to 10.

29. Click **OK**.

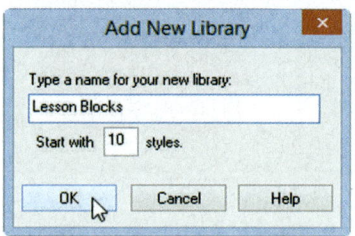

Steps 28-29

30. Now you will see My Custom Libraries. Click the **+ sign** in front of My Custom Libraries.

31. Click the **+ sign** in front of Lesson Blocks. We see the 10 Styles listed where we can add blocks.

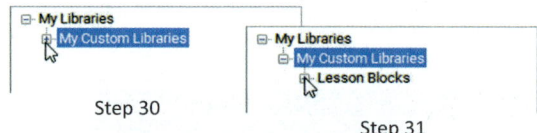

Step 30 Step 31

32. Click the name **Style 1** to highlight it. You will see "No blocks to display" until we add blocks.

33. Right-click on the style name and choose **Modify Style** from the context menu. The Style Name dialog box will appear.

34. Type **EasyDraw** and click **OK**.

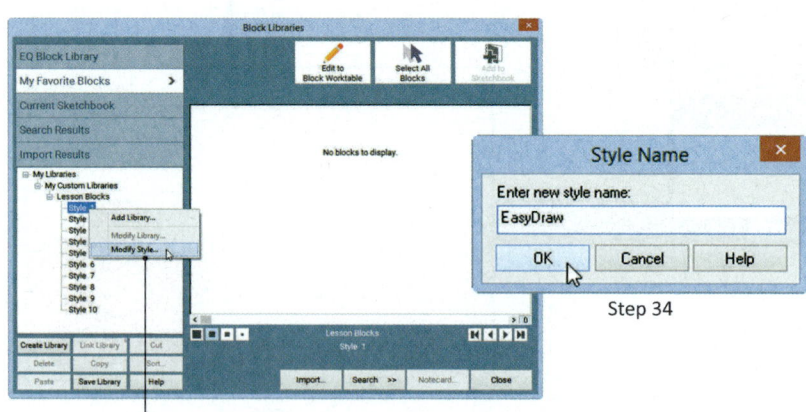

Step 33

Chapter 1: Learning the EQ8 Basics

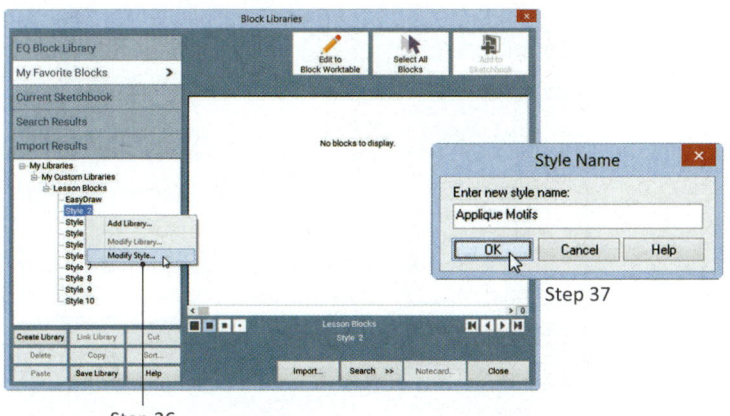

Step 37

Step 36

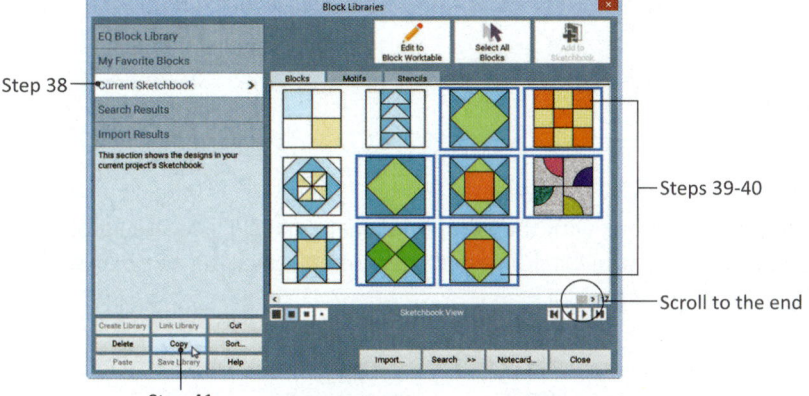

Steps 39-40

Scroll to the end

Step 41

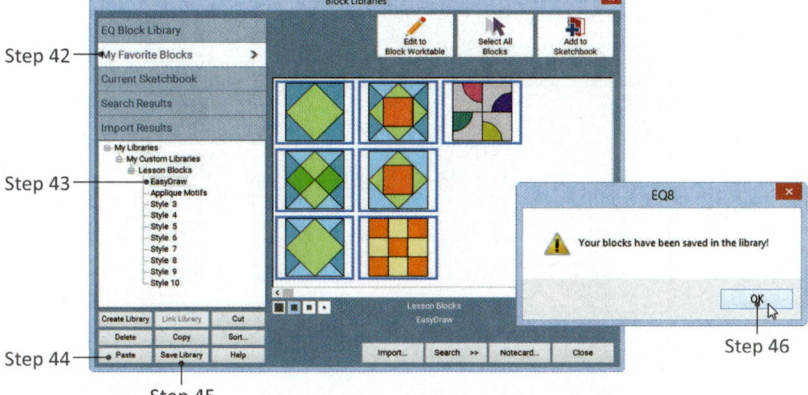

Step 42

Step 43

Step 44

Step 45

Step 46

Step 48

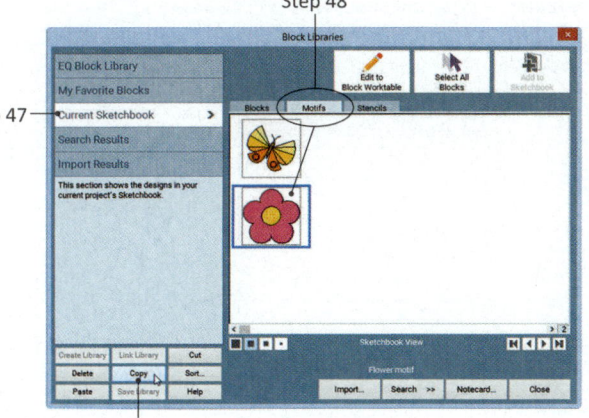

Step 47

Step 49

35. Click the name **Style 2** to highlight it.

36. Right-click on the style name and choose **Modify Style** from the context menu.

37. Type **Applique Motifs** and click **OK**.

The new library is created. Now we need to copy the blocks from the Sketchbook and paste them in the library.

38. Click **Current Sketchbook**. Scroll to the end or change the display so that you can see all the newly drawn blocks.

39. Click the first **Square in a Square** block that we drew.

40. Press and hold the **SHIFT** key and click on the **last block** in the Sketchbook. This will multi-select all the blocks in between.

41. Click the **Copy** button.

42. Click **My Favorite Blocks**.

43. Click the style name **EasyDraw**.

44. Click **Paste**. The blocks will appear.

45. Click **Save Library**. You'll see a message that your blocks have been saved in the library.

46. Click **OK**.

47. Click **Current Sketchbook**.

48. Click the **Motifs** tab and click directly on the **applique flower**. You might see a butterfly motif in here too. This is a design that's part of the default project.

49. Click the **Copy** button.

47

EQ8 Lessons for Beginners

50. Click **My Favorite Blocks**.

51. Click the style name **Applique Motifs**.

52. Click **Paste**. The motif will appear.

53. Click **Save Library**. You'll see a message that your blocks have been saved in the library.

54. Click **OK**.

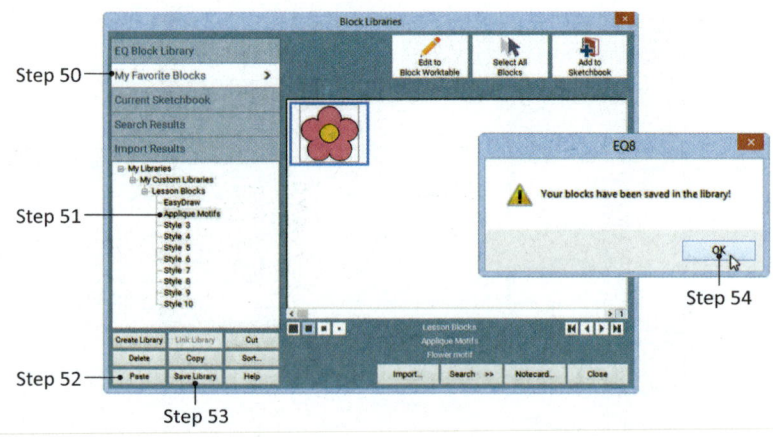

Creating a custom library is a great way to give you easy access to the blocks you've drawn or a place to store your favorite blocks. You can rename the libraries or the styles by clicking on the name you want to modify and using the right-click context menu.

Editing Blocks from the Library

When you draw your own blocks, you decide the size for the block along with the number of snap points. If you are editing an existing block, this work has been done for you. EQ will remember the block size and snap points. Let's edit some existing blocks from the library to see how the worktable changes when editing a block.

55. While still in the Block Library, click **EQ Block Library**.

56. Find the first block in **01 Classic Pieced > Compasses** and click on it to select it. If you float the cursor over it, you'll see its name is **Mariner's Star**.

57. Click the **Edit to Block Worktable** button.

58. Click the **Graph Paper** button to hide the graph paper.

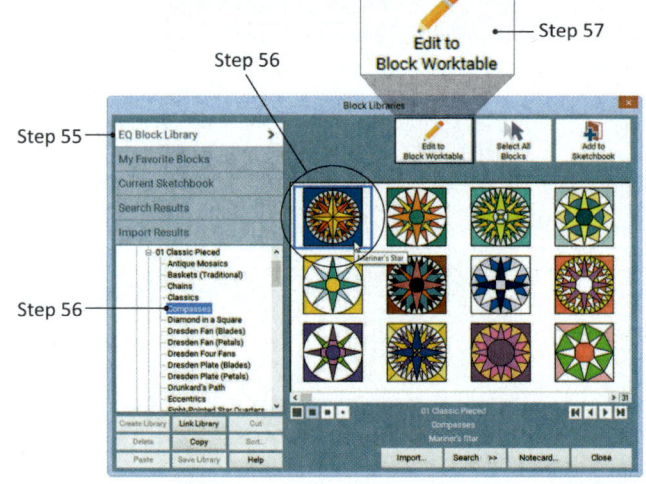

We can see from the palette that this is an EasyDraw block. We can see from the Precision Bar that it is 12 inches with 48 snap points. You can, if you like, change the block size and snap points, but you'll want to keep the new sizes a multiple of this size. This block was originally drawn using both straight lines and arcs. Do you wonder how this was done?

59. Click the **Edit** tool in the palette.

The Edit tool in EasyDraw lets you place nodes, using Partition and Stagger, on existing lines and arcs so that you can draw beautiful blocks like this one.

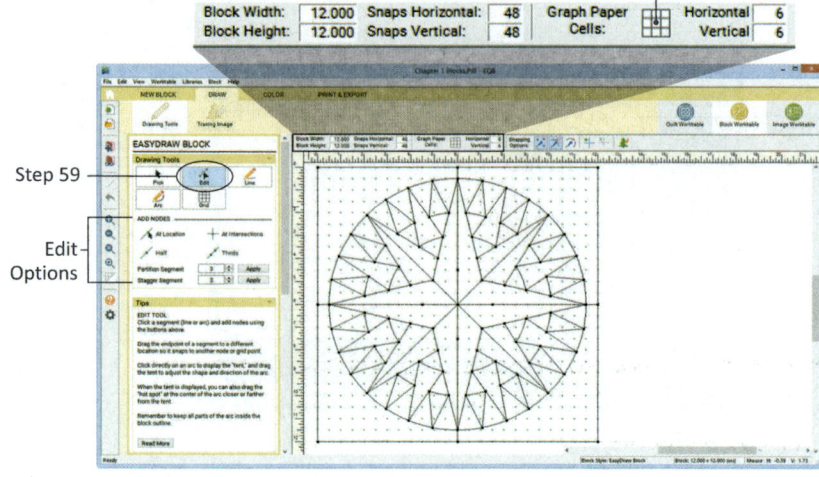

48

Chapter 1: Learning the EQ8 Basics

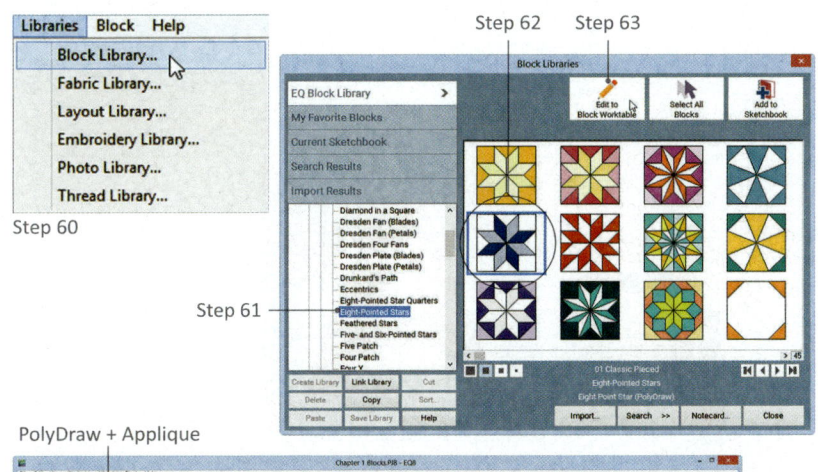

Step 60 / Step 61 / Step 62 / Step 63 / PolyDraw + Applique

60. Click **Libraries > Block Library**.

61. Scroll down the list to find **01 Classic Pieced > Eight-Pointed Stars**.

62. Click on the second block named **Eight Point Star (PolyDraw)**.

63. Click the **Edit to Block Worktable** button.

We can see from the palette that this is a PolyDraw + Applique block. There is only a pieced layer to this block – no applique. The pieced layer was drawn with the PolyDraw tools, not the EasyDraw tools. We'll learn about the PolyDraw tools in a future lesson.

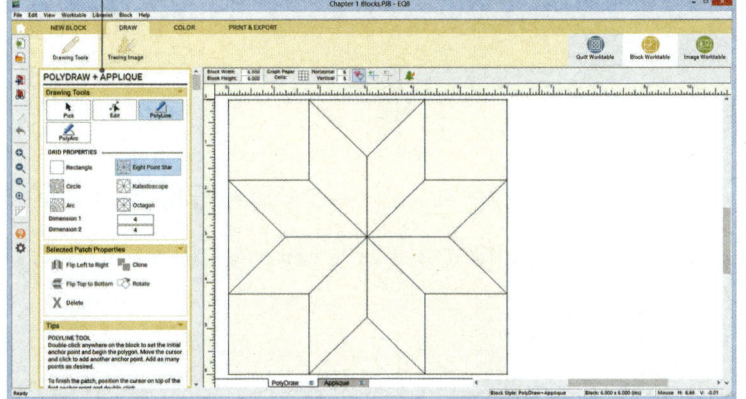

Step 64 / Step 65 / Step 66 / Step 67

64. Click **Libraries > Block Library**.

65. Scroll down the list to find **08 Overlaid**. Click the **+ sign** to open the Overlaid blocks.

66. Click **Embellished Alphabet** and click on the first block – A.

67. Click the **Edit to Block Worktable** button.

We can see from the palette that this is an EasyDraw + Applique block. The pieced layer of this block has been drawn with the EasyDraw tools.

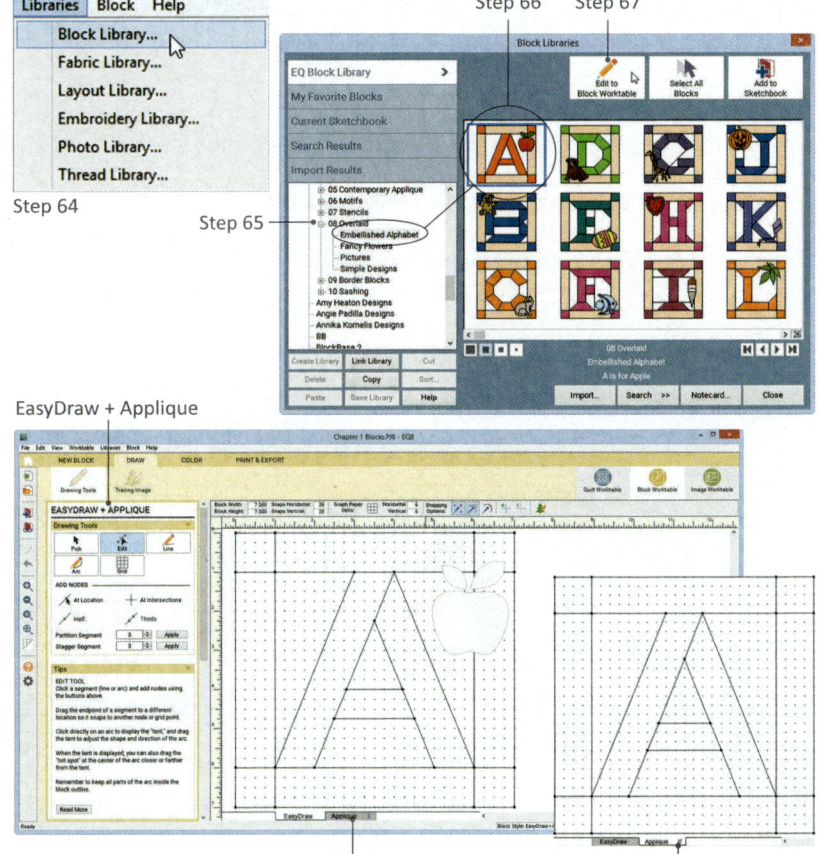

EasyDraw + Applique / Step 68 / Step 69

68. Click the **Applique** tab along the bottom of the block. Notice the small eye icon on the tab.

69. Click directly on the **eye** icon. This turns off the elements on the applique layer of the worktable. You'll find this useful when editing the pieced layer.

70. Click the **eye** icon again to turn on the visibility of the applique layer.

49

EQ8 Lessons for Beginners

71. Click the **COLOR** tab to see the colored version of our block.

72. Click the **Paintbrush** tool in the palette and click the **Fabrics** tab to display the default fabrics.

73. Recolor the block using any of the default fabrics. When coloring, there is no need to worry about layers. Recolor every patch in the block. Remember that you can use the Undo button or simply color over an existing color.

74. When you're happy with the coloring, click **Add to Project Sketchbook**.

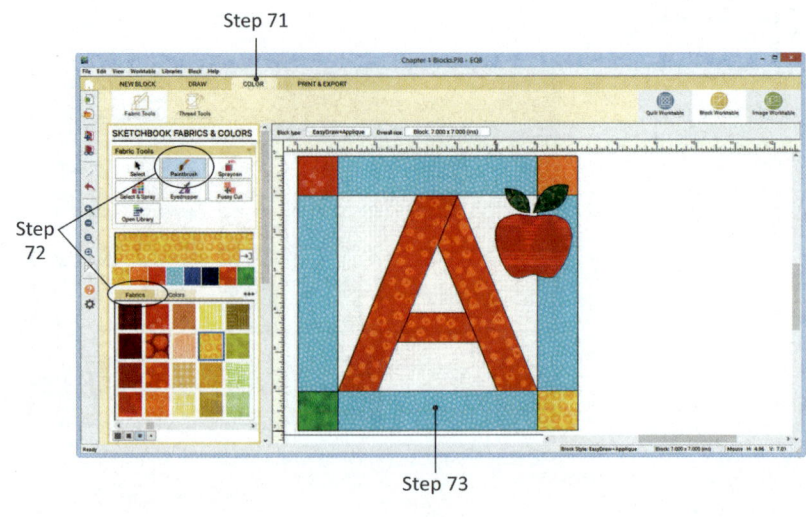

Step 71

Step 72

Step 73

Step 74

> **Coffee Break!**
>
> Break time! It's up to you whether you keep on truckin' or rest your eyes for a bit. Next we'll print patterns from the Block Worktable.
>
> If you want to continue on, jump to step 1 below.
>
> If you need to put EQ8 away for now, simply choose File > Exit. Your project is already saved and can be opened up again later to continue the lesson.

PRINTING PATTERNS

If you closed EQ8 after the last section, you'll need to open it again to get started with this next section of Chapter 1.

On the Home screen, click **Open an existing project**, choose **Chapter 1 Blocks** from the list, then click **OK**.

In the Sketchbook, click **Blocks**, then scroll to the end of the list to find your recolored **embellished A block**. Select it and choose **Edit** at the bottom of the Sketchbook.

Printing a Block

1. Click the **PRINT & EXPORT** tab.

2. Click **Print** in the ribbon.

3. Click the **Block** tool in the palette. The Print Block dialog box displays.

Just like the Quilt Worktable, when you print from the Block Worktable, the size of the block is automatically set for you. We'll leave the size at 7 x 7. To change the size, you would click Custom block size and type in new sizes.

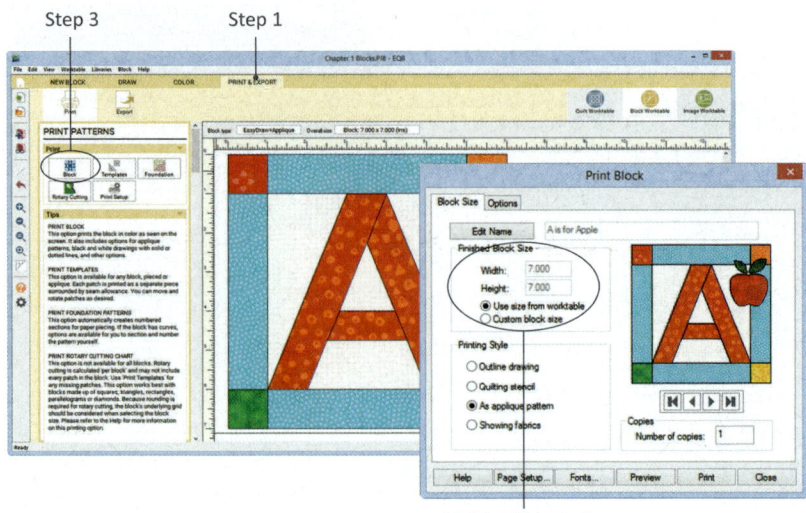

Step 3

Step 1

Finished block size

Chapter 1: Learning the EQ8 Basics

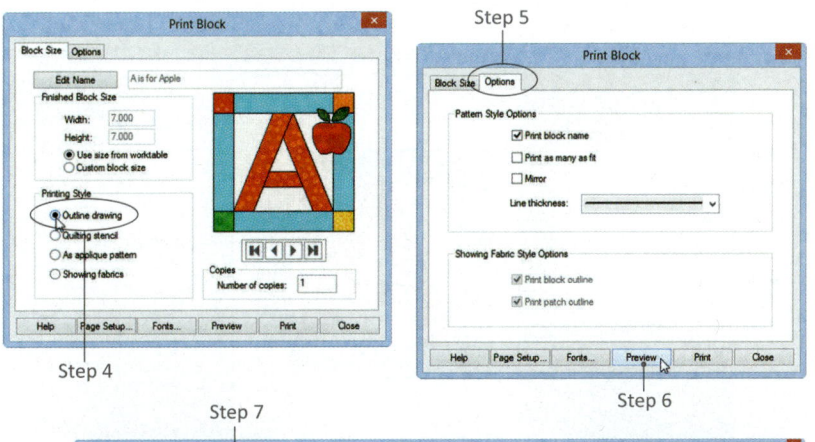

Step 5
Step 4

4. In Printing Style, click **Outline drawing**.

5. Click the **Options** tab at the top of the box. There are several options here. We won't make any changes.

6. Click **Preview**.

Step 6

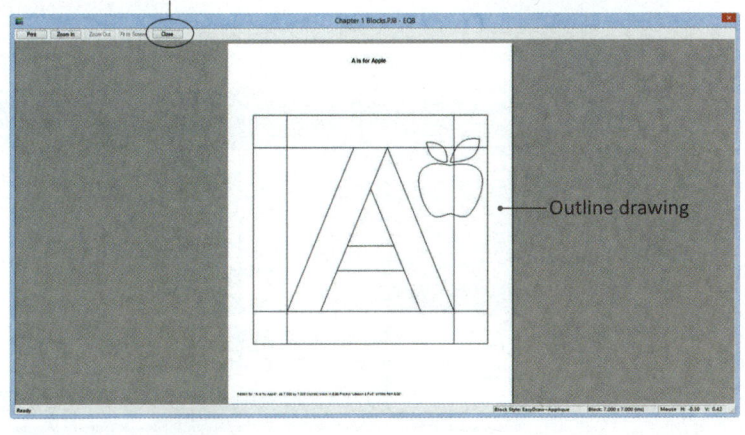

Step 7

When Outline drawing is selected, each patch is empty. We can see through the apple and leaves to the pieced part of the block below.

7. Click **Close**.

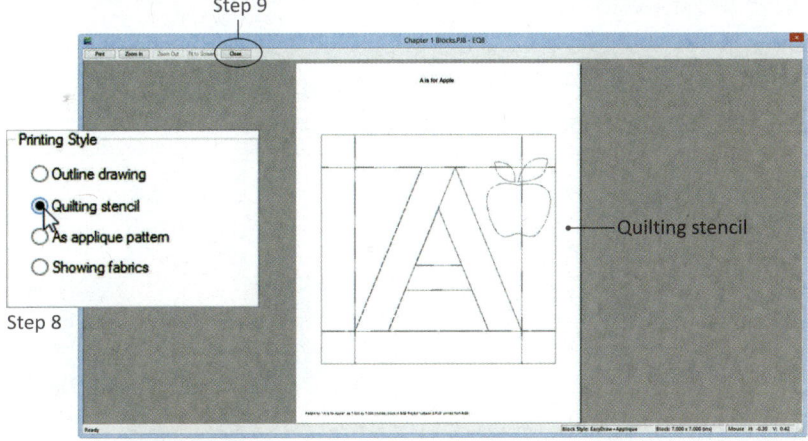

Step 9

Step 8

8. In Printing Style, click **Quilting stencil**, and click **Preview**.

This preview may not look much different, but when you print, the lines will be dashed like they have been stitched.

9. Click **Close**.

Step 11

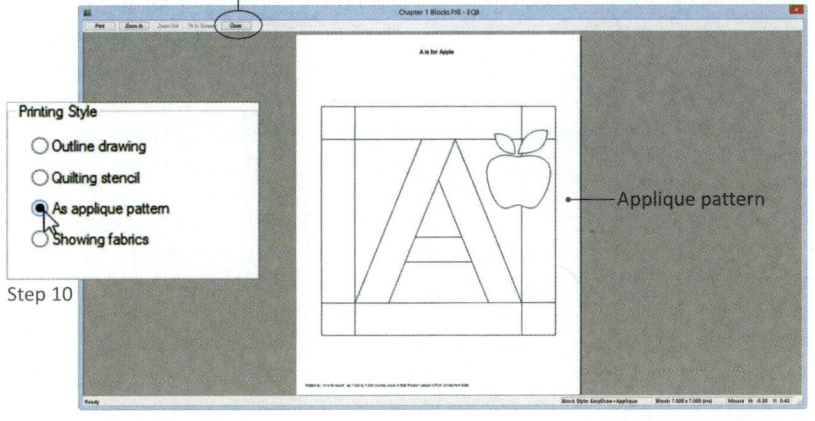

Step 10

10. In Printing Style, click **As Applique pattern**, and click **Preview**.

The patches here are filled. This type of pattern is useful for placement of applique patches.

11. Click **Close**.

EQ8 Lessons for Beginners

12. In Printing Style, click **Showing fabrics**, and click **Preview**.

13. Click **Print**.

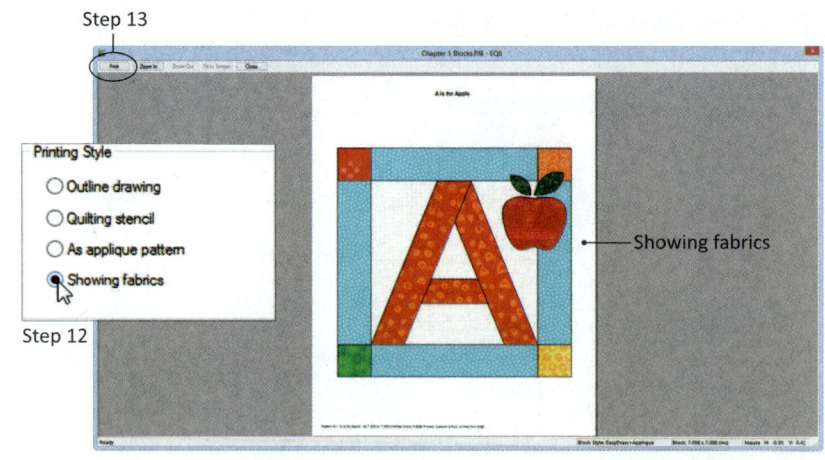

We've edited pre-drawn blocks directly from the library. We edit blocks from the Sketchbook in the same way.

14. Click **View Project Sketchbook**.

15. If you're still seeing the applique motif, click the **Blocks** tab along the top.

We see the blocks that we edited from the library have been automatically added to our project. Library blocks have two colorings by default. When we recolored the A block, it created a new block with 1 coloring.

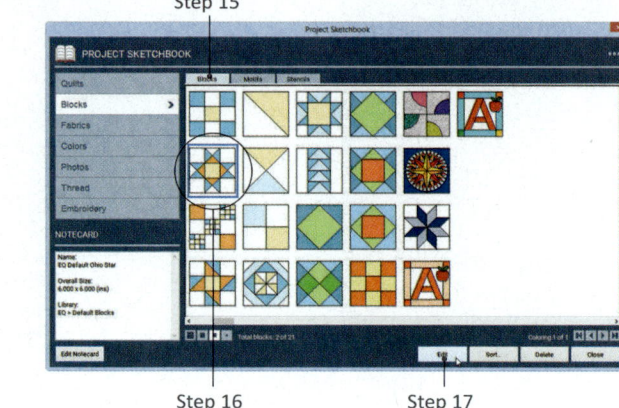

16. Click on the **EQ Default Ohio Star** block to select it.

17. Click the **Edit** button or double-click directly on the block to edit it back to the worktable DRAW tab. Notice that our settings go back to a 6 inch block with 24 snap points.

18. Click the **COLOR** tab to see the colored version of the block.

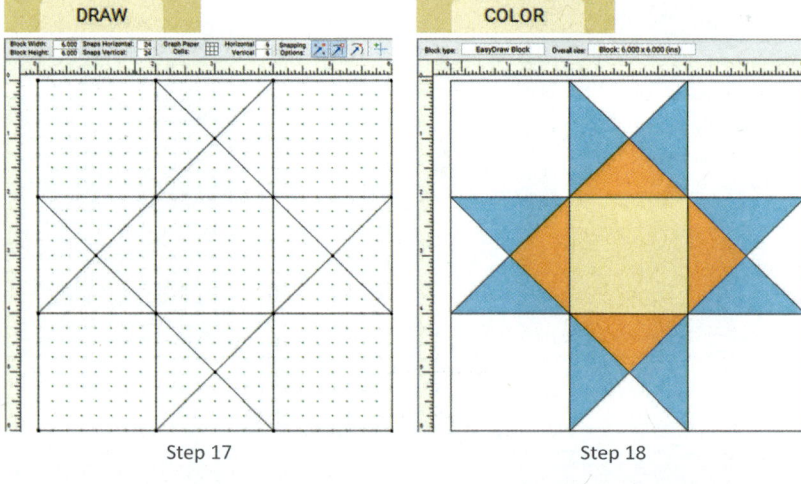

Printing Rotary Cutting Charts

19. Click the **PRINT & EXPORT** tab.

20. Click **Rotary Cutting** in the palette.

Rotary rulers show 1/8 markings. Block patterns printed from your computer can be any size so rounding (to get to a 1/8 increment) is unavoidable. Having several options for checking the "amount" of rounding for the pattern you are asking for will help you to make the best decision on the type of pattern that you want to use.

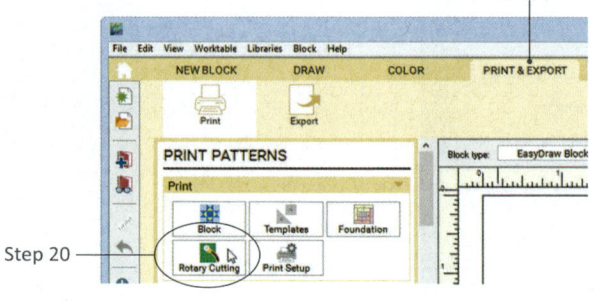

52

Chapter 1: Learning the EQ8 Basics

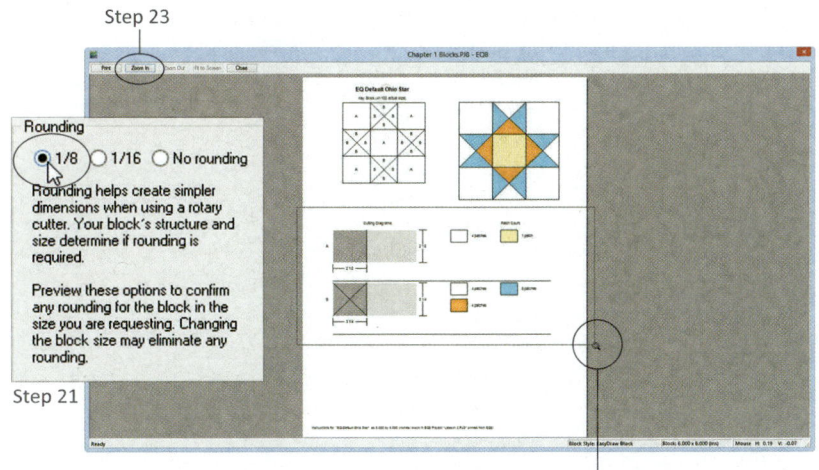

Step 23
Step 21
Step 24

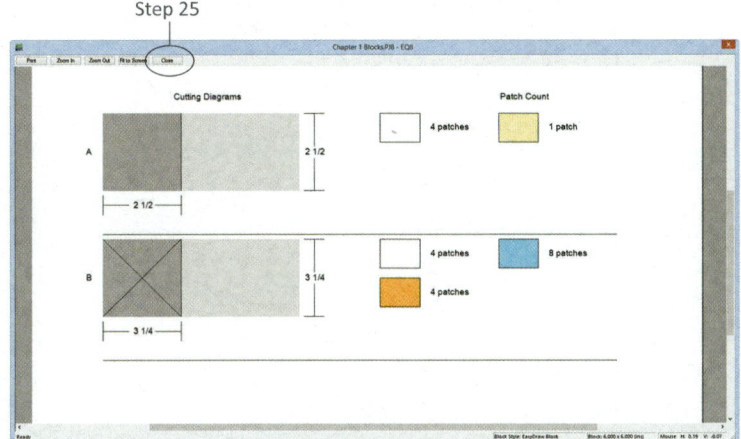

Step 25

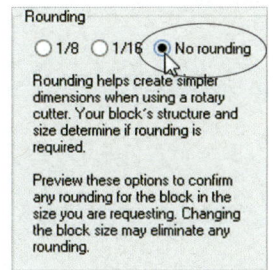

Step 26

Step 28

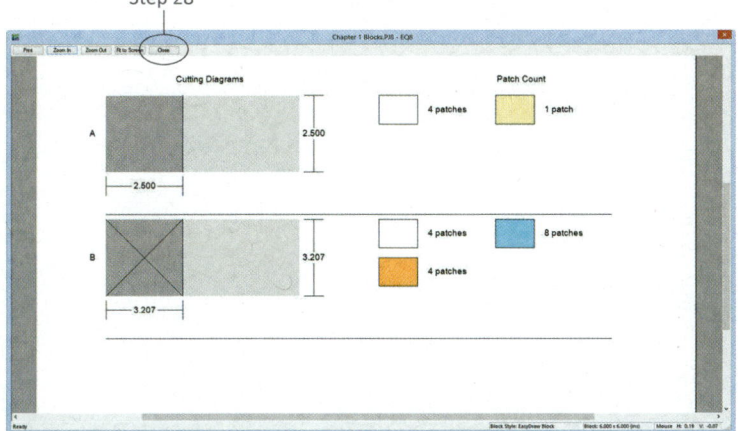

21. Click **1/8** for Rounding.

22. Click **Preview**.

23. Click the **Zoom In** button. The cursor will change to a magnifying glass.

24. **Drag diagonally across the center section of the page** to zoom in on the cutting diagram. A marquee box will appear as you drag to indicate the area that you want to zoom. When you release the mouse button, the screen will refresh in a zoomed view.

Patch A is 2½ by 2½ and Patch B is 3¼ by 3¼.

25. Click **Close**.

26. Click on **No rounding** in the dialog.

27. Click **Preview** and zoom in again if you need to see it more clearly.

Since we've turned off the rounding, the measurements are in decimal form. Patch A is unchanged. Patch B which is triangles has changed to 3.207 instead of 3.25. That's only a difference of 43/1000. That's a very, very small discrepancy. Using the Rotary Cutting Chart would be perfectly acceptable for this block at this size. To learn more about EQ's Rotary Cutting Charts, be sure to see Chapter 4, Lesson 4 in this book.

28. Click **Close** to Print Preview.

53

29. Click **Close** to the Rotary Cutting Chart.

30. Click **File > Exit** to close EQ.

This completes our lesson on the basics of the Block Worktable. This worktable is loaded with tools and techniques for drawing many different styles of blocks—from simple to sophisticated. We hope this lesson has made you comfortable in finding your way around the worktable, adding new blocks to your project, creating custom libraries and editing blocks back to the worktable.

Step 30

Here's what we learned in this lesson:

- The rules of EasyDraw
- Creating new EasyDraw blocks
- Using the Line tool, Arc tool and Grid tool
- Using and adjusting the graph paper
- How to delete lines in blocks
- Using undo
- Naming newly drawn blocks
- Creating a new applique motif
- Using the PosieMaker tool
- Centering and resizing patches in applique
- Creating a custom library of blocks
- Editing blocks from the library
- Editing blocks from the sketchbook
- Using the Paintbrush tool
- Printing blocks and templates

Chapter 1: Learning the EQ8 Basics

LESSON 3: BASICS OF THE IMAGE WORKTABLE

In this lesson, we will learn the basics of the Image Worktable. If you love fabric, as all quilters do, you'll want to learn the basics of importing your own fabric. Plus, it's easy to personalize any quilt, quilt label or craft project with a photo from your phone or camera. We'll show you how easy it is to print on printable fabric.

At the beginning of the book, we suggest that you restore the default settings of the program before completing the first three lessons. If you are continuing on from Lessons 1 and 2, you don't need to Restore Defaults. If you've been using the program for a time, you may want to Restore Defaults before starting this lesson. See page 7 for details.

The Home screen will display when you start EQ. If you don't see the Home screen, click the Home button in the upper-left corner of the EQ window.

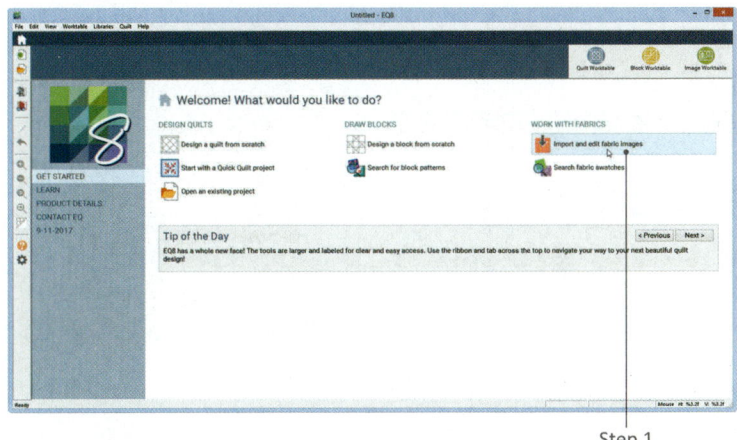
Step 1

1. Click **Import and edit fabric images** from the Home screen under WORK WITH FABRICS.

The Image Worktable is where you import fabric scans and photos. You can see that you're on the Image Worktable because its icon is pressed in the ribbon at the top-right of the screen. This worktable has a green color scheme. You will be surprised and impressed with the level of tasks that you can perform with the tools found here. It's a mini photo-editing program within EQ! Let's start by looking at how you can import your fabric scans.

IMPORTING A SCANNED FABRIC

We are on the IMAGE tab with Edit selected on the ribbon. The Edit Image palette is displayed and the only tool enabled is the one we want.

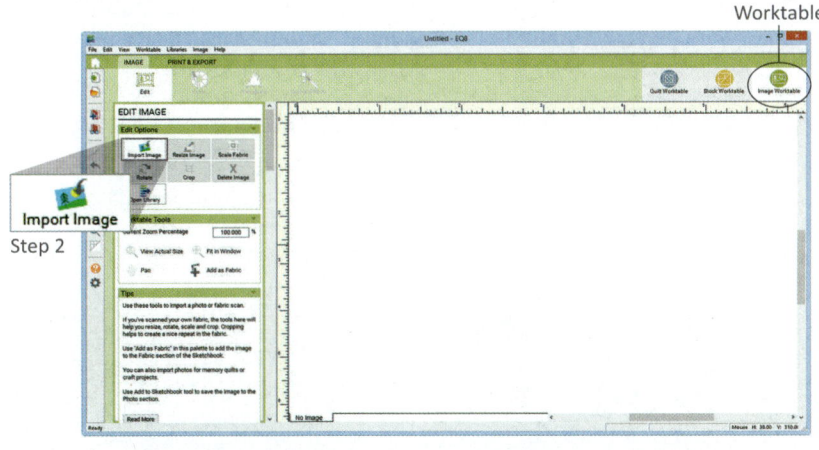
Step 2

2. Click the **Import Image** tool in the palette.

3. By default, the Import Image dialog box should open to **My EQ8\Images** folder. If it does not, navigate to find the folder.

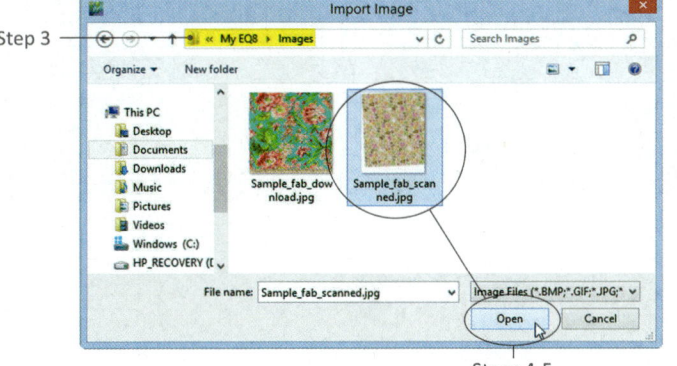
Steps 4-5

4. Find the file **Sample_fab_scanned.jpg** in the list, and click on it to select it.

5. Click **Open**. The fabric image appears on the screen.

55

EQ8 Lessons for Beginners

6. Click **View Actual Size**, and then click **Fit in Window** to observe the difference.

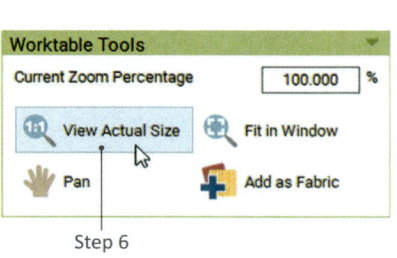
Step 6

Fabric image shown at actual size.

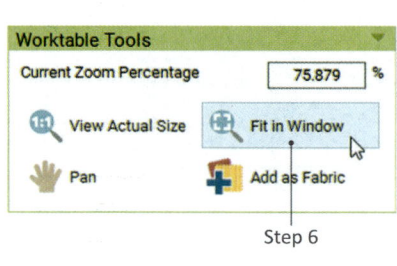
Step 6

Zoom level adjusted to show all of the fabric image.

7. Right-click over the image and choose **Image Info**. Here we see that the image was scanned at 75 pixels per inch. We also see that the size of the image is very close to 8.5 inches by 11 inches.

When scanning your own fabrics, set the scanner to 72 or 75 dpi. Either of these settings are fine and are typical options using most scanner software. If you follow this rule when scanning fabric, EQ will create an image of the fabric with the appropriate scale. In other words, if the fabric has polka dots, the fabric will scale to show the correct number and size of polka dots whether the fabric is in a 6 inch block or a 20 inch block.

8. Click **Close** in the Image Information dialog box.

Before we do any work to this fabric, let's add the image to the Sketchbook.

9. Click **Add to Project Sketchbook**.

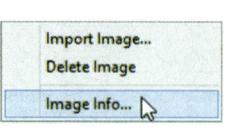
Step 7
Right-click on image to view this menu.

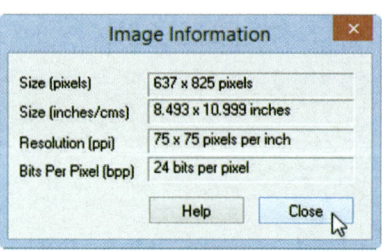
Steps 7-8
View the Image Information

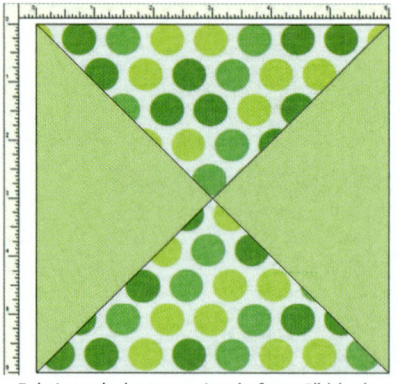
Fabric scaled appropriately for a 6" block.

Fabric scaled appropriately for a 20" block.

Step 9

56

Naming the Project

Since this is the first time we are adding something to the Project Sketchbook, you will see the Save As box. This allows you to name the project. The Save As box should be saving to **My EQ8\Projects** location.

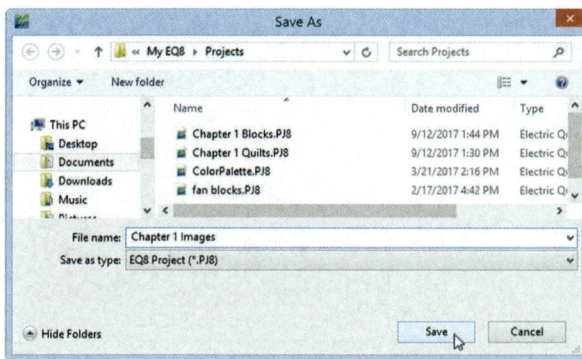
Steps 10-11

10. Type **Chapter 1 Images** in the File name box.

11. Click **Save**. The project has been named, and you may hear a sound indicating the image has been added to the Sketchbook.

Notice the project name now appears on the top title bar. Now that our project is named, every time that you click Add to Project Sketchbook, the Chapter 1 Images project automatically updates and saves. Let's look for this image in the Sketchbook.

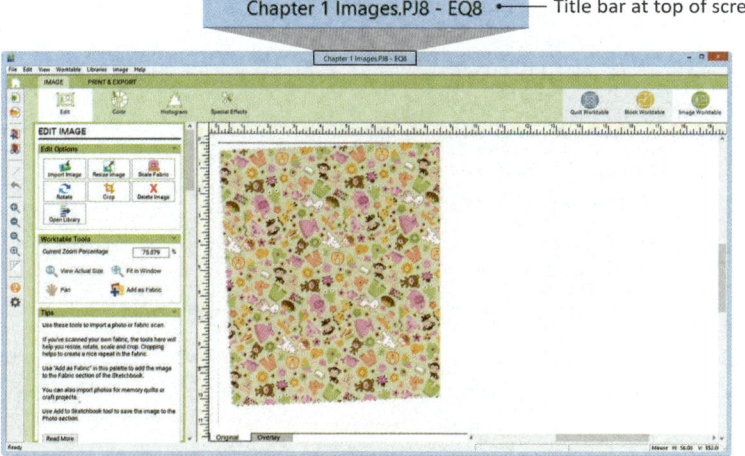

12. Click **View Project Sketchbook**.

13. Click the **Photos** button on the left.

Step 12

By default, any image on the Image Worktable gets saved to the Photos section of the Sketchbook. The image can be a photograph or any scanned image, like fabric. It's a good idea to save the fabric scan here first. If we need to re-crop or make some adjustment, we have it right in our Sketchbook. We won't need to import it again.

The name of the file will appear as the name on the Notecard. Display buttons are available to change the size and number of photos you see.

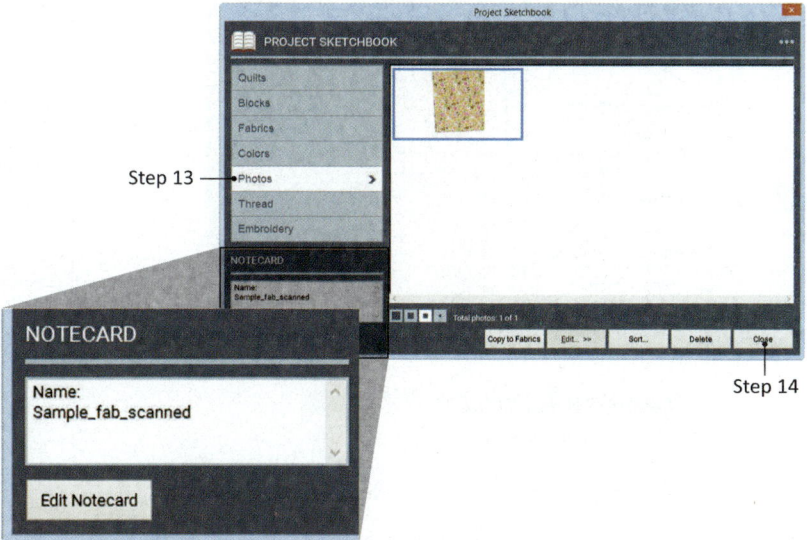
The image name appears on the Notecard.

14. Click **Close**.

We don't need the fabric to be this big. It's obvious that it was crooked on the scanner, so we need to do some work to it. When we are done editing the image, we will add it to our Project Sketchbook as a fabric instead of a photo.

EQ8 Lessons for Beginners

Using Straighten

First let's straighten it.

15. Click the **Rotate** tool.

If you knew exactly the number of degrees that you wanted to rotate the image, you could use any of the rotate options in the palette. Another way to rotate is to use the design that's printed on the fabric.

16. Find the **pink dresses** in the fabric that are horizontal from one another. If you had the actual piece of fabric in front of you, you could see that the dresses should be aligned on the same horizontal plane.

17. Click **Straighten** in the palette. This will allow you to draw a straight line on the image. EQ will adjust the image so that the line is perfectly horizontal or vertical. You can follow something in the design to help you straighten it.

18. **Draw a line from one pink dress to the other dress**.

If you don't like the line, you don't need to erase it. Just start redrawing a new line and the old line will disappear.

19. Click **Apply Straighten**.

The fabric will straighten and redraw at actual size.

20. Click **Fit in Window** so that the whole image fits in the screen again.

You'll notice that EQ filled in the background canvas with a color when the fabric was straightened. We will eventually crop that out, so don't worry about it right now. If you do not like the way the fabric straightened, do it again.

21. If you're happy with the straightening, click **Add to Project Sketchbook**.

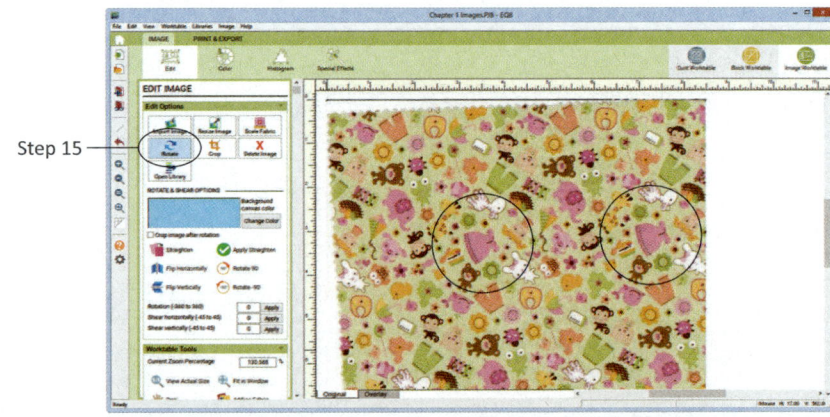
Notice the 2 pink dresses. The dress on the right is higher than the left, indicating that the fabric image is crooked. (This graphic is zoomed in to show detail.)

Step 18
Drag a line from the top of the left dress to the top of the right dress.

The fabric image is now straightened based on the line you drew on the worktable.

Step 20

Step 21

58

Cropping to the Fabric Repeat

Now we are ready to analyze the pattern repeat and crop it.

It's not always easy to find the pattern repeat. Sometimes the pattern is simply too big to include the whole repeat. Sometimes it helps to find the repeat by doing the cropping in two steps. The pink dresses that we used to straighten also give us the repeat horizontally.

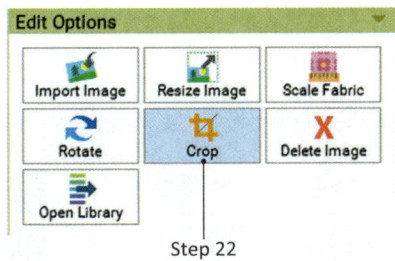
Step 22

22. Click the **Crop** button.

23. Drag the **middle node on the left side of the fabric**, to the bottom of the pink dress on the left side of the fabric. You'll know the cursor is in the correct position when you see the double-headed arrow appear. Drag in the direction of the arrow. Use the illustration as a guide.

24. Drag the **middle node on the right side of the fabric**, to the bottom of the pink dress that is horizontal from the first pink dress.

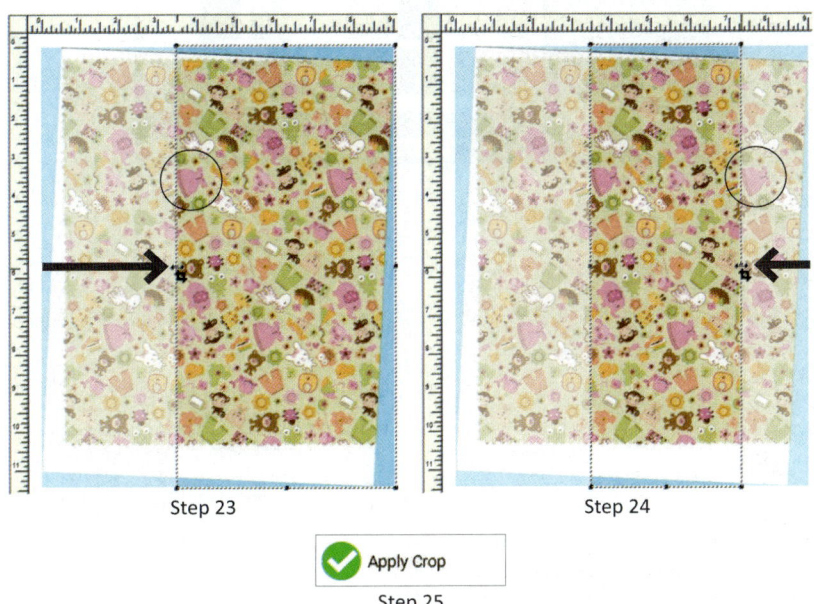
Step 23 Step 24 Step 25

25. Click **Apply Crop**.

Now let's look for a repeat of the pattern in the vertical direction. Find the brown monkey towards the top of the image.

26. Drag the **middle-top node** down to the top of the monkey's head.

27. Drag the **middle-bottom node** up to the top of the monkey's head that's close to the bottom of the fabric. Make sure it's the monkey that's in the same orientation as the one at the top.

Step 26 Step 27 Step 28

28. Click **Apply Crop**.

EQ8 Lessons for Beginners

Add to Sketchbook as a Fabric

29. Click **Add as Fabric** in the palette.

Step 29

Step 30

30. Click **View Project Sketchbook**.

31. Click **Fabrics**.

32. Scroll to the end of the fabrics. Newly added fabrics always appear at the end. Click on the **last fabric**.

Step 31 / Step 32 / Step 33

Notice the name on the notecard is the name of the image that you imported. If you want to change the name, click the Edit notecard button. We'll leave the name as it is now.

33. Click **Close**.

Let's see how the fabric looks in a block.

34. Click **Block Worktable** in the ribbon.

35. Click the **NEW BLOCK** tab.

36. Click **Pieced** on the ribbon.

37. Click **EasyDraw** in the palette.

Step 34 / Step 35 / Step 36 / Step 37

38. In the precision bar above the ruler, set the block size to **6 x 6** by typing in the entry boxes and pressing the **Enter** key on your keyboard.

39. Click the **COLOR** tab.

40. Click the **Paintbrush** tool in the palette.

41. Click the small **Detach** button in the fabric preview to separate it from the palette. (If your fabric preview is already detached, skip to step 43.)

42. Move the **Fabric Preview** to the right of the block, and resize it to make it larger.

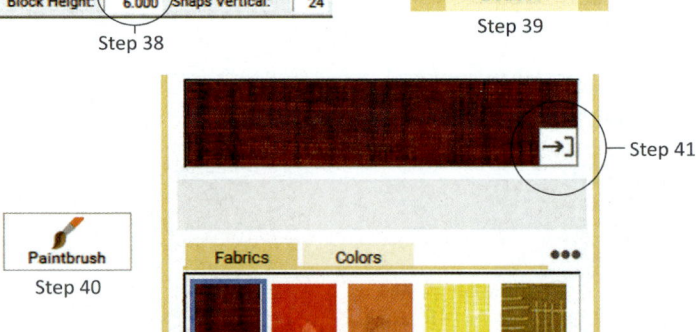
Step 38 / Step 39 / Step 40 / Step 41

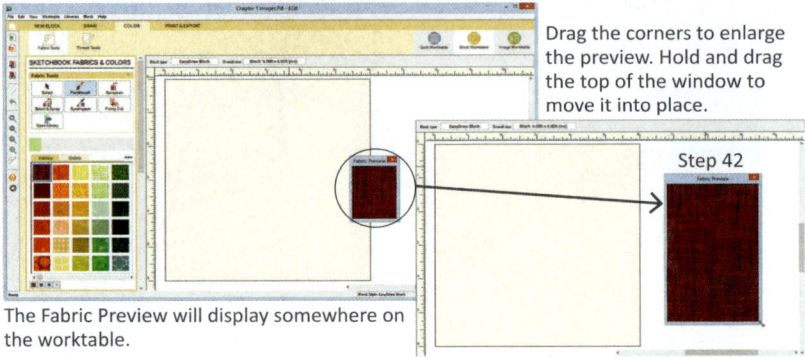
Step 42

Drag the corners to enlarge the preview. Hold and drag the top of the window to move it into place.

The Fabric Preview will display somewhere on the worktable.

60

Chapter 1: Learning the EQ8 Basics

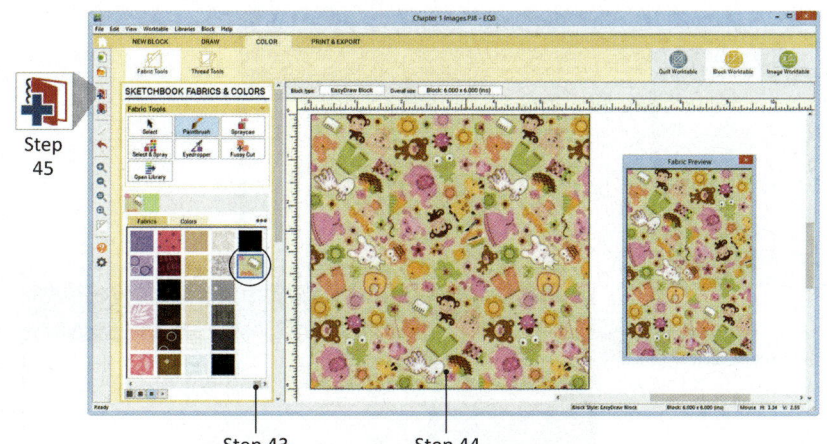

Step 43 Step 44

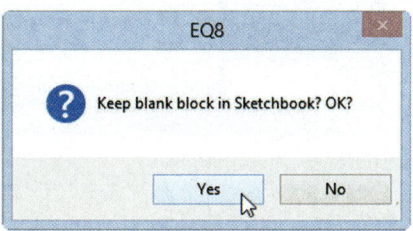

Step 46

Step 47   Step 48

Step 49

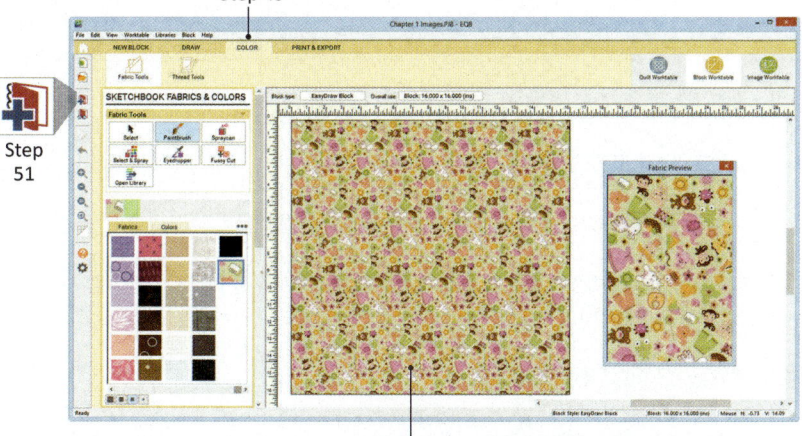

Step 50
Notice how the fabric changed now that the block size is larger.

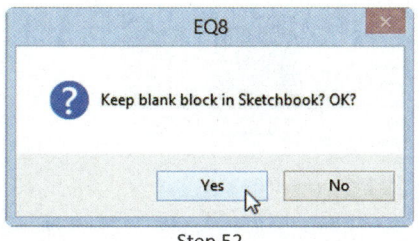

Step 52

43. At the bottom of the palette, drag the scrollbar to the right to display the last fabric.

44. Click to **set the fabric** into the 6 inch block.

45. Click **Add to Project Sketchbook**. You'll see a message, "Keep blank block in Sketchbook? OK?"

46. Click **Yes**.

47. Click the **DRAW** tab.

48. In the precision bar set the block size to 16 x 16 by typing in the entry boxes and pressing the **Enter** key on your keyboard.

49. Click the **COLOR** tab.

50. Now you will see much more of the repeat of the fabric in the block. This shows how EQ will automatically scale the fabric for the size of the block. Notice the Fabric Preview stays unchanged. Remember, this is just a sample.

51. Click **Add to Project Sketchbook**. You'll see the blank block message again.

52. Click **Yes**.

53. Click **View Project Sketchbook**.

Step 53

61

EQ8 Lessons for Beginners

54. Click **Blocks**.

55. Click the first newly added plain block. The Notecard says 6 x 6 inches.

56. Click the last block. The Notecard says 16 x 16 inches.

The blocks look identical in the Sketchbook because the fabric does not scale here. These images are simply too small to scale the fabric. You will always see the scaling on the worktable, but not in the smaller versions like the Sketchbook, palette and Fabric Preview window.

57. Click **Close**.

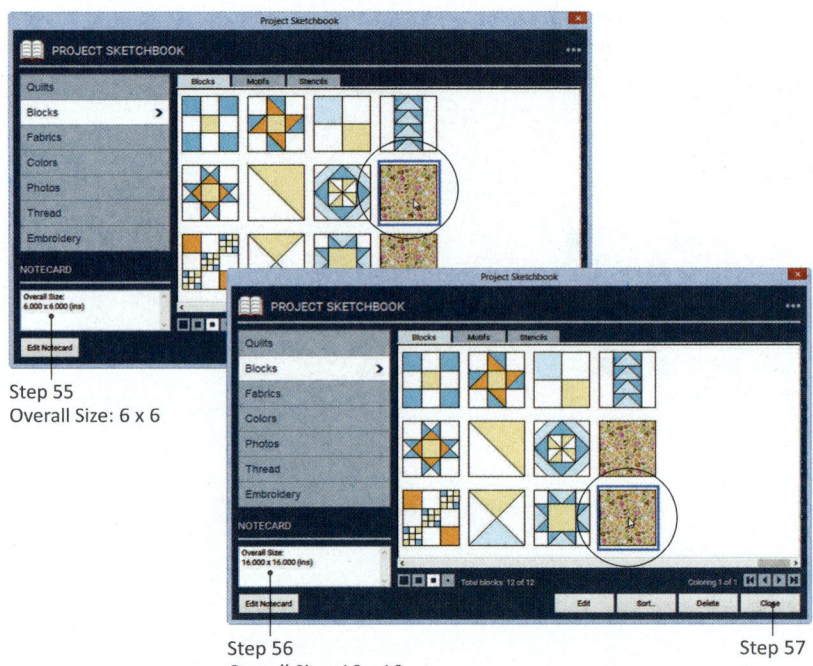

Step 55
Overall Size: 6 x 6

Step 56
Overall Size: 16 x 16

Step 57

Coffee Break!
Way to go! You'll love being able to use your own fabric stash in EQ8—it's one of the software's most popular features!

If you want to continue on, jump to step 1 below.

If you need to put EQ8 away for now, simply choose File > Exit. Your project is already saved and can be opened up again later to continue the lesson.

IMPORTING A FABRIC FROM THE INTERNET

If you closed EQ8 after the last section, you'll need to open it again to get started with this next section of Chapter 1.

On the Home screen, click **Open an existing project**, choose **Chapter 1 Images** from the list, then click **OK**. Click the **Close** button to close the Sketchbook. The title bar at the top will say Chapter 1 Images.PJ8.

What if you don't have a scanner to scan your own fabric? You could search for the fabric on the internet and save the image, or you could take a photo of your fabric with your smart phone or digital camera.

1. Click **Image Worktable** at the top.

2. Click **Import Image**.

3. Find the file **Sample_fab_download.jpg** in the list, and click on it to select it.

4. Click **Open**. The fabric image appears on the screen.

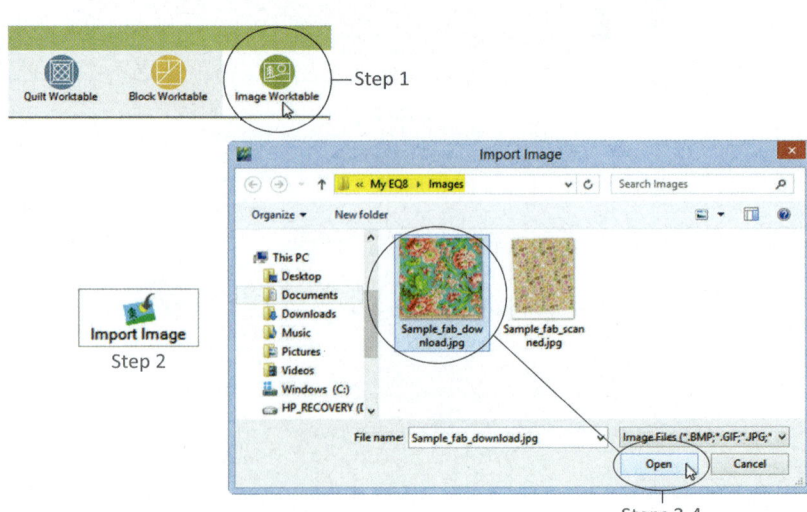

Step 1

Step 2

Steps 3-4

62

Chapter 1: Learning the EQ8 Basics

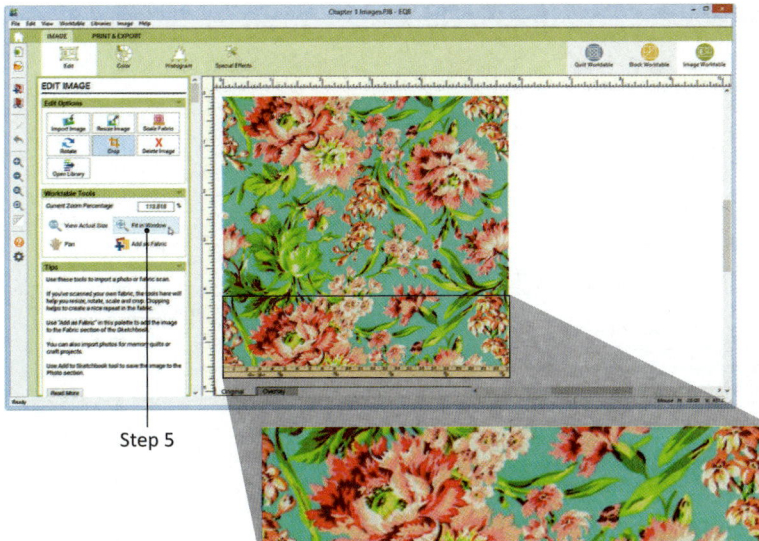
Step 5

Many web images will include a ruler as part of the image. If you take a photo of your own fabric, be sure to also include a ruler in your photo to ensure the scaling is accurate.

Step 6

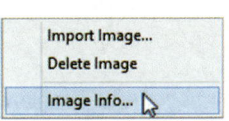
Step 7
Right-click on image to view this menu.

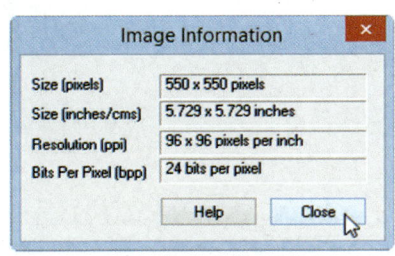
Steps 7-8
View the Image Information.

Step 10
Drag a box around the bottom ruler to zoom in.

Ruler shows the fabric is 23 inches, but the EQ8 ruler shows it's almost 5.75 inches.

Step 11

5. Click **Fit in Window**.

Many of the fabrics on the internet that you can download have a ruler along the edge like this one. This ruler is important because it helps scale the fabric to the appropriate size in EQ. **If you want to take a photo of fabric, place a ruler on the fabric before you take the photo**. Then you can follow the same instructions below for scaling.

When you find an image on the internet that you want to try in EQ, you need to save the image to your computer. Position the mouse over the image and right-click to display the context menu. Choose "Save Image As….." Make sure you are saving the image in the **My EQ8 > Images** folder. You can change the name if you like, or leave it. Many times the images from the web will have long and cryptic names. Once you've saved it to the Images folder, you're ready to import.

Before we do any work to this fabric, let's add the image to the Sketchbook.

6. Click **Add to Project Sketchbook**.

7. Right-click over the image and choose **Image Info** to observe the size.

8. Click **Close** in the Image Information dialog box.

Many times the fabric images will be fairly small. Sometimes they are fairly large. In this image, the ruler part of the image gives a size much larger than the rulers on the Image Worktable.

If we make the rulers match, then our fabric will scale appropriately when used in a quilt.

9. Click the **Zoom In** button on the left side of the screen.

10. **Drag a marquee box around the ruler at the bottom of the image**. When you release the mouse, the image will be zoomed in to that area. This allows us to take a closer look at the image and observe that the ruler shows 23 inches.

11. Click **Fit in Window** in the palette.

63

Scaling the Fabric

Now let's scale the fabric.

12. Click the **Scale Fabric** button in the palette. Take a minute to read the tip in the palette. This explains how you would measure your fabric if you didn't have a ruler as part of your image.

We know the width of this fabric is 23 inches by the ruler that's part of the image.

13. Type **23** in the entry in the palette.

14. Click **Apply Scale**. The image will resize and display at actual size.

15. Click **Fit in Window** in the palette.

Take a moment to look at the rulers that are part of the Image Worktable. They should show that the fabric image is now 23 inches wide. Our fabric is now the proper scale. We can crop any way we choose, and the fabric will scale appropriately no matter what size of patch it is placed in.

This fabric is a large print. We may not be able to crop it in a way that will show a nice repeat.

16. Click the **Crop** button in the palette.

17. Drag the **middle node from the bottom** up to crop off the ruler. We don't want the ruler to show when we use this in our designs.

18. Click **Apply Crop**.

19. Click **Add as Fabric** in the palette.

20. Click **View Project Sketchbook**.

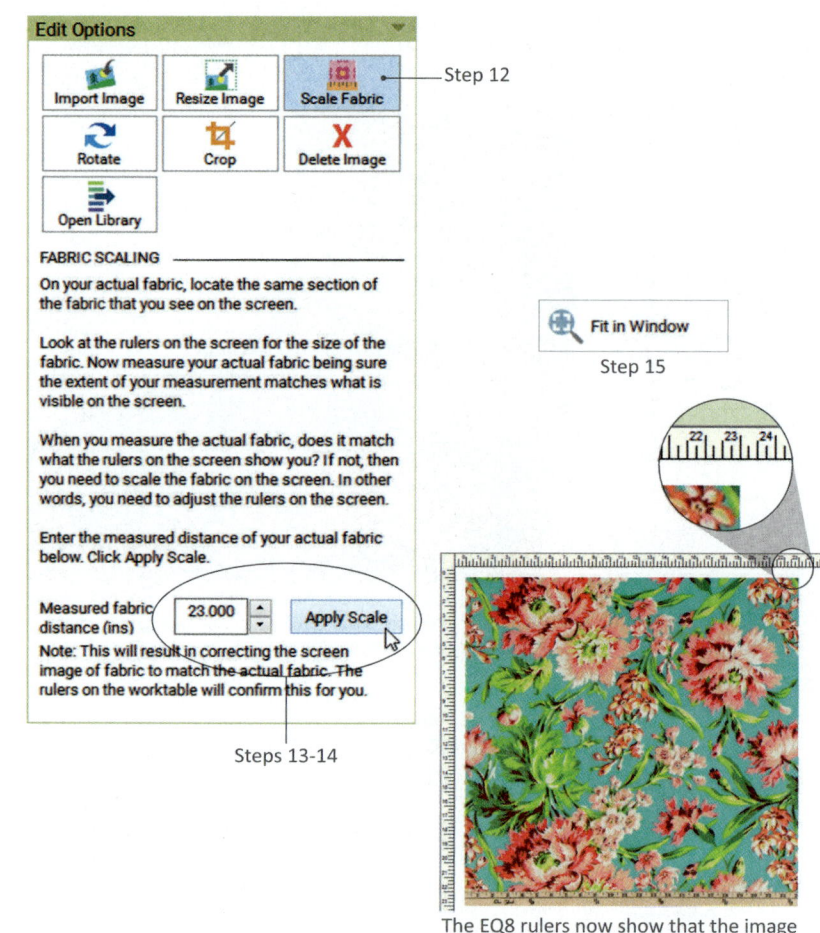

Step 12

Steps 13-14

Step 15

The EQ8 rulers now show that the image is 23 inches, and scaled properly.

Step 16

Step 17
Crop out the ruler.

Step 18

Step 19

Step 20

Chapter 1: Learning the EQ8 Basics

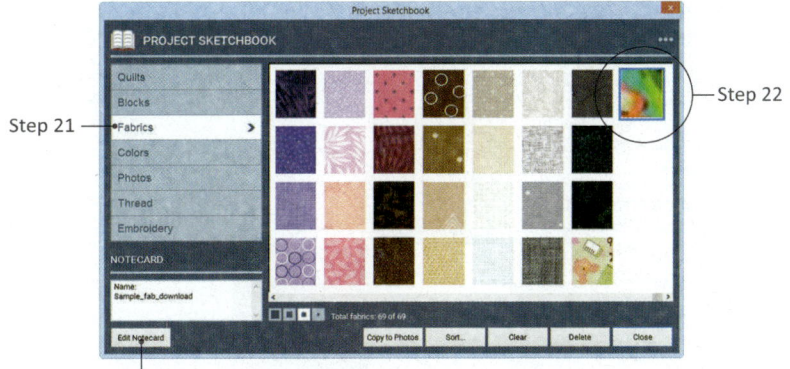

Step 21
Step 22
Step 23

Step 24
Step 25
Step 26

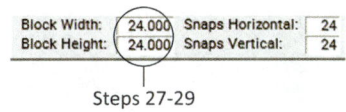

Steps 27-29

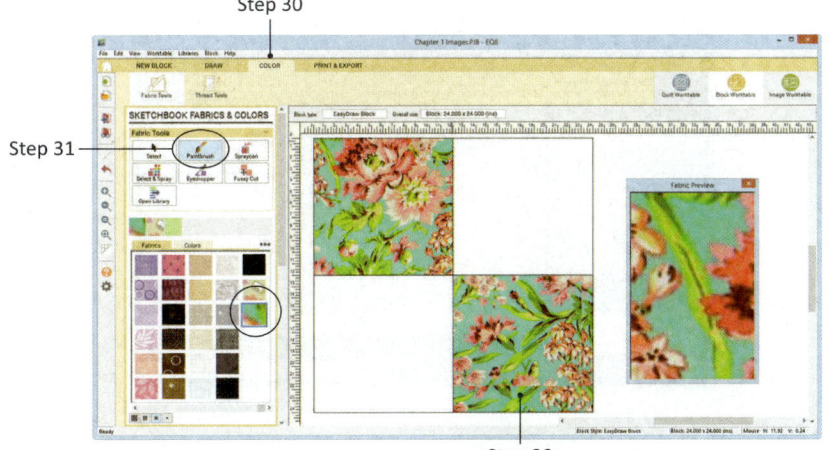

Step 30
Step 31
Step 32

21. Click **Fabrics**.

22. Scroll to the end of the fabrics to see the new fabric. Since we resized the image and made it much bigger, we only see a small portion of it in the Project Sketchbook.

23. If you wanted to change the notecard, click the **Edit Notecard** button, make changes and close the Notecard.

To see the fabric set in a block, let's edit a block from the Sketchbook.

24. Click **Blocks**.

25. Click the **Four Patch** block to select it.

26. Click **Edit**.

We can see from the rulers and the precision bar that this block is 6 inches. We won't see much of the large fabric print at this size. Let's make the block bigger.

27. Double-click in the Block Width box and type **24**.

28. Press the **Tab** key and type **24**.

29. Press the **Enter** key. Now our block is 24 by 24. This means each square will be 12 inches.

30. Click the **COLOR** tab.

31. Click the **Paintbrush** tool and scroll to the end and click on the last fabric to select it.

32. Click to **place the fabric in the two colored squares** of the block.

65

EQ8 Lessons for Beginners

Let's look at one more tool.

33. Click the **Fussy Cut** tool in the palette. This tool allows you to move the fabric inside the block or patch.

34. Take a minute to read about the tool in the palette.

35. Position the cursor over a patch with the fabric. **Press the left mouse button and drag.** It's as if the cursor has picked up the fabric and is sliding it in any direction that you want. You'll find this very useful on fabrics with large prints that you want to 'fussy' the fabric's design into position within a patch.

36. Click **Add to Project Sketchbook**.

37. Click **View Project Sketchbook**.

38. Click **Blocks**.

39. Scroll to the end to see the block. Remember that you won't observe the fabric in the same scale here.

40. Click **Close**.

If you designed a new quilt with 24 inch blocks, when you set this block into the quilt, the fussy cut of the fabric would be remembered and shown. If you set this block in any size other than 24, you'd need to use the Fussy Cut tool again to make adjustments for the new size.

Coffee Break!
Are you loving the different ways to get fabric into your EQ8? We hope so!

If you want to continue on, jump to step 1 on the next page.

If you need to put EQ8 away for now, simply choose File > Exit. Your project is already saved and can be opened up again later to continue the lesson.

Before Fussy Cut

After Fussy Cut

Step 36

Step 37

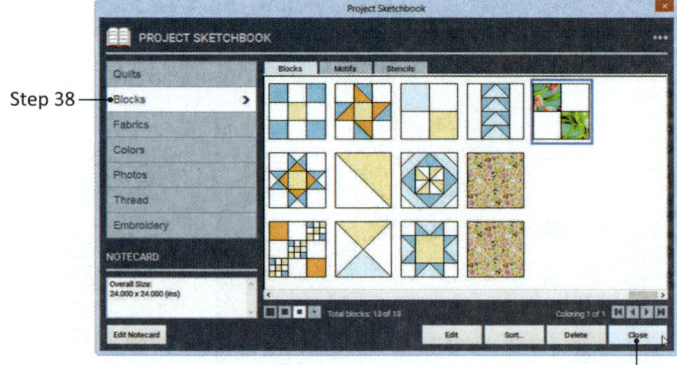
Step 40

USING THE LIBRARIES

If you closed EQ8 after the last section, you'll need to open it again to get started with this next section of Chapter 1.

*On the Home screen, click **Open an existing project**, choose **Chapter 1 Images** from the list, then click **OK**. Click the **Close** button to close the Sketchbook. The title bar at the top will say Chapter 1 Images.PJ8.*

Creating a Custom Fabric Library

In the last lesson, we created a custom library for the blocks we drew. Let's do the same with our fabrics.

1. Click **Libraries > Fabric Library**.

2. Click **My Favorite Fabrics**.

3. Click **Create Library**. The Add New Library dialog box will display.

4. Type **Lesson Fabrics**. We'll leave the number of styles set to 10.

5. Click **OK**.

6. Now you will see My Custom Libraries. Click the **+ sign** in front of My Custom Libraries.

7. Click the **+ sign** in front of Lesson Fabrics. We see the 10 Styles listed where we can add fabrics.

8. Click the name **Style 1** to highlight it.

9. *Right-click* on the style name and choose **Modify Style** from the context menu. The Style Name dialog box will appear.

10. Type **Fabric Scans** and click **OK**.

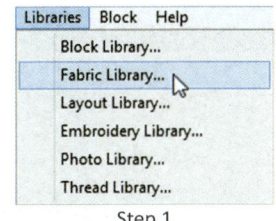
Step 1

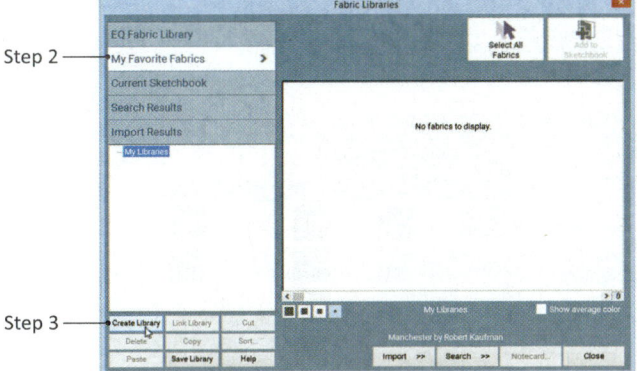
Step 2
Step 3

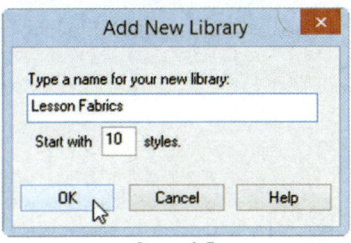
Steps 4-5

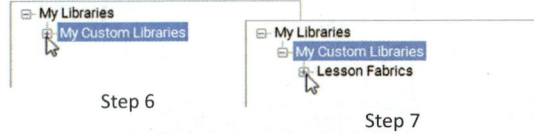
Step 6
Step 7

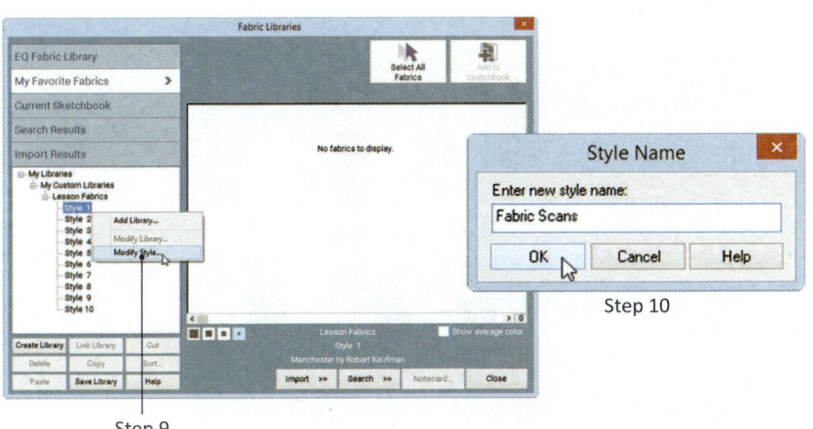
Step 9
Step 10

11. Click the name **Style 2** to highlight it.

12. Right-click on the style name and choose **Modify Style** from the context menu.

13. Type **Internet Downloads** and click **OK**.

The new library is created. Now we need to copy the fabrics from the Sketchbook and paste them in the library.

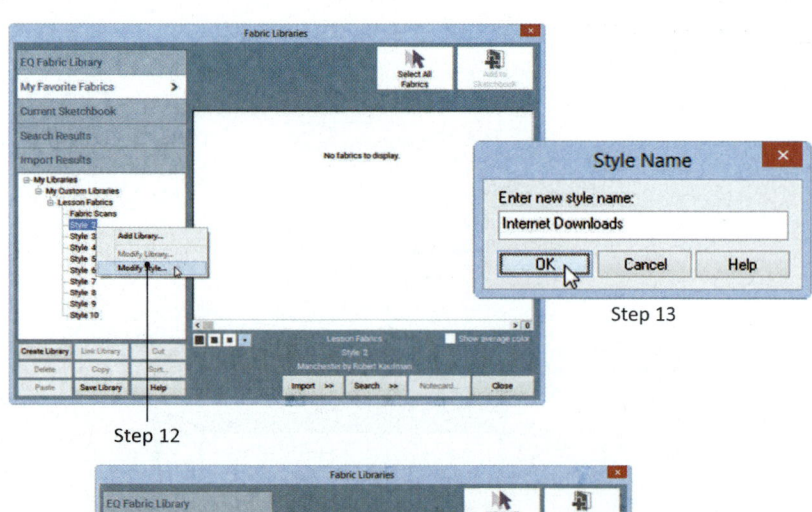
Step 12
Step 13

14. Click **Current Sketchbook**. Scroll to the end or change the display so that you can see the fabrics at the end of the list.

15. Click the **second to last fabric**.

16. Click the **Copy** button.

17. Click **My Favorite Fabrics**.

18. Click the style name **Fabric Scans**.

19. Click **Paste**. The fabric will appear.

20. Click **Save Library**. You'll see a message that your fabrics have been saved in the library.

21. Click **OK**.

22. Click **Current Sketchbook**.

23. Scroll to the end and click on the **last fabric in the list**.

24. Click the **Copy** button.

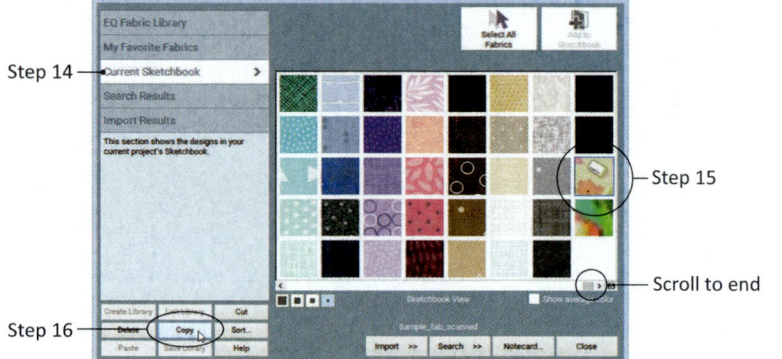
Step 14
Step 15
Scroll to end
Step 16

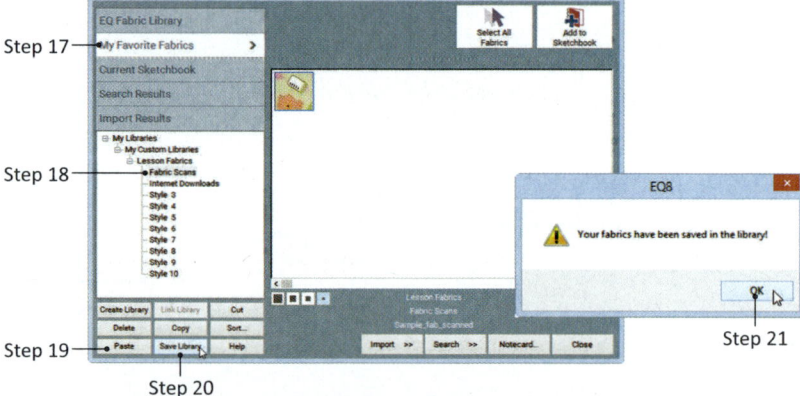
Step 17
Step 18
Step 19
Step 20
Step 21

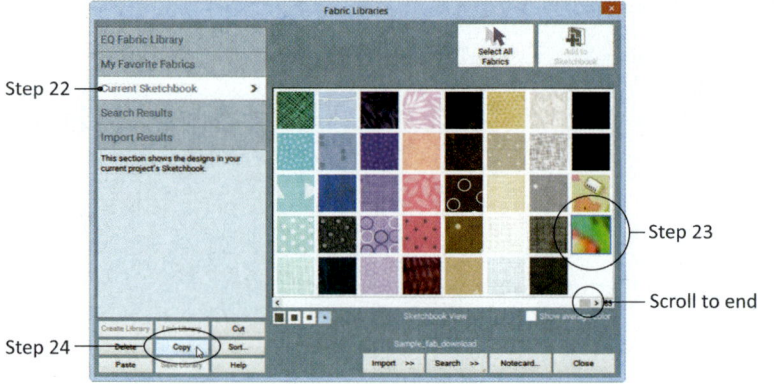
Step 22
Step 23
Scroll to end
Step 24

Chapter 1: Learning the EQ8 Basics

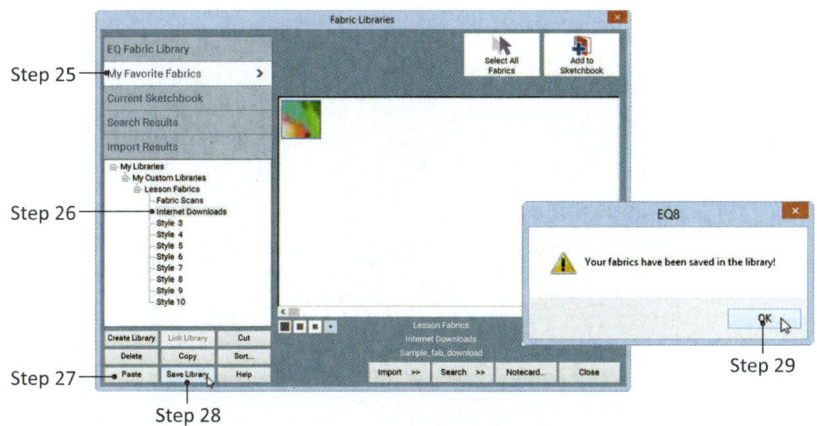

25. Click **My Favorite Fabrics**.
26. Click the style name **Internet Downloads**.
27. Click **Paste**. The fabric will appear.
28. Click **Save Library**. You'll see a message that your fabrics have been saved in the library.
29. Click **OK**.

If you like scanning in your own fabrics, you'll want to become familiar with these steps for creating nice scans and building them into a library.

You don't have to make individual scans this much work. It's all up to you. If you like to be very precise, then you know the steps. If you're just looking for a representation of the fabric color, it's really not necessary to fuss over each fabric.

Importing Several Fabrics at Once

You can import fabric images (JPG, PNG, GIF, TIF and BMP) all at once using the Fabric Library. One way to collect fabric images from the web would be to right-click on the web image and choose Save Image. Be sure you are saving all of these images in one place so you know where to find them.

Alternatively, many of the fabric manufacturers found in our Fabric Library offer zip files of their fabrics on their websites. A zip file is a single computer file that contains several "zipped" or compressed files. This is done so that you can download them faster. Plus, you typically will get a complete fabric line in one download. **Because these are zipped, they need to be unzipped before you can use them.** Once downloaded, you unzip the files into a folder. (On Windows, right-click on the file and choose Extract All. On a Mac, the files get unzipped automatically.) Now you're ready to import them into EQ8.

30. Feel free to take a few minutes to go online and **save some fabric web images**, or find a **zip file of fabrics** from a fabric manufacturer. Several of the fabric manufacturers in the EQ Fabric Library provide these files on their websites. Be sure to unzip the file before moving onto the next step.

31. Still in the Fabric Library, click the **Import** button and choose **From Image Files**.

32. **Navigate to the location** that contains your newly downloaded images.

33. **Select all the fabrics** (CTRL+A on Windows or Command+A on a Mac), and click the **Open** button.

69

EQ8 Lessons for Beginners

The fabrics will appear in Import Results. They are not yet part of your project.

34. Click the **Select All Fabrics** button, or hold the CTRL key (Command on a Mac) and click to individually select the ones that you want.

35. Click **Add to Sketchbook**, then **Close**.

At this point, you can use them from the project or you can copy them to a custom library. It's up to you. This method works for a single fabric or for a group of fabrics. It's important to remember that the scale of the fabric may not be correct when you are importing from the internet as a group.

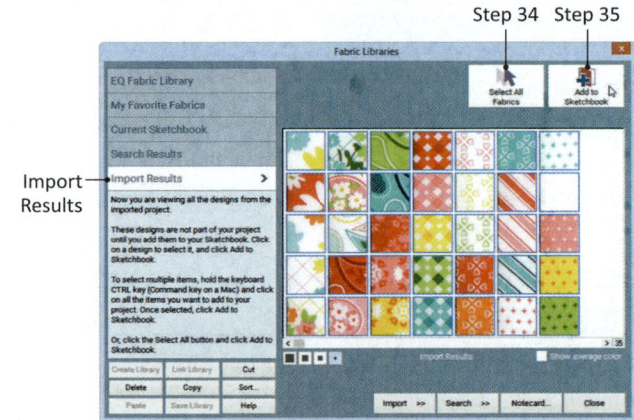

After importing, you must select the fabrics you want, then click Add to Sketchbook.

Coffee Break!

Did you go to a fabric manufacturer's website to find some fun fabrics to download? We know how much you love fabric, and how easy it is to get distracted, but don't forget to come back to this book! There's lots more to learn!

If you want to continue on, jump to step 1 on the next page.

If you need to put EQ8 away for now, simply choose File > Exit. Your project is already saved and can be opened up again later to continue the lesson.

EDITING PHOTOS

If you closed EQ8 after the last section, you'll need to open it again to get started with this next section of Chapter 1.

On the Home screen, click **Open an existing project**, choose **Chapter 1 Images** from the list, then click **OK**. Click the **Close** button to close the Sketchbook. The title bar at the top will say Chapter 1 Images.PJ8.

Using the Photo Library

The Image Worktable also has many photo editing abilities. Let's get a couple photos from EQ's Photo Library.

1. Click **Libraries** on the main menu.

2. Click **Photo Library**.

Remember to click the + to open a library and click on a style name to see the photos in that style.

3. Click **01 Red** in the Colors library.

4. Click the **Red Tricycle** photo, and click the **Add to Sketchbook** button.

5. Click the **Red Chair** photo, and click the **Add to Sketchbook** button.

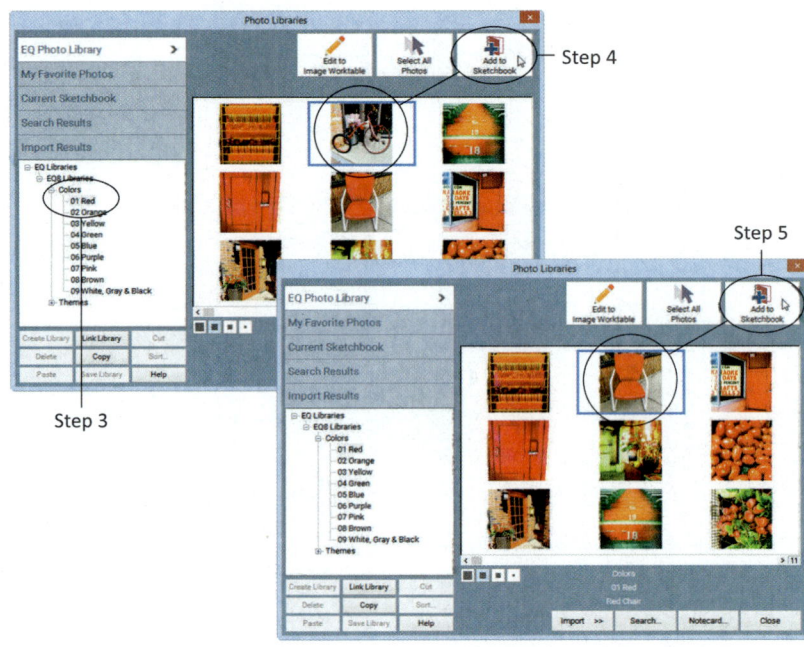

70

Chapter 1: Learning the EQ8 Basics

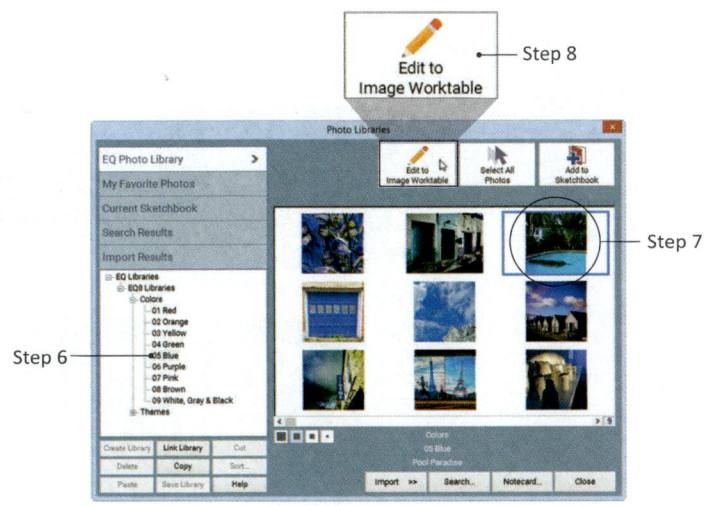

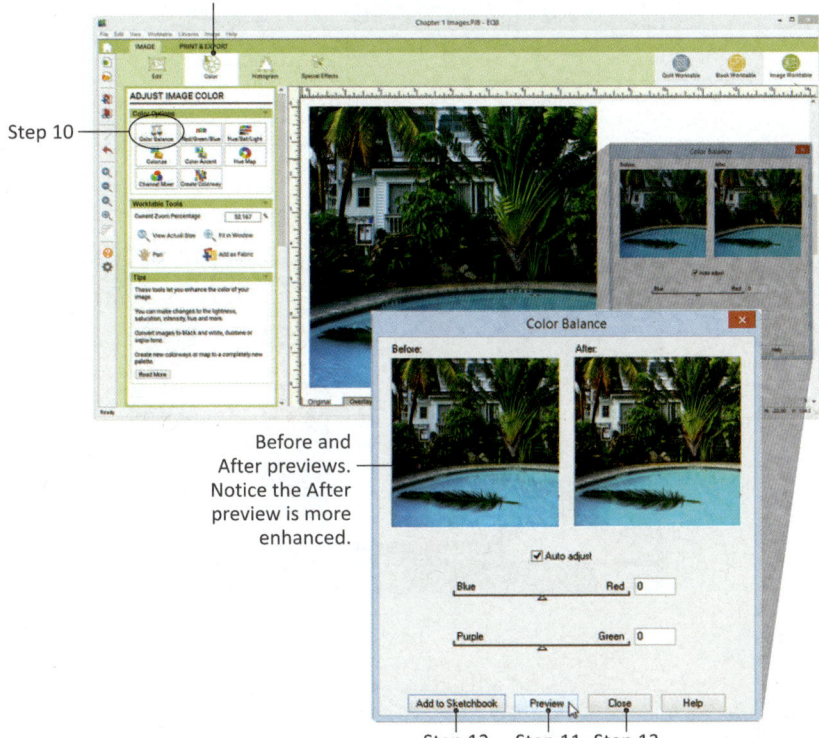

6. Click **O5 Blue**.

7. Click the third photo from the end, **Pool Paradise**.

Instead of adding it to the Sketchbook, let's edit it directly to the worktable.

8. Click the **Edit to Image Worktable** button.

This added the photo to the Sketchbook and placed it on the worktable with just a click.

Adjusting the Color Balance of a Photo

9. Click **Color** on the ribbon.

10. Click the **Color Balance** tool in the palette. The Color Balance dialog box will display.

The Color Balance dialog will automatically adjust color levels in the image. It will make the dark pixels darker and light pixels lighter. The result will enhance shadows and brighten the image.

11. The dialog box shows the "Before" and "After" and you can see the image on the worktable when you click Preview. Click the **Preview** button in the Color Balance dialog box.

12. Click **Add to Sketchbook** in the Color Balance dialog box.

13. Click **Close** in the Color Balance dialog box.

14. Click **View Project Sketchbook**.

15. In the Photos section, click the **Red Tricycle** photo to select it.

16. Since we are already on the Image Worktable, another way to edit the photo is to simply double-click on it. **Double-click the photo** to edit it to the Image Worktable.

71

Changing a Color Photo to Black and White

17. Click the **Hue/Sat/Light** tool in the palette. The Hue/Saturation/Lightness dialog box displays.

If you want to turn a color photo into a grayscale photo, this is the tool to use. Saturation refers to the intensity of the image's colors.

18. Drag the **Saturation** slider to the left until it reads **-120**. When the slider is at the minimum value, -120, the colors are desaturated so no hue is dominant. In other words, the image looks grayscale.

19. Click **Add to Sketchbook** in the Hue/Saturation/Lightness dialog box.

20. Click **Close**.

Applying Special Effects

21. Click **View Project Sketchbook**.

22. **Double-click the Red Chair photo** to edit it to the worktable.

23. Click **Special Effects** on the ribbon.

24. Click the **Effects** tool in the palette. The Apply Effects dialog box will display.

25. In the menu at the top of the dialog choose **Artistic > Oil Painting**. You will see four difference samples display.

26. Click on **one of the samples** to select it. This effect applies an oil painting look to the image. The larger the number, the less detail in the photo.

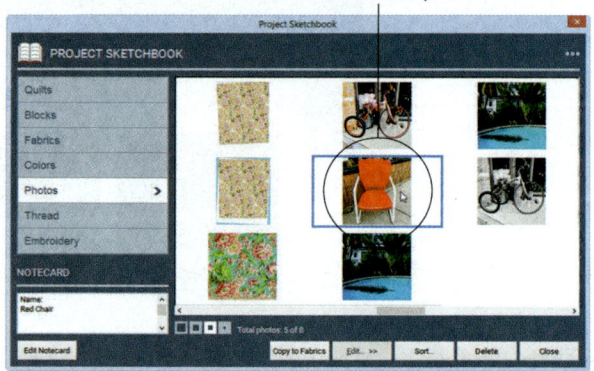

***Mac users**: When the Special Effects dialogs are open, their menu options appear at the top of the screen, not at the top of the dialog, as shown in these images.

Chapter 1: Learning the EQ8 Basics

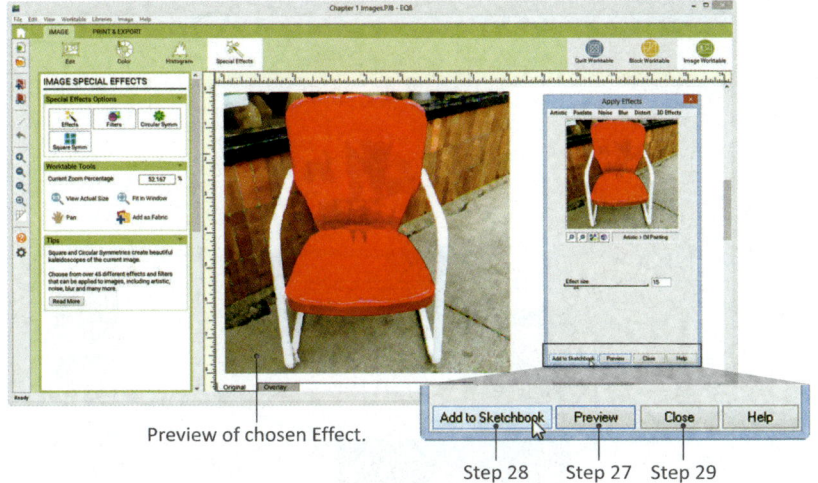

Preview of chosen Effect.

Step 28 Step 27 Step 29

Step 31 Step 30

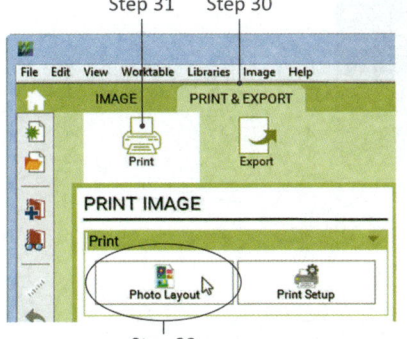

Step 32

Step 34

Step 33

Use the scrollbar to see all the images.

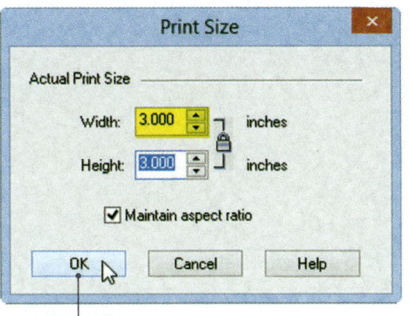

Step 36

27. Click the **Preview** button to see the image on the worktable.

28. Click the **Add to Sketchbook** button in the Apply Effects dialog box.

29. Click **Close** in the Apply Effects dialog box.

There are many, many tools available for editing photos, including 54 different effects and filters. We've briefly looked at a few of them. The final feature of the Image Worktable that you'll want to become familiar with is Photo Layout.

Printing Photos Using the Photo Layout

30. Click the **PRINT & EXPORT** tab.

31. Click **Print** on the ribbon.

32. Click the **Photo Layout** tool in the palette. You will see a white rectangle that represents the preview of the page that will print. All the images from the Photo section of the Sketchbook appear on the right.

33. **Drag an image to the page**. If the image is larger than the page, a message will display asking if you want EQ to resize for you. If you see the message, click Yes.

Whenever you drag an image onto the page, it will be selected for you. If you happened to deselect it, click on it to select it.

34. Click the **Resize** button to display the Print Size dialog box.

35. Change the Width to **3 inches**. The Height will change automatically.

36. Click **OK**.

37. Continue to resize the photo by dragging on one of the nodes.

73

38. There are several tools along the top for rotating, flipping and positioning the photo. Click on several of them to see the results.

EQ lets you customize your printout by resizing, rotating and printing several different photos at once. You will find this very helpful if printing on fabric because it helps prevent waste.

39. **Drag another photo** to the page.

40. Practice moving and resizing the photos.

41. If you want to print the photos, click the **Print** tool.

42. Click **File > Close Photo Layout**.

43. Click **File > Exit** to close EQ.

This completes our lesson on the basics of the Image Worktable. We realize these first three lessons have been long and packed with information. Great job for finishing them! The rest of the book has shorter task-oriented lessons on various topics. Feel free to skip around and do the ones that interest you.

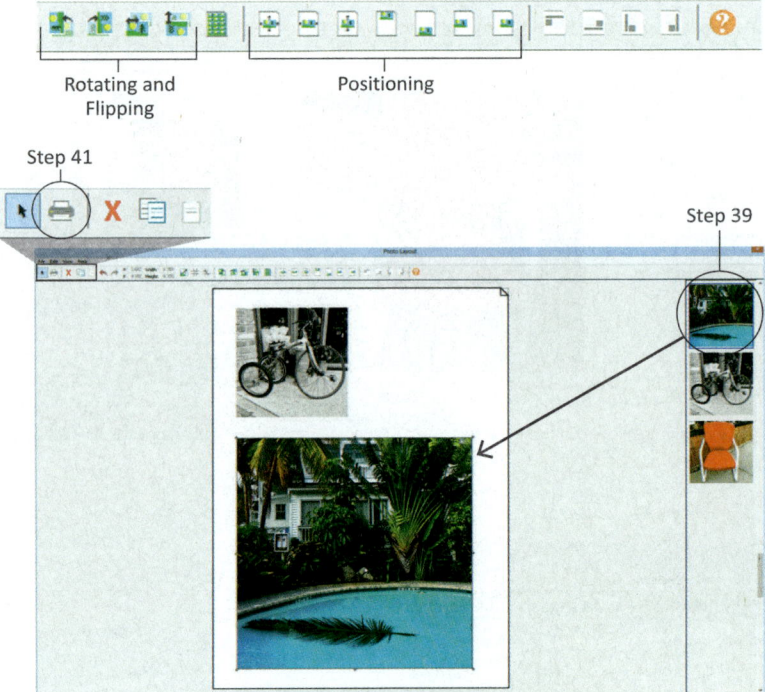

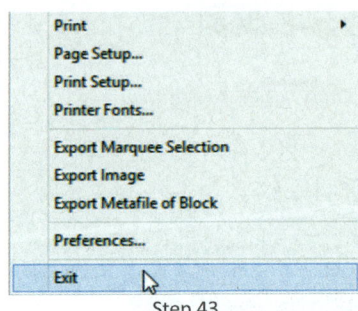

Step 43

Here's what we learned in this lesson:

- Import image
- See image info
- Add to Photo section of the Project Sketchbook
- Straighten fabric
- Crop fabric
- Add to Sketchbook as Fabric
- Apply fabric scale
- Fussy cut the fabric into position
- Build a custom Fabric Library
- Use the Photo Library
- Apply color balance
- Change a color photo to grayscale
- Apply oil painting Special Effect
- Use Photo Layout

CHAPTER 2

Quilt Worktable: After the Basics

You'll be back on the Quilt Worktable for this chapter. These lessons explore more of the quilt layout styles including, custom quilts and quilt labels. Feel free to skip around or skip over any lesson. We do suggest you complete Lesson 1 on Layers.

Lesson 1: Understanding Layers in EQ..76

Lesson 2: Creating a Custom Quilt Layout from Scratch....................................81

Lesson 3: Creating a Custom Quilt from a Block..85

Lesson 4: Making A Quilt Label 87

Lesson 5: Using Pre-designed Quilt Labels 90

Lesson 6: Making a T-Shirt Quilt 92

EQ8 Lessons for Beginners

LESSON 1: UNDERSTANDING LAYERS IN EQ

We've all read comparisons of quilts to sandwiches. The fabric front and back are the bread and the batting in the middle is the filling of the sandwich. The whole idea is to talk about the layers that make up a quilt. In EQ, we use layers as well. Layer 1 holds the blocks of our design. Layer 2 is for motifs, which are appliques with no background patch, and for applique text. Layer 3 is for quilting stencils or embroidery images. Stencils represent the stitching that goes through all 3 layers of a real quilt sandwich. The Photo tool and Thread tools can be used on any layer. Let's make a quilt using all three layers.

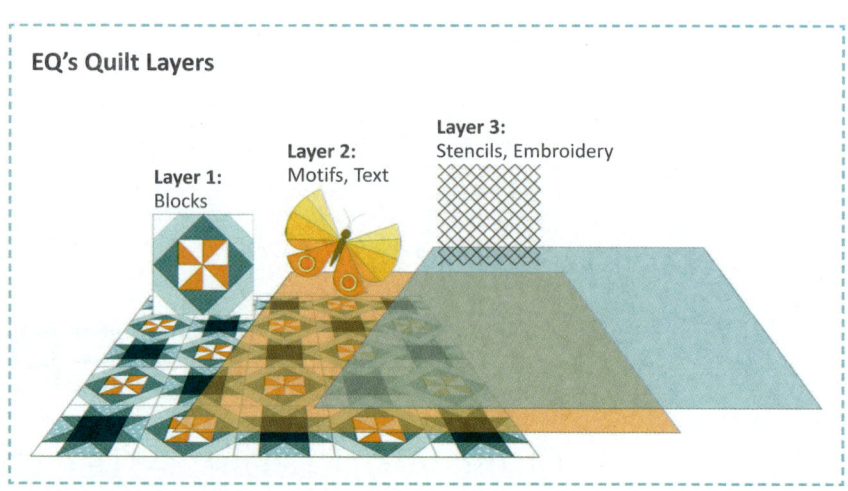

1. Click **File > New Project**, or click on the **New Project button** on the Main Toolbar.

2. Type **Chapter 2 Quilt with Layers** on the **Create a new project tab**, and click **OK**. This process created the project file Chapter 2 Quilt with Layers.PJ8 on your computer.

3. Click **Libraries > Layout Library**.

Using layouts from the library is another way to get started with a quilt layout. There are two libraries. One is organized by size and the other by style.

4. Click **Layouts by Size > Wall**.

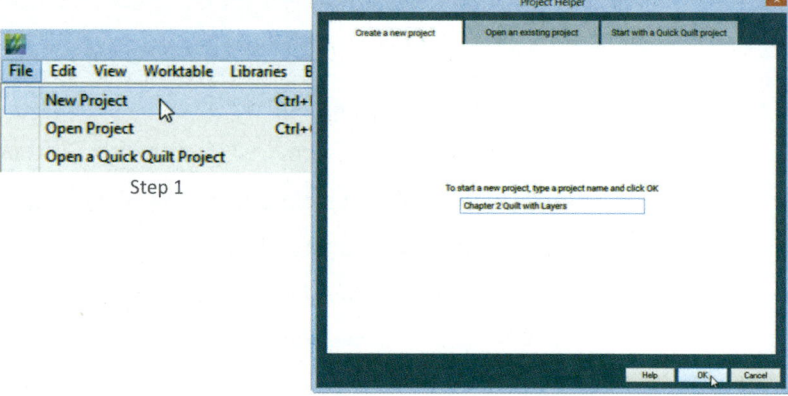

As you click on different layouts, you'll find information about the number of blocks, block size and so on at the bottom of the dialog box.

5. Click on the **on-point layout with sashing and 6 inch blocks**.

6. Click **Edit to Quilt Worktable**.

This is a fast way to get a layout without building it from scratch. Of course this does not mean that we can't make changes to it. You can always edit any layout. Let's change the borders.

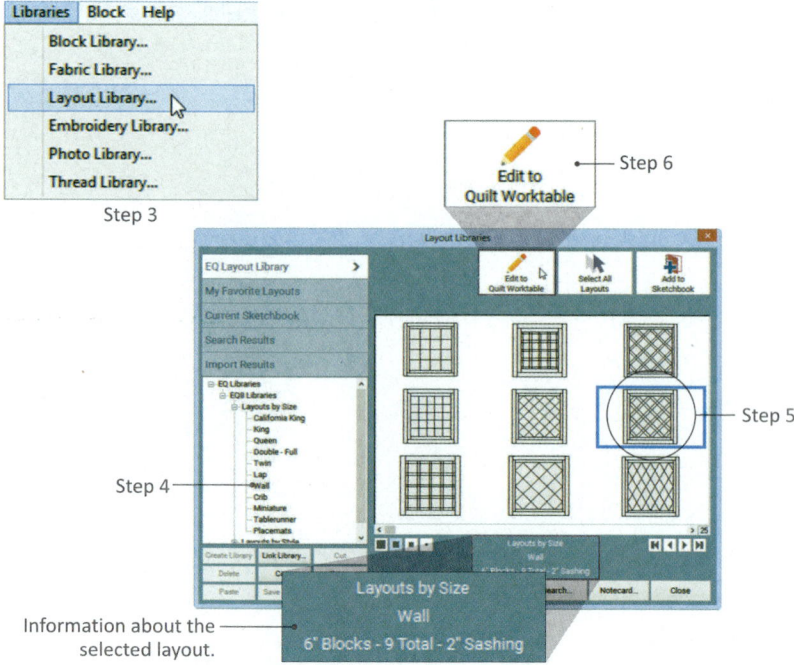

76

Chapter 2: Quilt Worktable: After the Basics

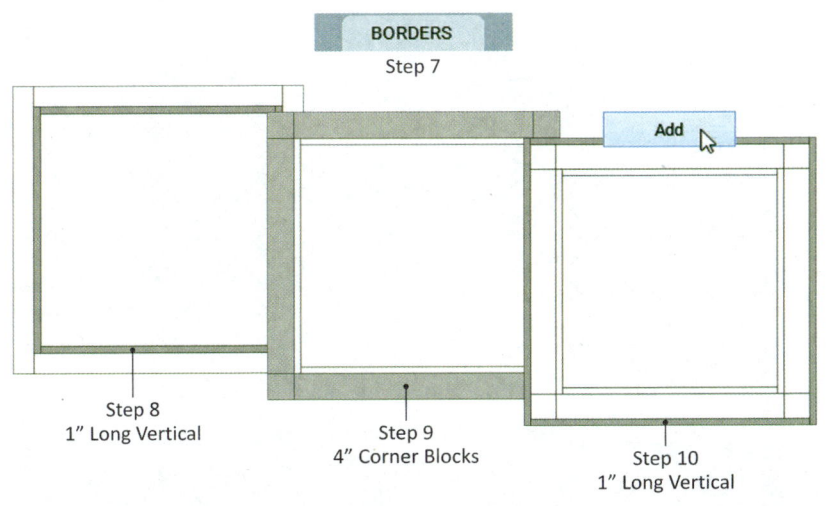

Step 7 BORDERS

Step 8
1" Long Vertical

Step 9
4" Corner Blocks

Step 10
1" Long Vertical

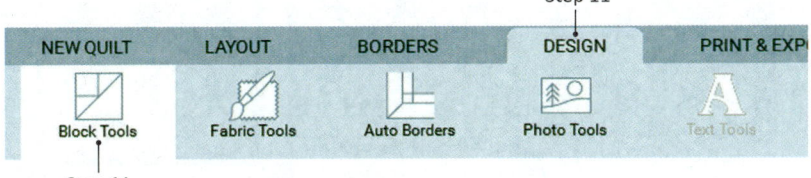

Step 11

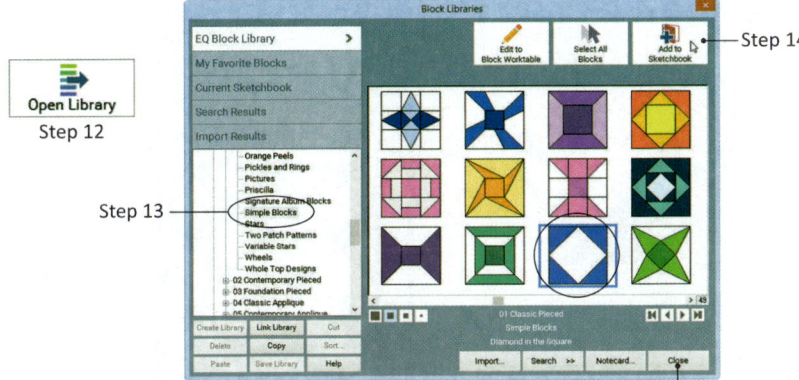

Step 12 Open Library

Step 13

Step 14

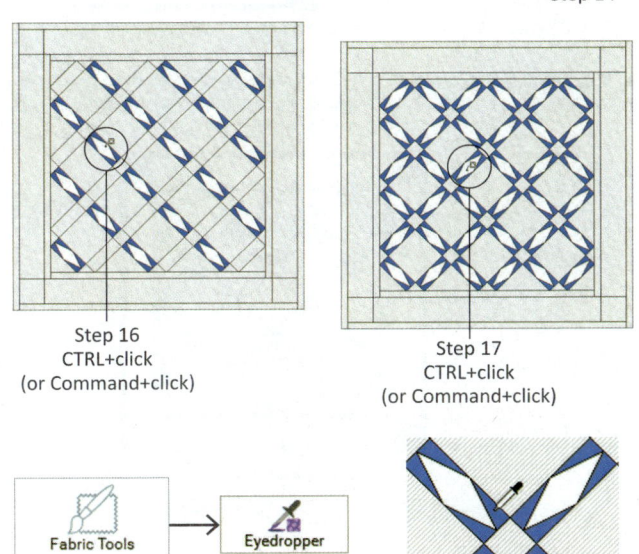

Step 16
CTRL+click
(or Command+click)

Step 17
CTRL+click
(or Command+click)

Step 18 Fabric Tools → Eyedropper

Step 19

7. Click the **BORDERS** tab.

8. Click on **Border 1** and change the size to **1 inch**. We will leave the style as Long Vertical.

9. Click on **Border 2** and change the style to **Corner Blocks** and make it **4 inches**.

10. Click **Add** to add a third border and change the style to **Long Vertical**. Leave the size a 1 inch.

11. Click **DESIGN > Block Tools > Set Block tool**.

12. Click the **Open Library** tool.

13. Scroll to **01 Classic Pieced > Simple Blocks > Diamond in the Square**. Depending on your display, you may need to scroll to find the block. Click directly on the block.

14. Click the **Add to Sketchbook** button, and then click **Close**.

15. Click the **Diamond in the Square** block in the palette.

16. Press and hold the **CTRL key** (Command) and click in one of long sashing locations.

17. Continue to hold **CTRL** (Command) and click in the other long sashing location.

18. Click **Fabric Tools > Eyedropper**.

19. Click on the **blue color in the sashing** to find the color and select it in the palette.

77

EQ8 Lessons for Beginners

20. Click the **Paintbrush** tool.

21. Press and hold the **CTRL key** (Command) and click in one of the cornerstones of the sashing. Half of the cornerstones will fill with blue.

22. **CTRL+click** (Command) to color the remaining cornerstones with blue.

Tip: Remember that if you click in the wrong location, click the Undo tool on the left toolbar.

23. **CTRL+click** (Command) in the first border.

24. **CTRL+click** (Command) in the corner squares of the wide border.

25. **CTRL+click** (Command) in the narrow third border.

26. Click the **Eyedropper** tool and click on the white color in the sashing to select the white color in the palette.

27. Click the **Swap Color** tool and click on the wide border to fill all the empty spaces with white.

28. Click **Add to Project Sketchbook**.

This completes Layer 1 of our quilt. Notice that the Text Tools and Embroidery Tools in the ribbon are disabled. They are not available for use on Layer 1.

29. Click **Layer 2** below the quilt.

30. Click **Block Tools > Set Block > Motifs tab** above the blocks.

31. Drag the **butterfly motif** to the upper-right corner of the quilt and drop it.

32. Drag a second **butterfly** to the same area of the quilt. It doesn't matter where these motifs land on the quilt. We'll adjust them.

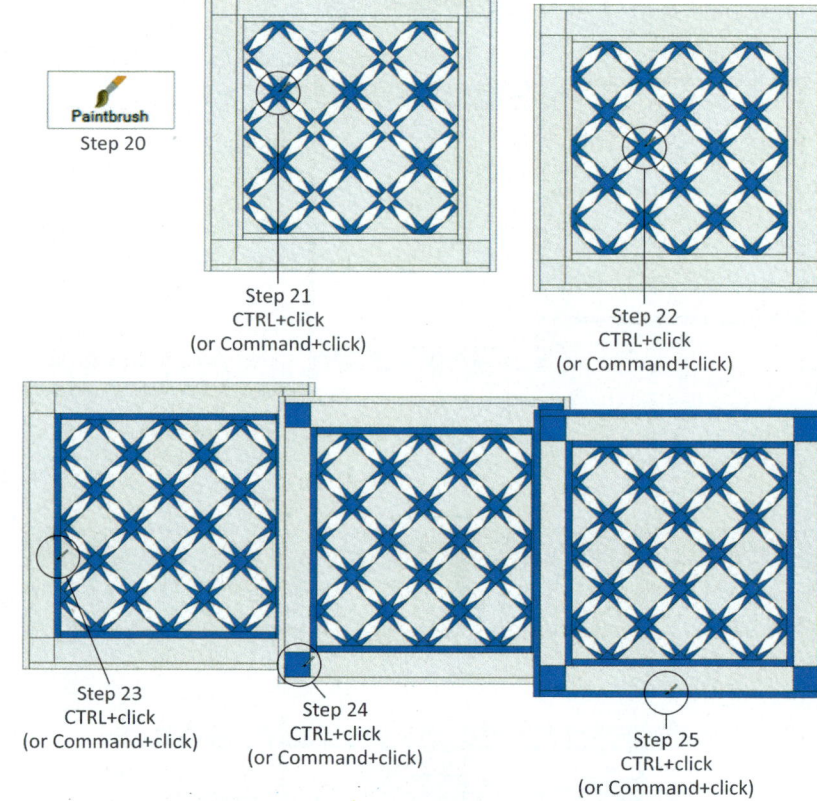

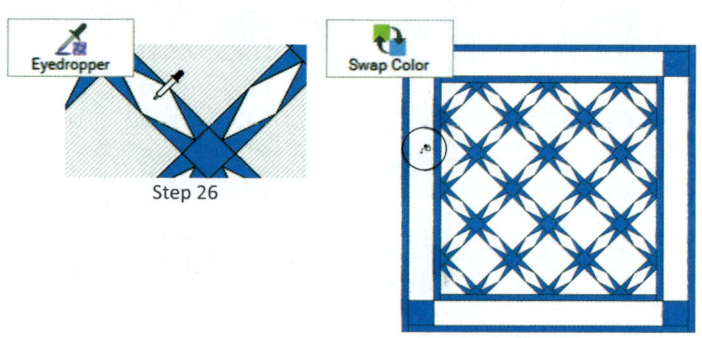

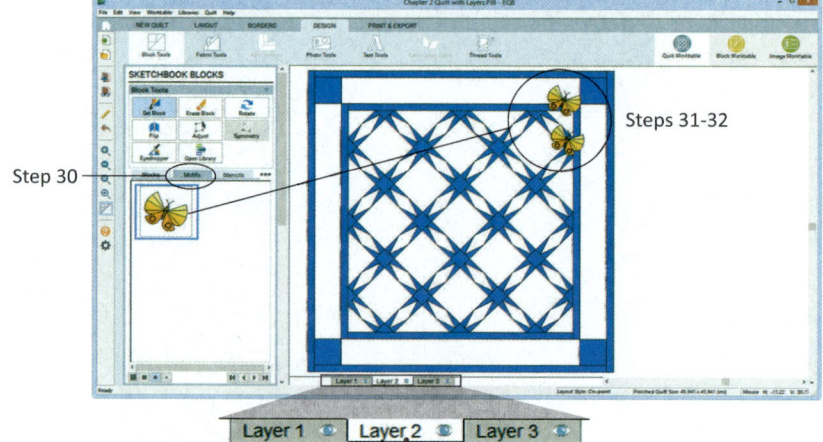

Chapter 2: Quilt Worktable: After the Basics

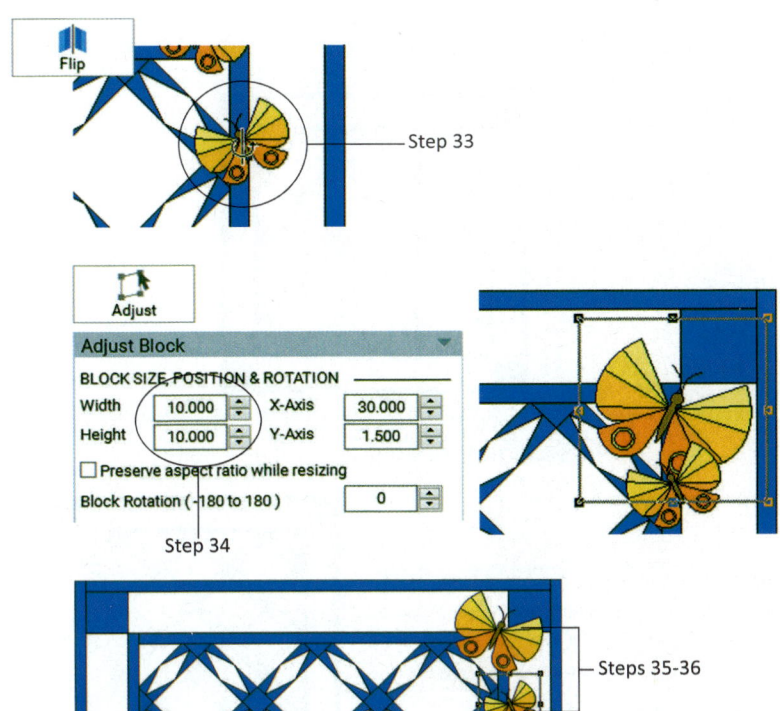

Step 33

Step 34

Steps 35-36

Step 37

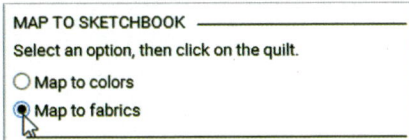

Step 38

Step 39
Click directly on the butterfly with the Randomize tool.

The solid colors will be replaced with fabrics from your Sketchbook.

Step 40

Quilt with patch lines on

Quilt with patch lines off

Step 41

33. Click the **Flip** tool and flip one of the butterfly motifs.

34. Click the **Adjust** tool and resize one of the butterflies to 10 inches by typing **10** in the Width and Height boxes in the palette, then clicking Enter on your keyboard.

35. **Position the larger butterfly** so that it overlaps the first two borders on the top and right of the quilt.

36. **Position the lower one** in a pleasing position underneath the first.

This completes Layer 2. Notice that Text Tools in the ribbon is now enabled and the Embroidery Tools are still disabled. Before we go to Layer 3, let's convert all of these solid colors into fabrics.

37. Click **Fabric Tools > Randomize tool**.

38. Click to select **Map to fabrics** under MAP TO SKETCHBOOK.

The tip in palette tells us to click on the quilt. Since we're on Layer 2, we need to click on one of the butterflies on Layer 2 to activate this feature.

39. **Click directly on a butterfly**. The entire quilt is now colored with fabrics with a single click. The fabrics are very close in color to the solids so you may not notice a dramatic change.

One way to make the quilt on the computer screen look more realistic is to turn off the dark lines that surround the patches.

40. Click the **Hide/show quilt patch lines** button along the left a couple of times to observe how this changes the look of your quilt. Leave the patch lines turned off.

41. Click **Add to Project Sketchbook**.

79

EQ8 Lessons for Beginners

42. Click **Layer 3** below the quilt.

43. Click the **Set Block tool > Stencils tab** above the blocks.

44. **Drag the stencil block** to the quilt and drop it.

45. Click the **Adjust** tool and move and resize the stencil to cover the entire quilt except for the outer-most border. Use the controls in the palette to fine tune it to **44 inches x 44 inches** at **-5.00 for both X and Y Axis**.

We can make the quilting look more realistic by giving it a thread color.

46. Click **Thread Tools > Spray Thread**.

47. Select a thread color like **medium blue**.

48. Under Thread Properties, check Style and choose **dashed**. Check Weight and choose the **thickest weight** so that we can see it more easily.

49. Click on the **stencil**. Since these lines are thin, it make take more than one click to get the stencil colored. Since we're using the Spray Thread tool and we sized the single block to cover the entire quilt, all the lines in this block will color at once.

You may find it useful when designing to turn off the visibility of one or more layers.

50. Click the **Eye icon** on the **Layer 3** tab. This turns off the stencil on Layer 3.

51. Click the **Eye icon** on the **Layer 2** tab. This turns off the butterfly motifs on Layer 2.

52. Click the **Eye icon** on the **Layer 1** tab. This dims the blocks on Layer 1 so that you can still use them as a reference when working on Layers 2 and 3.

53. Click each of the **Eye icons** to turn on all the layers.

54. Click **Add to Project Sketchbook**.

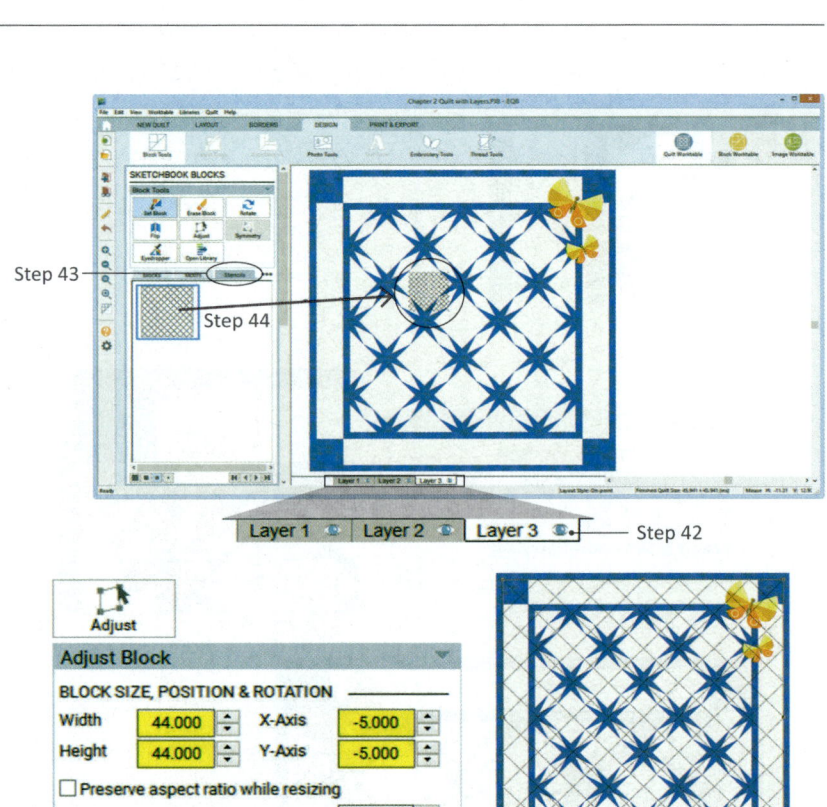

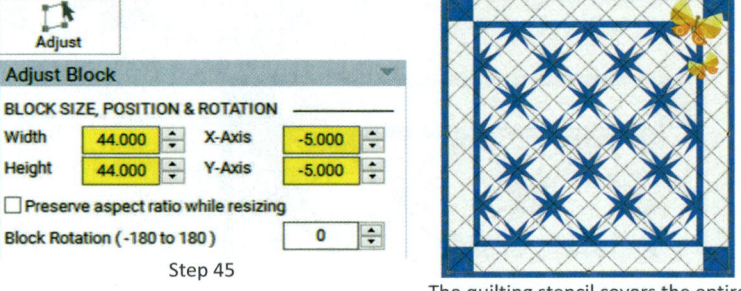

The quilting stencil covers the entire quilt, except the outside border.

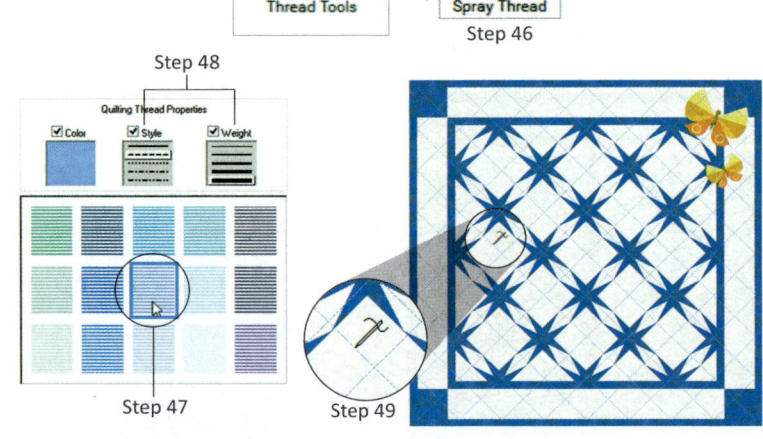

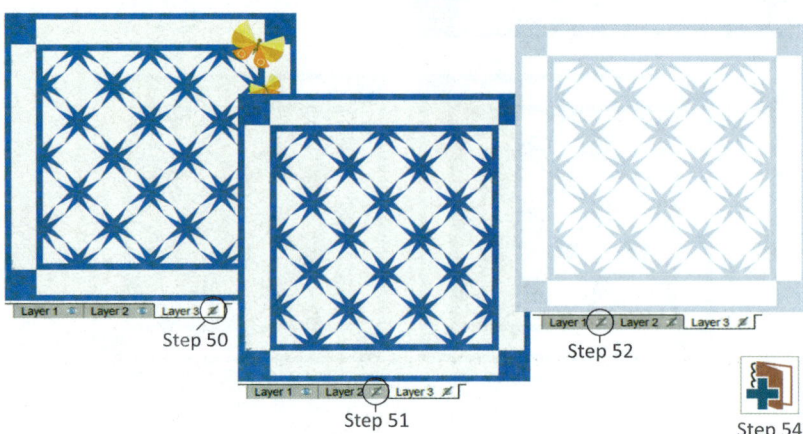

80

Chapter 2: Quilt Worktable: After the Basics

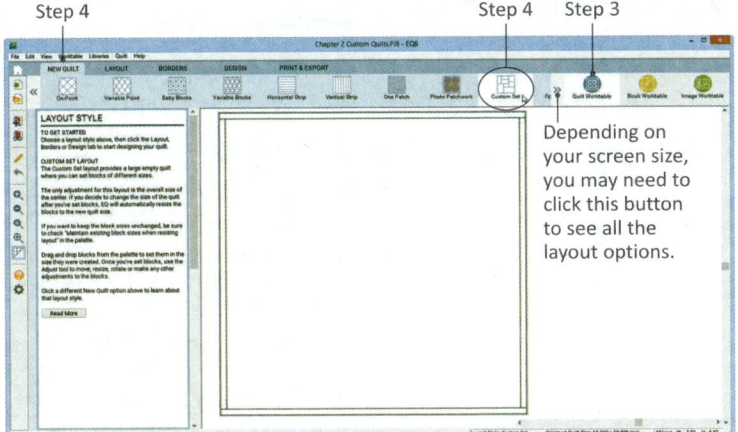

Step 1
Step 2
Step 4
Step 4
Step 3

Depending on your screen size, you may need to click this button to see all the layout options.

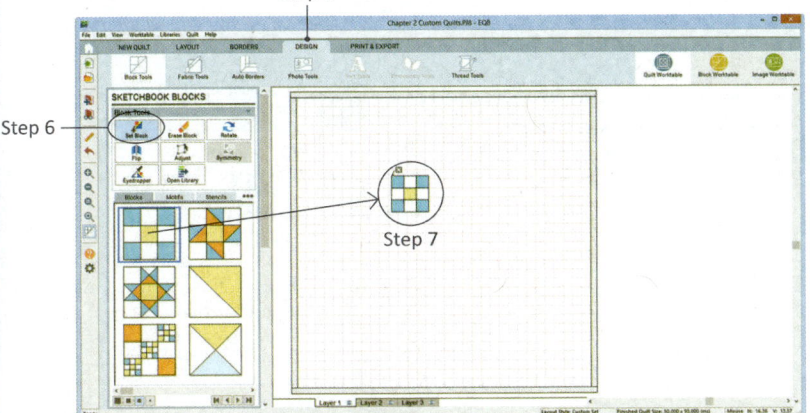

Step 6
Step 6
Step 7

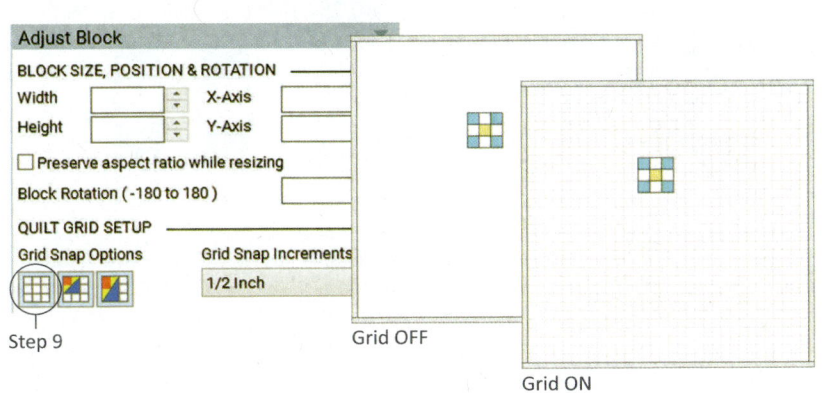

Step 9
Grid OFF
Grid ON

LESSON 2: CREATING A CUSTOM QUILT LAYOUT FROM SCRATCH

If you want to place blocks of different sizes next to one another in a quilt, then the Custom Layout is the best choice.

1. Click **File > New Project**, or click on the New Project button on the Main Toolbar.

2. Type **Chapter 2 Custom Quilts** on the **Create a new project tab**, and click **OK**.

3. Click **Quilt Worktable** on the ribbon.

4. Click **NEW QUILT > Custom Set**. You may need to scroll the ribbon to see it.

5. Click the **LAYOUT** tab.

The Custom Set layout is one large rectangle. Blocks can be placed anywhere in this rectangle.

6. Click the **DESIGN tab > Block Tools > Set Block** tool.

7. **Drag and drop** any block onto the worktable. The block will be the size that it was drawn when you drop it.

8. Click the **Adjust** tool in the palette.

Before we move and resize this block, let's look at the grid, the grid size and snapping options.

9. Click the **Show Grid** button a couple of times to observe how this button turns on and off the red grid lines in the quilt.

10. Float the cursor over the two snapping buttons to **read the tool tip** and make sure they are turned on.

The second button will snap the block to the grid. The third button will make the size of the block snap to the grid when resizing.

81

EQ8 Lessons for Beginners

The size of the grid can be adjusted easily using the drop-down control in the palette.

11. Click the down arrow and click **12 inches** for Grid Snap Increments. Notice that the grid is now 4 x 4. The overall size of our quilt was 48 inches, and 12 times 4 equals 48, so this makes sense.

12. Click on the block and **move it just a bit**, then release the mouse. You'll see how the block snaps to the grid. Now look in the palette at the numbers for the block size and position.

13. **Drag the corner node of the block** just a bit and then release the mouse to see the size of the block snap to the grid. Observe the new block size in the palette.

14. If the position of the block adjusted slightly when resizing, then move the block again just a bit and notice how the numbers in the palette change.

When making a custom quilt, be sure to pay attention to the numbers in the palette for the size and position of the blocks. This will keep your layout "perfect"—without gaps or overlap that you may not be able to see if you are just looking at the quilt.

15. Click the down arrow and click **1 inch** for Grid Snap Increments. Notice that there are many more red grid lines—too many to count.

16. Click on the block and **move it several times** letting it snap in several locations.

Depending on your screen, the block may not always snap to a red line. This is because the grid may not "show" a red line every 1 inch, but the snapping is set to 1 inch. Grid lines do not draw for the smaller snapping increments. So even though you don't see a red line, the grid is still snapping. The numbers in the palette will verify that the block is snapping every inch.

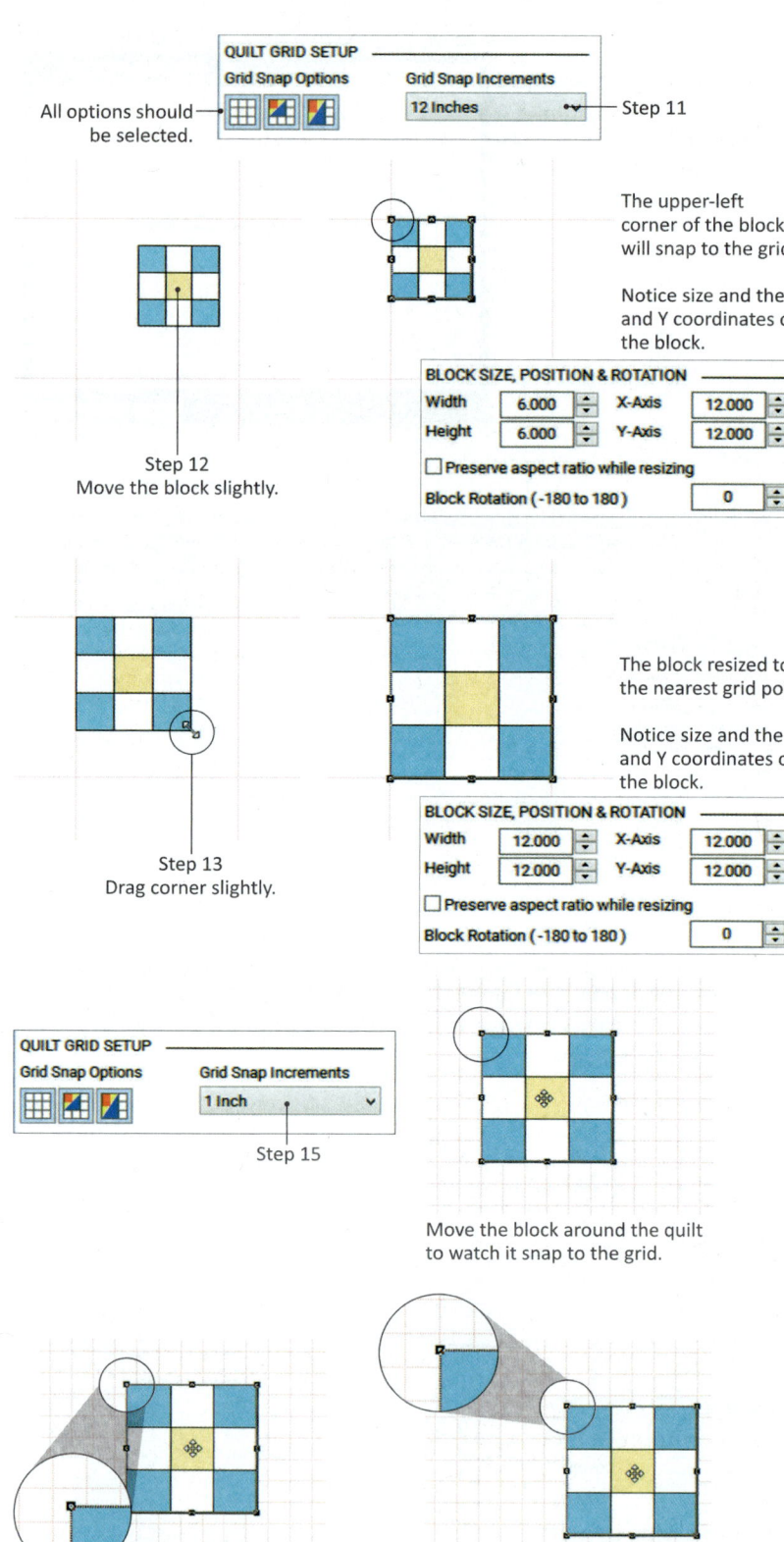

Chapter 2: Quilt Worktable: After the Basics

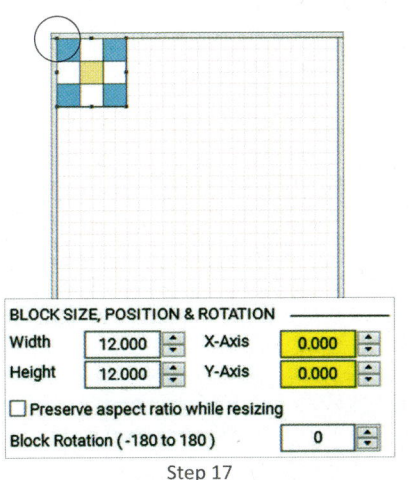

Step 17
Move the block to X-Axis 0.000 and Y-Axis 0.000.

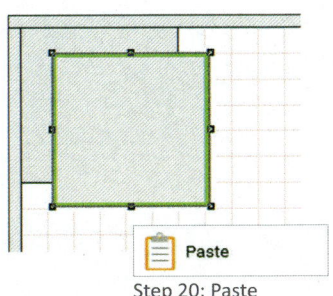

Step 18
Click to delete the design within the block space.

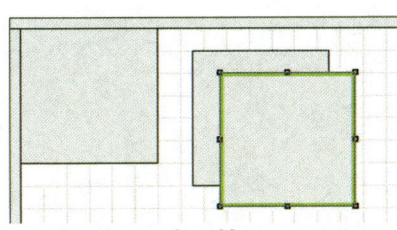

Step 20: Copy   Step 20: Paste

17. Move the block to the upper-left corner of the quilt and snap it to **X and Y position of 0 for both entries**.

18. Click the **Erase Block** tool in the palette and click on the block to erase the design.

Sometimes you will want to build your layout without the design of the blocks influencing you, and sometimes you'll want to leave the block design. Let's design the layout with empty blocks.

19. Click the **Adjust** tool and select the block.

20. Click **Copy** and then **Paste** in the palette.

21. Move the new block to another position in the quilt.

22. With the block still selected, press **CTRL+C** (Command+C) and then **CTRL+V** (Command+V) to use the keyboard to copy and paste.

23. Resize the new block by dragging one of the nodes. Make it **6 x 12** in size.

24. **Copy** and **paste** this vertical strip. **Position** both of these vertical strips next to the 12 inch blocks. Make sure to move the 12 inch blocks if you need to. No blocks should overlap.

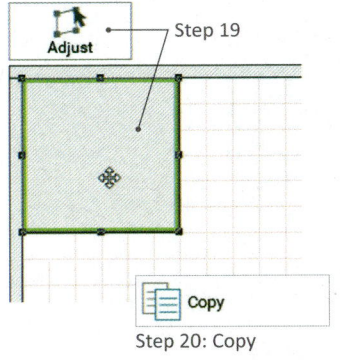

Step 22
CTRL+C then CTRL+V to copy and paste.
(Command+C and Command+V on a Mac)

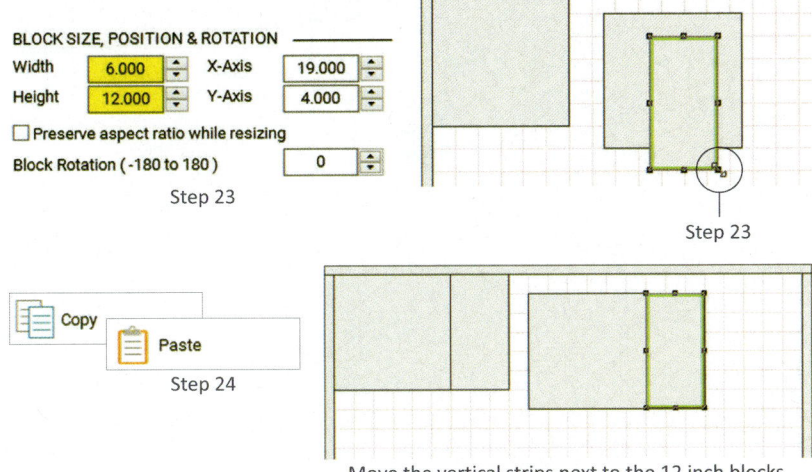

Move the vertical strips next to the 12 inch blocks.

83

EQ8 Lessons for Beginners

25. Continue to **create new blocks of various sizes and position them in the quilt** until the entire center is filled with empty blocks. Remember to use the numbers in the palette to help with sizes and position.

Tip: You can select more than one block to copy and paste by holding the SHIFT key as you select blocks.

26. Use the **Block Tools** to set blocks into several of the locations.

27. Use the **Fabric Tools** to fill any empty block with color.

28. When you're happy with your design, click **Add to Project Sketchbook**.

Tip: When you spend the time to create a custom layout, it's a good idea to save the layout to the Layout Library under My Favorite Layouts. We created a Favorites library in Chapter 1, Lesson 2 and in Lesson 3. Refer to those if you need help in creating another one. Saving the layout in the library will give you easy access to it the next time you want to use it.

Below are some sample layouts that you can imitate or create your own.

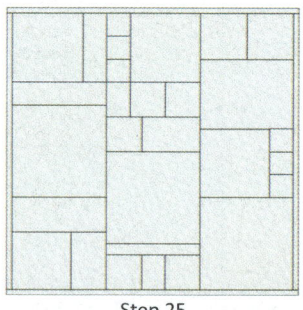
Step 25

Step 26

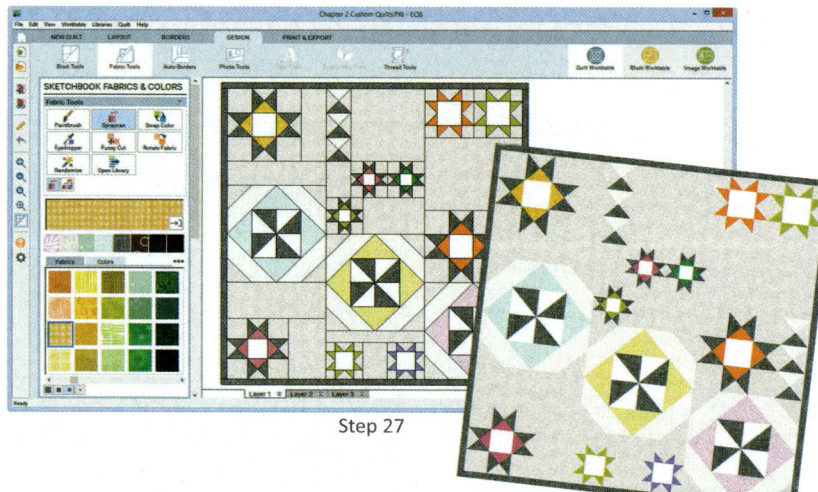
Step 27

Finished quilt with patch lines turned off.

Step 28

84

Chapter 2: Quilt Worktable: After the Basics

LESSON 3: CREATING A CUSTOM QUILT FROM A BLOCK

EQ has a feature called "Create Quilt From Block" that will turn any pieced block made up of rectangles and squares into a quilt. The blocks are required to have horizontal and vertical lines only—no diagonals. Here's how to do it.

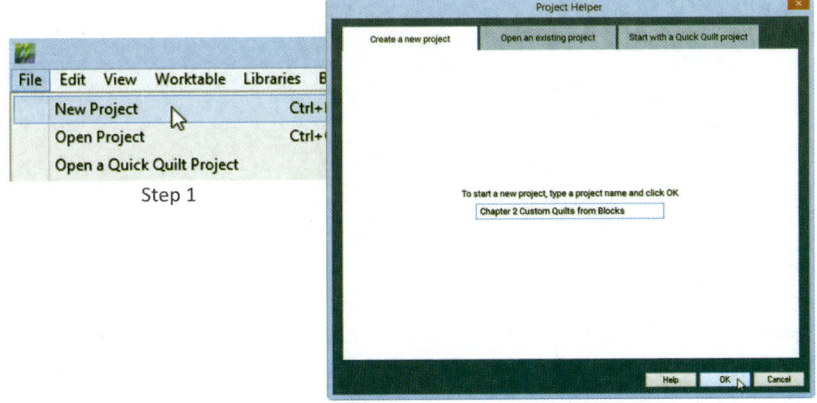
Step 1
Step 2

1. Click **File > New Project**, or click on the New Project button on the Main Toolbar.

2. Type **Chapter 2 Custom Quilts from Blocks** on the **Create a new project tab**, and click **OK**.

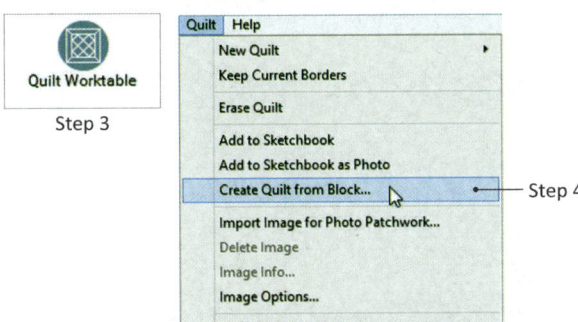
Step 3
Step 4

3. Click **Quilt Worktable** on the ribbon.

4. Click **Quilt** on the main menu and choose **Create Quilt from Block**.

5. Some of the default blocks are made up of horizontal and vertical lines only. They will show up in the box on the left. Click the **Nine Patch Chain** block.

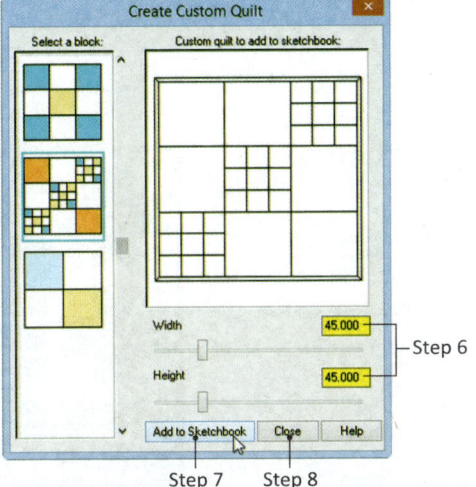
Step 6
Step 7   Step 8

The overall size of the custom quilt is set to 48 inches by default. It's always a good idea to think about the grid of the block design and the overall size. In this case, we have nine small blocks that fit horizontally and vertically so it would be helpful if the overall size of the quilt's center could be divided by 9.

6. Let's change the overall size to **45** by dragging the sliders or by typing 45 in both the boxes.

7. Click **Add to Sketchbook**.

8. Click **Close**.

9. Click **View Project Sketchbook** and click the **Quilts** section.

10. Click the **Nine Patch Chain** layout and then click the **Edit** button.

Step 9

Step 10

85

EQ8 Lessons for Beginners

11. Click the **LAYOUT** tab. You see this is a Custom Set layout that is 45 x 45.

12. Click the **DESIGN tab > Block Tools > Adjust tool**.

13. Click on several of the blocks in the quilt. The large blocks are 15 inches and the small ones are 5 inches.

Your custom layout is ready to be filled with blocks and fabrics. Use the Block Tools and Fabric Tools to color in your quilt.

14. Click **Add to Project Sketchbook**.

Tip: The Block Library has over 400 blocks that work with this feature! Block Library > Search > By Category > Rectangles Only > Search.

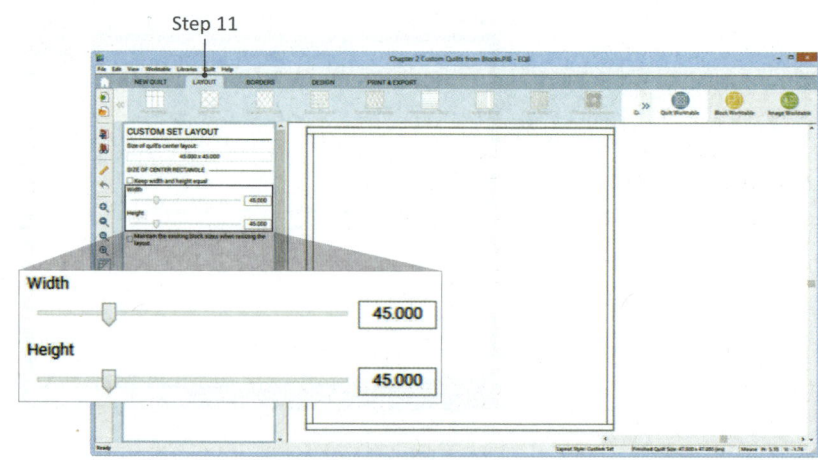
Step 11

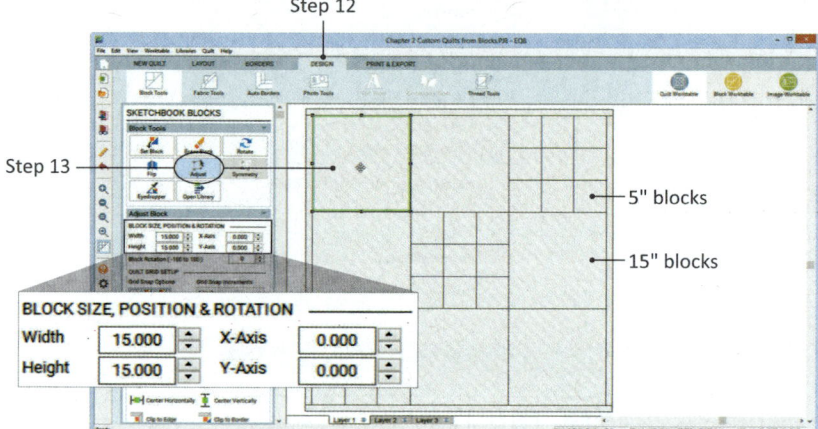
Step 12

Step 13

Set blocks into the layout.

Add fabrics.

Step 14

86

Chapter 2: Quilt Worktable: After the Basics

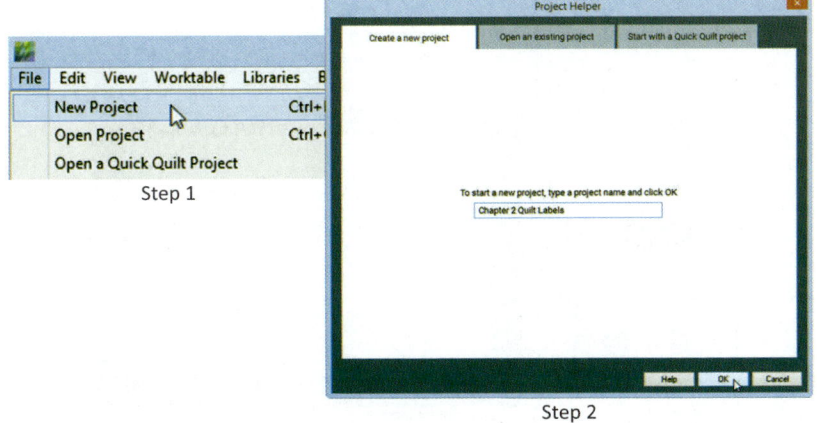

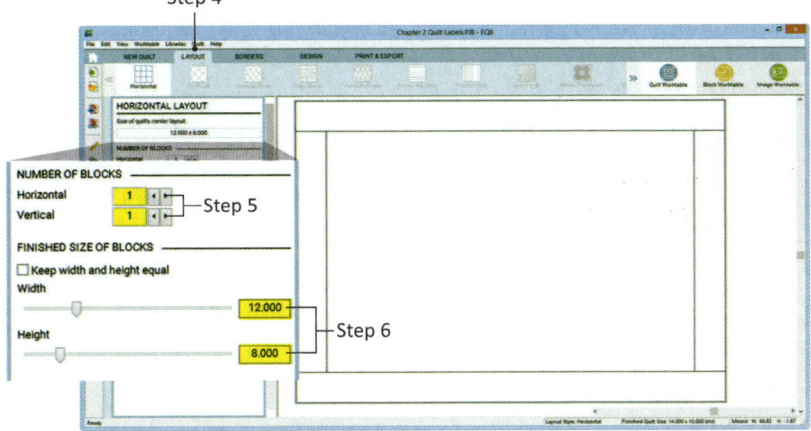

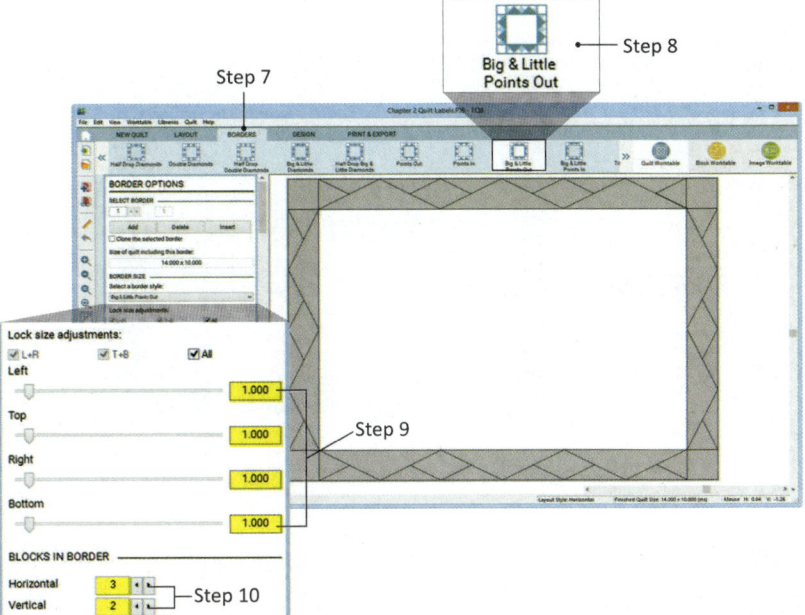

LESSON 4: MAKING A QUILT LABEL

Quilt labels personalize your quilts and provide important information for any future owners of your handiwork. They are the perfect finishing touch to any quilt. Here are the steps to make a simple label that can be printed directly onto printable fabric.

1. Click **File > New Project**, or click on the New Project button on the Main Toolbar.

2. Type **Chapter 2 Quilt Labels** on the **Create a new project tab**, and click **OK**.

3. Click **Quilt Worktable** on the ribbon.

4. Click **NEW QUILT > Horizontal > LAYOUT tab**.

5. Set number of blocks to **1** for **Horizontal** and **Vertical**.

6. Set the block size to **Width 12** and **Height 8**.

We don't really need to worry about the actual size of this quilt. We will resize it when we print it.

7. Click the **BORDERS** tab.

8. Set the border style to **Big & Little Points Out**. You may need to scroll the ribbon to see this option.

9. Set the border size to **1 for all sides**.

10. Set the number of blocks in the border to **3 Horizontal** and **2 Vertical**.

87

EQ8 Lessons for Beginners

11. Click the **DESIGN tab > Fabric Tools > Paintbrush tool**.

12. **Color the quilt with solid colors**, and use the **CTRL key** (Command) to help color patches in the border. **Make sure that the center of the quilt is a light color.**

13. Select a dark color in the palette to use for the text color.

14. Click **Layer 2**. This will enable the Text Tools on the ribbon.

Applique text is only available on Layer 2 of a quilt.

15. Click **Text Tools > Set Text tool**.

16. Set **Arial**, **1.500** for size and formatting to **centered**.

17. **Click on the quilt.** You'll see a blue note reminding you that you need to hold the SHIFT key to create the text box.

18. Press and hold the **SHIFT** key as you **drag out a box** on top of the quilt.

Don't worry about the size or position of the text box. We can make adjustments after we type the words for the label.

19. Type: **Made with Love** [press Enter to create a new line] **by Sophie** [press Enter twice to create two new lines] **November 2017**

20. Click the **Adjust** tool in the palette, and click on the text to select it.

21. Click **Center Horizontally** in the palette, and then **Center Vertically**.

22. Click **Add to Project Sketchbook**. This puts a copy of the quilt in the Quilts section of the Sketchbook.

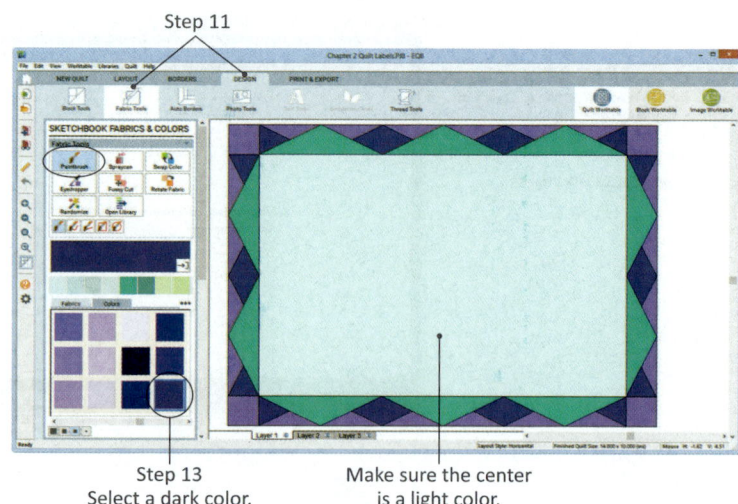

Step 11

Step 13
Select a dark color.

Make sure the center is a light color.

Step 14

Step 15

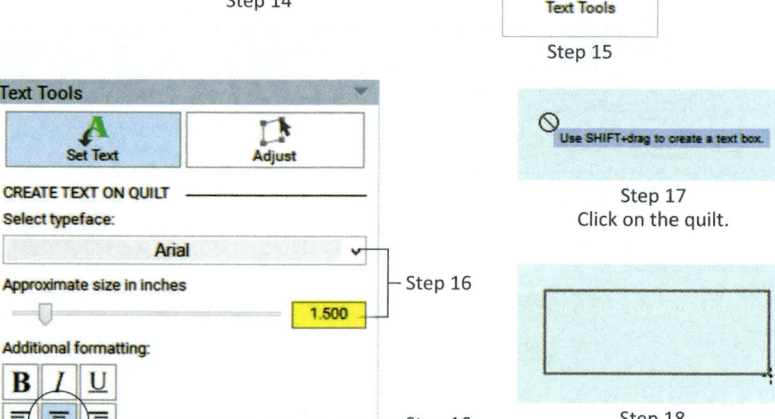

Step 16

Step 17
Click on the quilt.

Step 16

Step 18
Hold SHIFT and drag a box.

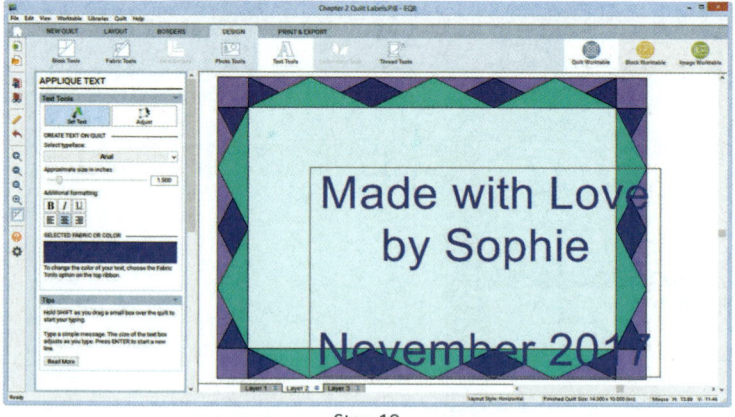

Step 19
Type your text. It's okay if it extends off the edge of the quilt.

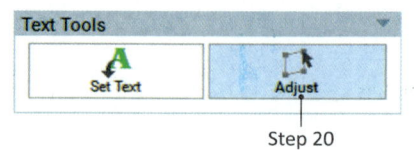

Step 20

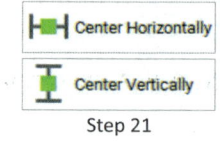

Step 21

Step 22

Chapter 2: Quilt Worktable: After the Basics

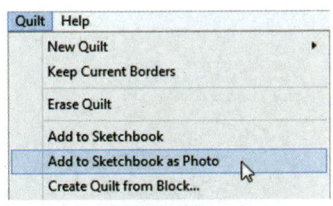
Step 23

Label in Quilts section

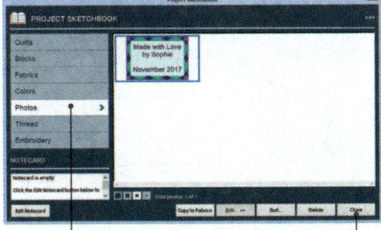
Label in Photos section

Step 26

Step 27

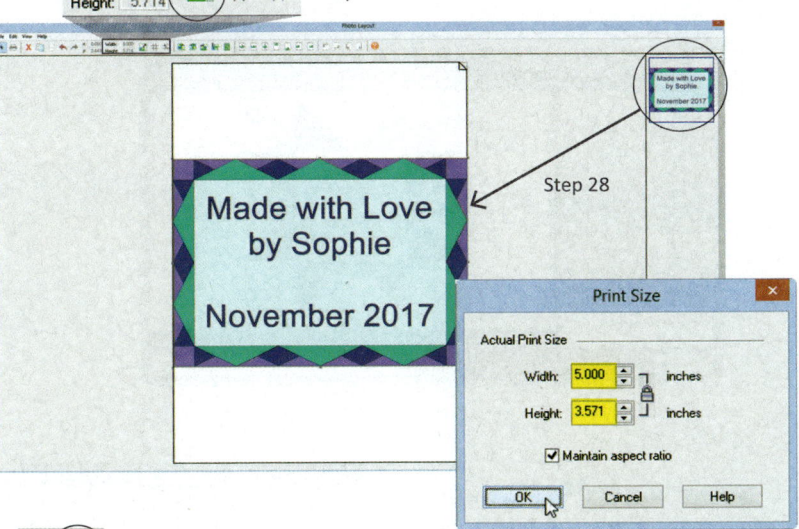
Step 29 / Step 28 / Steps 30-31

Step 32

23. Click Quilt on the main menu, then click **Add to Sketchbook as Photo**. This puts a copy of the quilt in the Photos section of the Sketchbook.

24. Click **View Project Sketchbook**. You will find the quilt in the Quilts section and a photo of the quilt in the Photos section.

25. Click **Close**.

26. Click **Image Worktable** on the ribbon.

27. Click the **PRINT & EXPORT tab > Photo Layout tool**.

28. **Drag the image of the quilt label onto the page**. If you get the message asking if you want it resized, click **Yes**.

29. Click the **Resize dialog** button. If the tool is disabled, click on the quilt label to enable the tools.

30. Change the Width to **5 inches**. The Height will adjust automatically to keep the same proportions as the original.

31. Click **OK**.

32. **Position** anywhere on the page and **print** a sample label on paper.

33. Click **File > Close Photo Layout**.

When using printable fabric, you'll want to plan your printout so that you can print several images at the same time to make the most of your printable fabric.

89

EQ8 Lessons for Beginners

LESSON 5: USING PRE-DESIGNED QUILT LABELS

EQ comes with several pre-designed quilt labels. Simply adjust the text, and your label is complete. Let's learn how to do it.

1. Click **Home > Start with a Quick Quilt project**.

2. Click **Quilt Labels.TP8** in the list, and click **OK**.

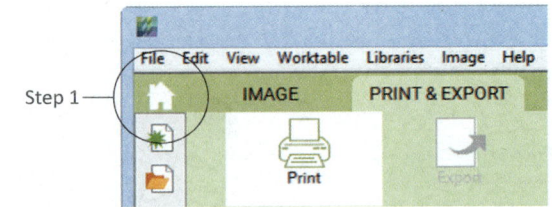

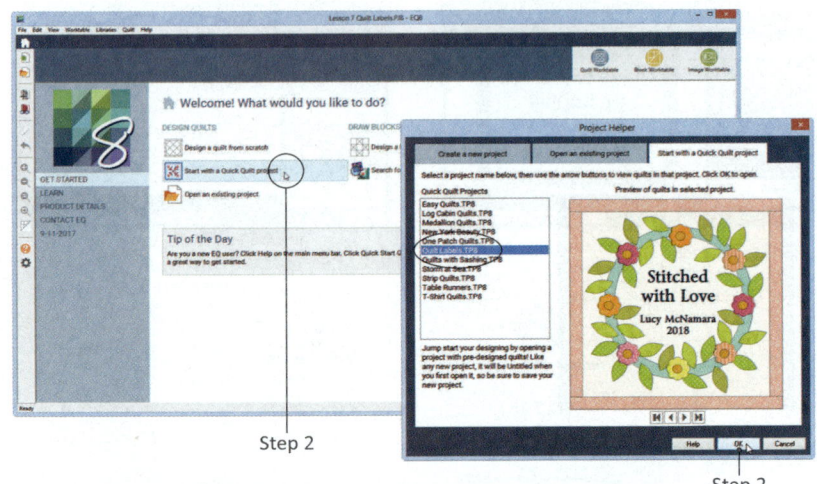

3. The Project Sketchbook will display. Click **Quilts** and scroll through all the quilts to see them.

4. Click **Sawtooth Star Quilt Label**, and click **Edit**.

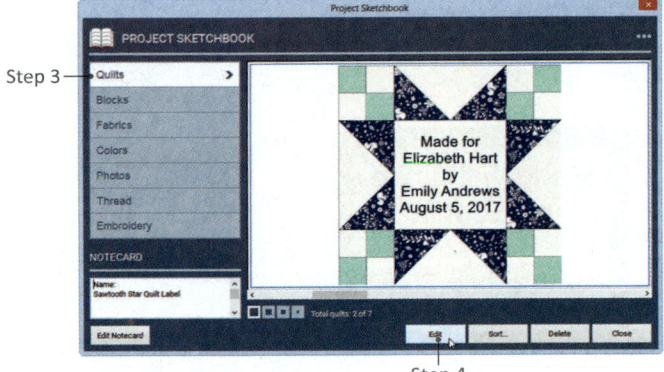

5. Click **Fabric Tools > Swap Tool** and recolor the quilt.

6. Click **Layer 2 > Text Tools > Set Text**.

7. **Click on the existing text to select it**. You may see a message if a font was used in the original design that does not exist on your computer.

8. Use the **Backspace** and **Delete** keys on your keyboard to remove the existing text.

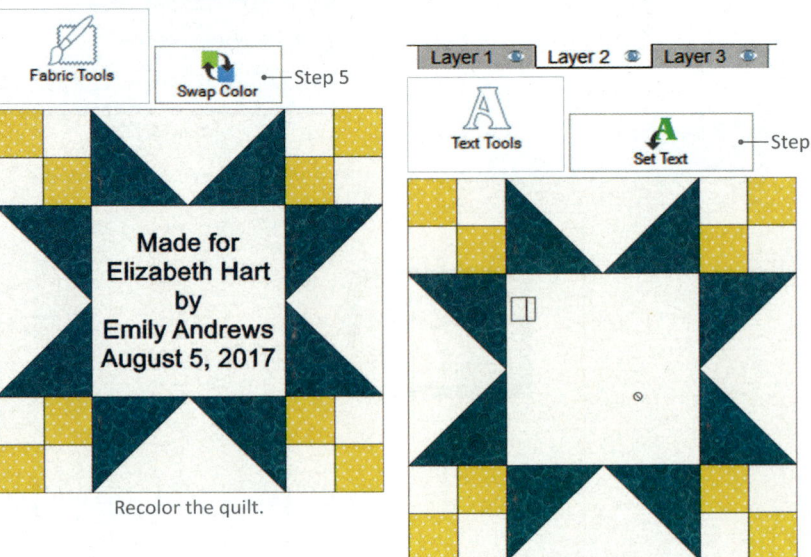

Recolor the quilt.

Step 8
Delete the text from the text box.

Chapter 2: Quilt Worktable: After the Basics

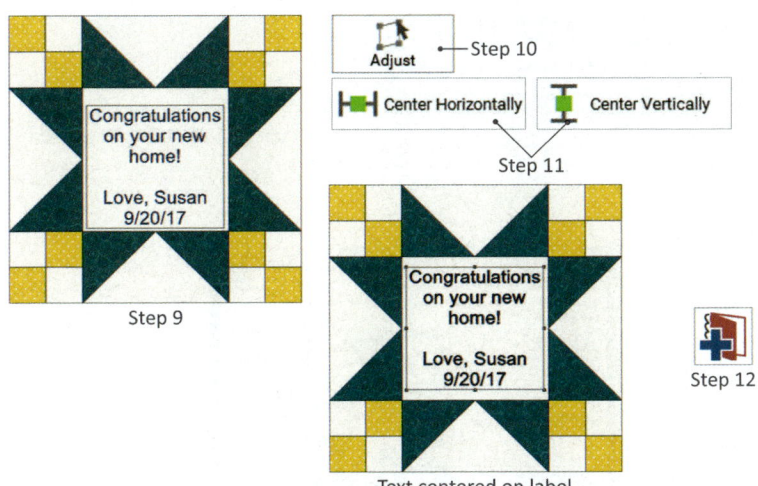

Step 9

Step 10
Step 11

Text centered on label
Step 12

9. **Type a new phrase**. Remember to use the Enter key to start a new line. There is no word wrap. You can adjust the font and size in the palette.

10. Click the **Adjust** tool in the palette, and click on the text to select it.

11. Click **Center Horizontally** in the palette, and then **Center Vertically**.

12. Click **Add to Project Sketchbook**. You'll see the Save As dialog for naming a project. This is because Quick Quilt projects always open as Untitled projects. Let's name the project.

13. Type **Chapter 2 Quick Quilt Labels** in the File name box.

14. Click **Save**. The project has been named.

15. Click **Quilt** on the main menu, then click **Add to Sketchbook as Photo**.

16. Click **Image Worktable** on the ribbon.

17. Click the **PRINT & EXPORT tab > Photo Layout tool**.

18. **Drag the image of the quilt label onto the page**. If you get the message asking if you want it resized, click **Yes**.

19. Click the **Resize dialog** button, and set the size you want for the label.

20. Click **OK**.

21. Drag the label to **position it** anywhere on the page.

22. If you like, **print** a sample label on paper.

23. Click **File > Close Photo Layout**.

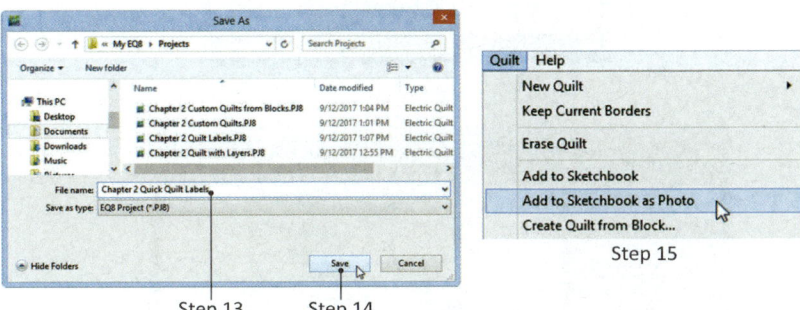

Step 13 Step 14
Step 15

Step 16 Step 17

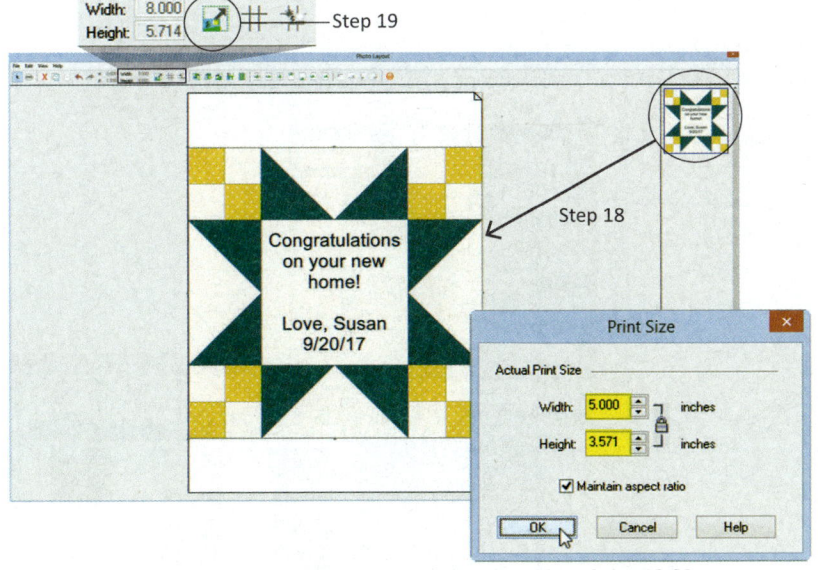

Step 19
Step 18
Steps 19-20

Step 22

91

LESSON 6: MAKING A T-SHIRT QUILT

You've cut your t-shirt logos into squares and rectangles of various sizes and stabilized them. You're ready to design the quilt. EQ has several pre-designed layouts to help you.

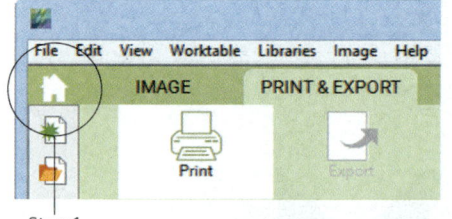
Step 1
Home

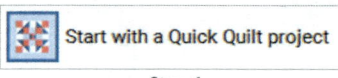
Step 1

1. Click **Home > Start with a Quick Quilt project**.

2. Click **T-Shirt Quilts.TP8** in the list, and click **OK**.

3. The Project Sketchbook will display. Scroll through all the quilts to see them.

4. Edit the first quilt, **T-Shirt Quilt with Mixed Sizes**.

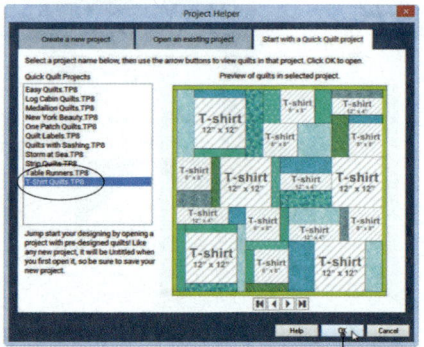
Step 2

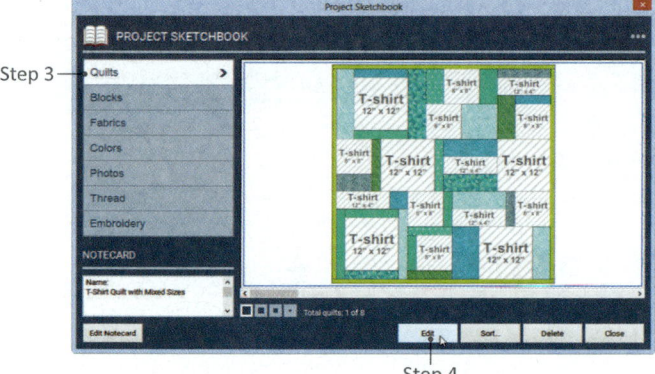
Step 3

Step 4

5. Click **Photo Tools > Set Photo**.

We see 4 photos that represent our t-shirt images. You can take photos of your t-shirt images and import them. Let's get a photo from the Photo Library to make some "fake" t-shirt images that we can use in this lesson.

6. Click **Open Library** in the palette.

7. Click **Colors > 09 White, Gray & Black** and find the second to last photo – Open Sign.

8. Click on the **Open Sign** photo, and click **Edit to Image Worktable**.

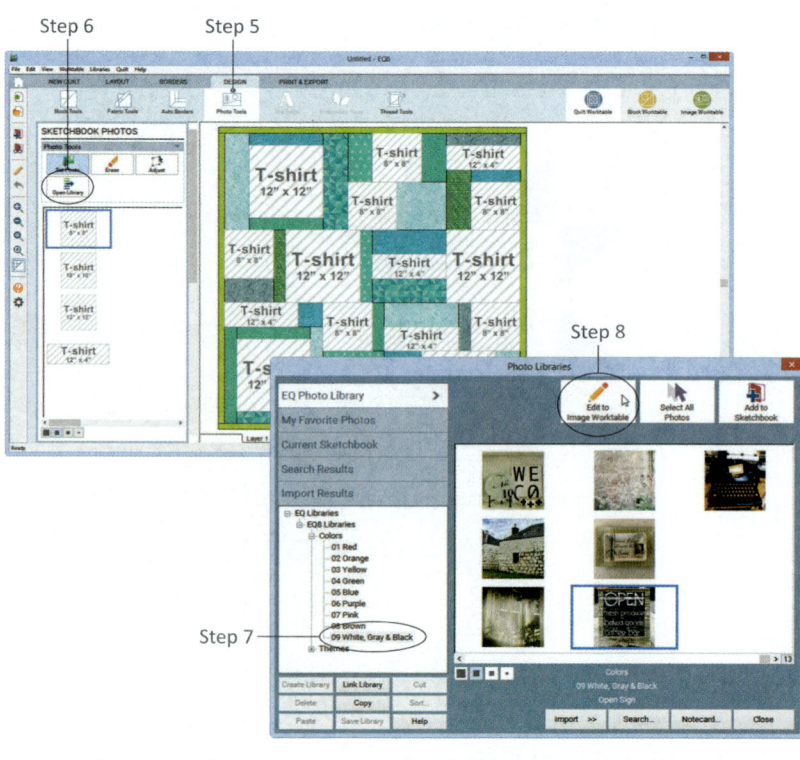
Step 6 Step 5

Step 8

Step 7

92

Step 9

Step 10

Step 11

Step 12

Step 13

Step 13

Step 14

Step 15

Three new photos have been added.

Step 17

9. Click **IMAGE > Crop** tool and adjust the sides to show just the words on the image.

10. Click **Apply Crop**.

11. Click **Add to Project Sketchbook**.

Since this is the first time we've use Add to Project Sketchbook and our Quick Quilt project is Untitled, the Save As dialog will display.

12. Type **Chapter 2 Quick Quilt T-Shirt Quilts** and click **Save**. The project has been named.

13. Adjust the sides to remove everything except *fresh produce* and **Apply Crop**.

14. Click **Add to Project Sketchbook**.

15. Click **View Project Sketchbook**, then click **Photos**. We've added 3 new images to the Photos section. If you had imported photos or scans of your t-shirt blocks, they would appear here.

16. Click **Close**.

17. Click **Quilt Worktable** on the ribbon.

We should return to the Photo Tools with the Set Photo tool selected. Our new photos that represent our t-shirts appear in the palette.

18. Set the first image in the 12 x 12 locations, the second image in the 8 x 8 locations, and the last image in the 12 x 4 locations.

Step 18

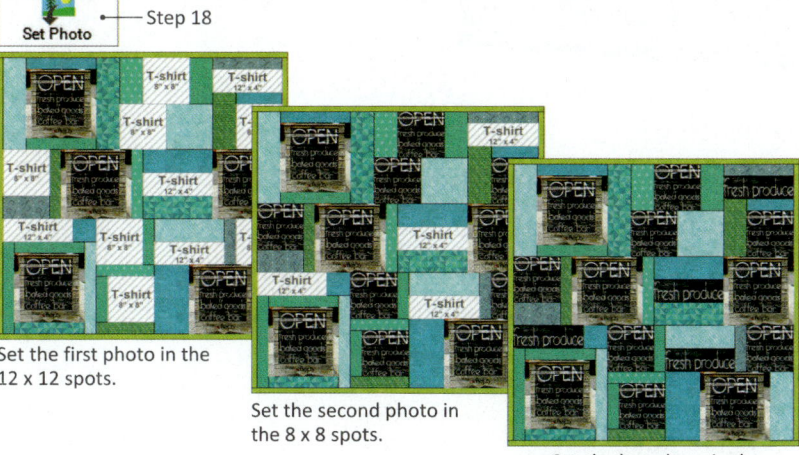

Set the first photo in the 12 x 12 spots.

Set the second photo in the 8 x 8 spots.

Set the last photo in the 12 x 4 spots.

EQ8 Lessons for Beginners

19. Click **Add to Project Sketchbook**.

Step 19

What if your t-shirt blocks are not the same size as in this quilt? You can create a custom quilt from scratch or you can adjust an existing layout like this one.

20. **Right-click over the quilt** to display the context menu.

21. Click **Erase Quilt**. Now we can see the layout of this custom quilt.

22. Use the **Adjust** tool in the palette to resize blocks.

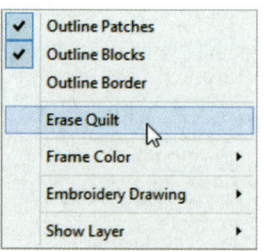
Step 21

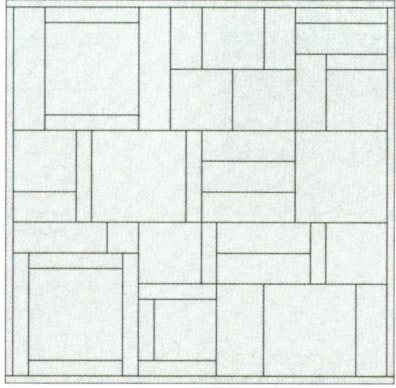
Quilt with all blocks erased, leaving empty spaces for blocks, fabrics or photos.

Block sizes are visible in the palette. Keeping all the snapping buttons turned on is helpful. Practice resizing some blocks. If you make blocks bigger, you'll need to resize the neighboring blocks to make room. If you make blocks smaller, you'll need to resize the neighboring blocks to fill in the gaps.

Tip: These layouts are great for memory quilts as well. Substitute your photos for the t-shirt locations in the quilt.

CHAPTER 3

Block Worktable: After the Basics

In Chapter 1 you learned how to use EasyDraw for drawing pieced blocks. In this chapter you'll learn to draw pieced blocks with the PolyDraw tools, and you'll have fun using several PatchMaker tools to draw applique blocks.

Lesson 1: PolyDraw Basics for Pieced Blocks 96

Lesson 2: Eight Point Star Grid and the PolyLine Tool 100

Lesson 3: Drawing Arcs with the PolyArc Tool 103

Lesson 4: Drawing Basics for Applique Blocks 106

Lesson 5: Applique Motif vs. Applique Block 110

LESSON 1: POLYDRAW BASICS FOR PIECED BLOCKS

In Lesson 2 of Chapter 1, we learned a lot about using EasyDraw. Now let's explore the PolyDraw tools for drawing pieced blocks. PolyDraw works differently than EasyDraw. PolyDraw builds blocks by drawing complete patches. The patches can be easily cloned and rotated to create the entire block. EQ has six special grids to aid you in drawing. Snapping is always automatic. It does not matter where you start to draw a patch as long as you remember to return to that same point to end the patch.

Let's begin by practicing the technique. Since we're just practicing, **we do not need to save a project for this lesson**. You can continue to work in whichever project you currently have open.

1. Click **Block Worktable** on the ribbon.

2. Click **NEW BLOCK > Pieced > PolyDraw**.

The PolyDraw tools appear in the palette. There will be two tabs along the bottom of the block. One says Applique. Since we want to draw a pieced block, we will stay on the PolyDraw tab.

3. Click **Rectangle** under GRID PROPERTIES. This block looks a lot like an EasyDraw block except there is no dark outline for the edge of the block. This is because edges of a PolyDraw block get created by completely filling the block with closed patches.

4. Click the **PolyLine** tool. Drag down the palette scrollbar to read about the PolyLine tool.

A double-click is two quick consecutive clicks of your left mouse button. When using the PolyDraw tools, *double-click* will **start** a drawing. *Double-click* will **end** a partial drawing and erase it at the same time. *Double-click* will **close** and complete the polygon if the mouse cursor is on top of the original starting point. Let's practice.

5. **Double-click** anywhere on the worktable, **release** the mouse button and **move** the mouse cursor. There is no need to press and hold the left mouse button when drawing with the PolyDraw tools.

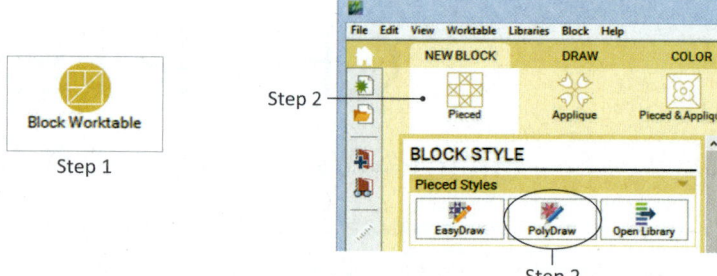
Step 1
Step 2

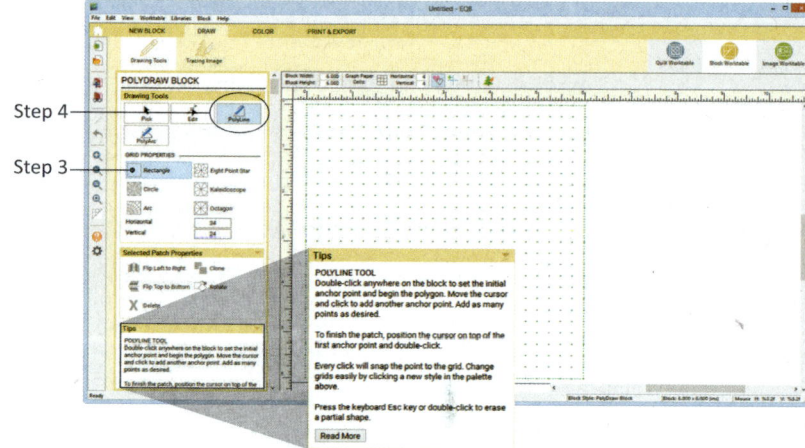
PolyLine tip

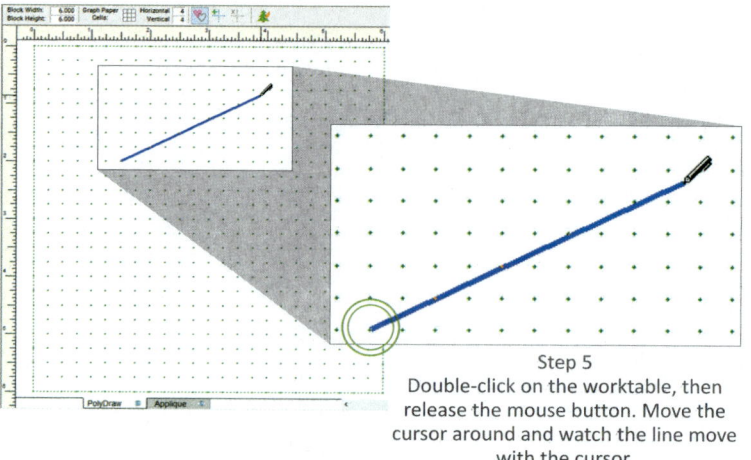
Step 5
Double-click on the worktable, then release the mouse button. Move the cursor around and watch the line move with the cursor.

In the most current version of EQ8, you will see a large green square appear after double-clicking to anchor your first line. This green square helps you know where to start and stop your drawing. If you do not see the green square, be sure to update your version of EQ8.

Chapter 3: Block Worktable: After the Basics

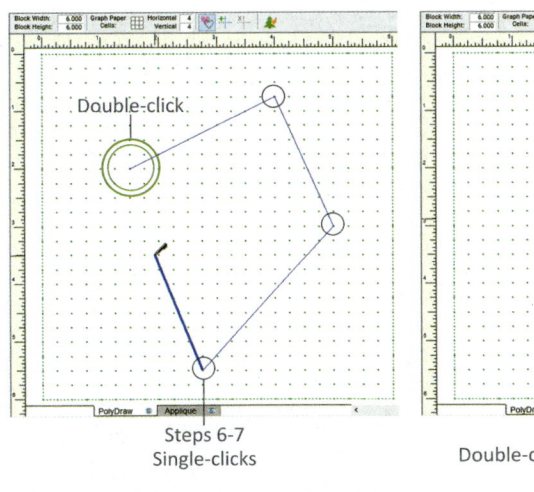

Steps 6-7
Single-clicks

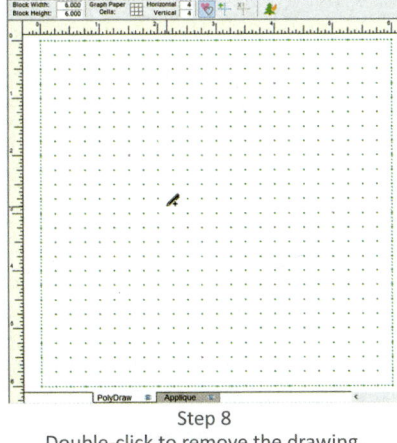

Step 8
Double-click to remove the drawing.

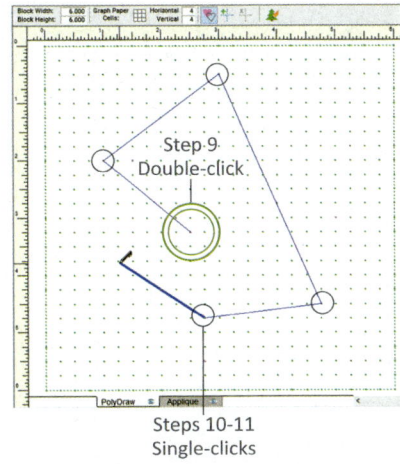

Steps 10-11
Single-clicks

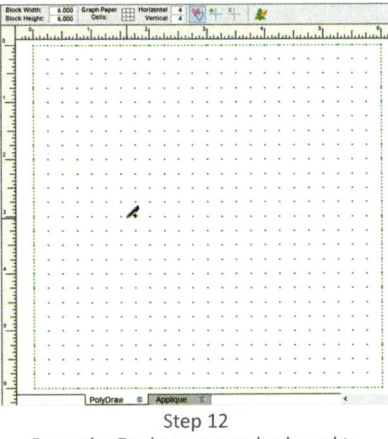

Step 12
Press the Esc key on your keyboard to remove the drawing.

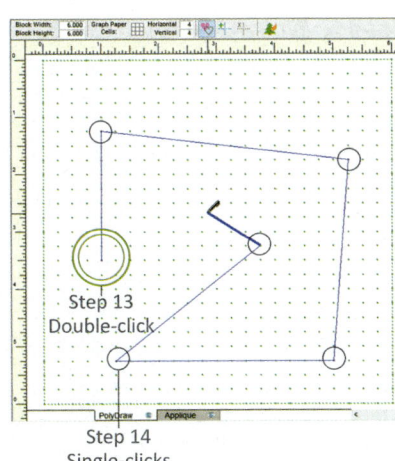

Step 14
Single-clicks

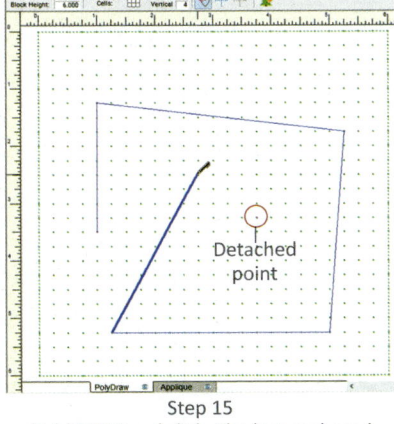

Step 15
Hold SHIFT and click. The last anchored point gets detached from the drawing.

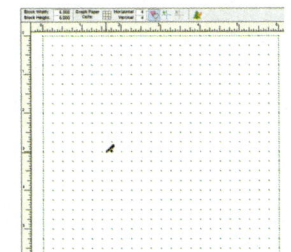

Step 17
Double-click to remove the drawing.

6. **Single-click and release** the mouse button on any space on the worktable. This anchors a second point for your shape.

7. Continue to **move** the mouse and **click** to anchor a segment.

8. Once you've anchored three or four points, **double-click anywhere on the worktable**. The partial drawing will be removed because no closed shape was created.

9. **Double-click** anywhere on the worktable to start a new drawing.

10. **Move** the cursor to a new position and **click**.

11. Continue to anchor 3 or 4 more points.

12. Press the **Esc** key on the keyboard to erase the drawing.

13. **Double-click** anywhere on the worktable to start a new drawing.

14. **Click 4 or 5 times** to anchor several points in different locations on the worktable.

15. Press the keyboard **SHIFT** key and click anywhere on the worktable. This will remove the last anchored point which turns two segments into one. In other words, it deletes the last-drawn segment.

16. Continue to hold the **SHIFT** key and click on the worktable. With each click, the nodes will detach and the drawing collapse.

17. **Double-click** to erase the partial drawing.

18. **Double-click** anywhere on the worktable to start a new drawing.

19. **Click 4 or 5 times** to anchor several points.

20. **Return to the starting point and double-click**. The polygon will close, and the patch will fill with cream to indicate it is closed. The patch will automatically be selected allowing you to move, rotate or clone the patch.

21. Position the cursor over the **four-headed arrow** in the center of the patch. Click, hold and **drag the patch** to move it.

22. Click outside the patch to deselect it.

23. Click the **Edit** tool in the palette.

The Edit tool allows you to add and remove nodes and move the position of any node.

24. Position the cursor over one of the anchored nodes and click on it. This will select it and draw the node larger.

25. Click, hold and **drag the node** to a new location and drop it. It will snap to a new snap point. Remember that snapping is automatic and always turned on.

26. Practice moving a couple more nodes.

27. Now **position the cursor over a straight line segment** between two nodes.

28. **Double-click on the segment**. A new node will be added.

29. Click, hold and **drag the newly added node** to a new location and release the mouse to snap it to a point.

30. Click on the worktable away from the node to de-select it.

31. Now **position the cursor over that newly added node and double-click**. The node will delete.

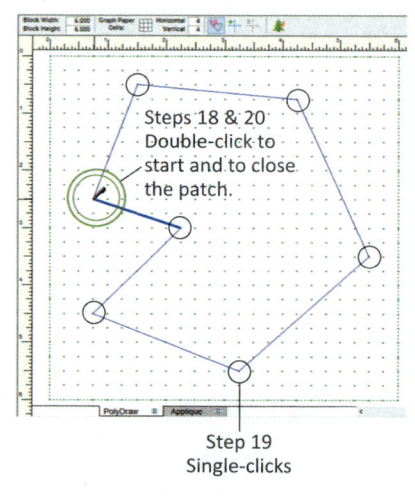

Step 19
Single-clicks

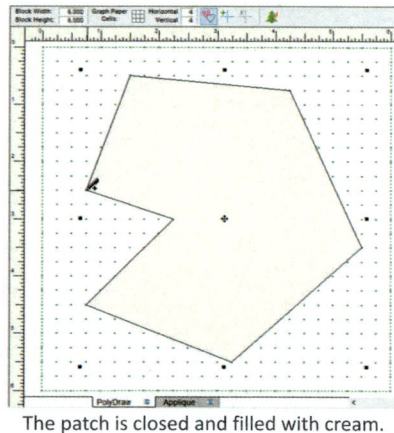

The patch is closed and filled with cream.

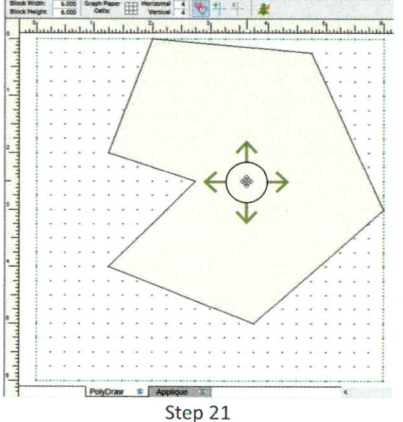

Step 21
Drag to move the patch on the worktable.

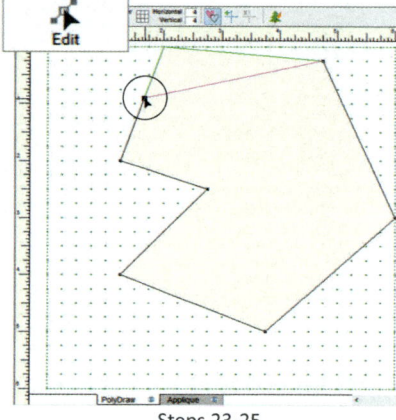

Steps 23-25
With the Edit tool, drag a node to a new position.

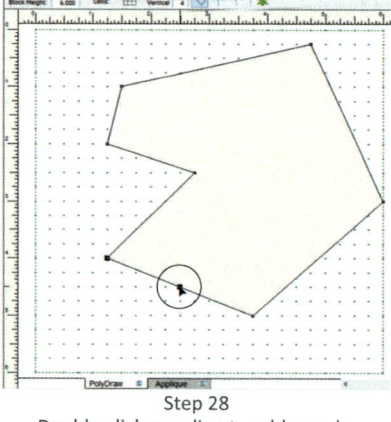

Step 28
Double-click on a line to add a node.

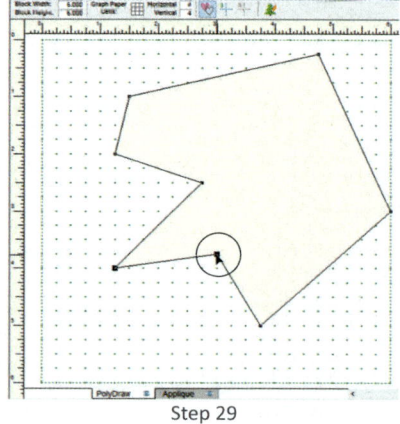

Step 29
Drag the node to a new position.

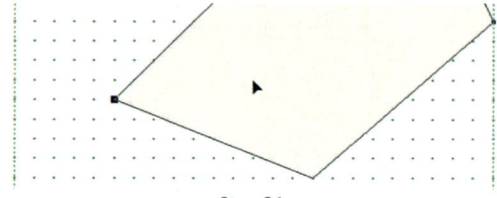

Step 31
Double-click on the node to delete it.

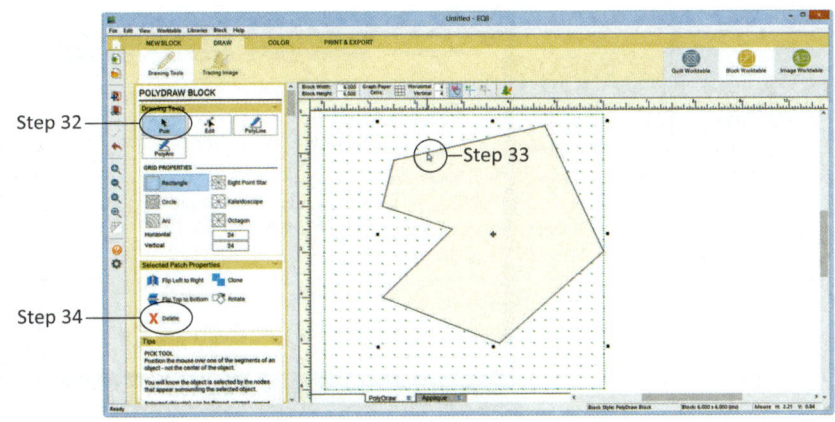

Step 32
Step 33
Step 34

32. Click the **Pick** tool in the palette.

33. Position the cursor on one of the segments of the patch, and click to select it.

Note: When using the Pick tool, the cursor must be on one of the segments, not in the center of the patch, to select it. Once it is selected, then the cursor needs to be in the center of the patch to move it.

34. Click the **Delete** button in the palette or press the keyboard's Delete key. The entire patch is deleted.

Here's a review of using the PolyDraw tools for drawing pieced blocks.

- Double-click to start drawing a patch.
- Double-click or press Esc to erase a partial drawing.
- Hold the SHIFT key to release the last anchor point.
- Double-click to close a patch.
- Newly drawn patches can be moved, cloned, rotated or deleted, otherwise use the Pick tool.
- Add, delete or move nodes using the Edit tool.

The rectangular grid will allow you to draw about any rectangular block you can think up. It's as easy as connecting the dots. The graph paper is very helpful when you build a rectangular block. Remember to make your snap points a multiple of the block size and make sure your graph paper falls on a snap point.

To learn to use the PolyArc tool, see the lesson Using the PolyArc Tool and a Special Grid.

LESSON 2: EIGHT POINT STAR GRID AND THE POLYLINE TOOL

EQ has six special grids to aid you in drawing. The best part of using the special grids is cloning and rotating patches. Let's get a special grid and draw a block.

1. Click **File > New Project**, or click on the New Project button on the Main Toolbar.

2. Type **Chapter 3 Eight Point Star** on the Create a new project tab, and click **OK**.

3. Click **Block Worktable** on the ribbon.

4. Click **NEW BLOCK > Pieced > PolyDraw**.

5. Click **Eight Point Star** under GRID PROPERTIES. The worktable will display guides showing an eight-pointed star on the block.

6. Set the block size in the precision bar to **12 for Width** and **12 for Height**.

7. Make sure the **Graph Paper** is turned **OFF** in the precision bar.

8. Click the **PolyLine** tool.

9. Position the cursor in the **center of the block** and **double-click** to start the drawing.

10. Move and click to anchor points to create the diamond that appears in the grid at the one o'clock position.

11. When you're back to the center of the block, **double-click** to complete the diamond. The patch will fill with cream and become selected.

12. Click **Clone** in the palette. The first patch will deselect and the newly created clone will be selected.

13. Click **Rotate** in the palette.

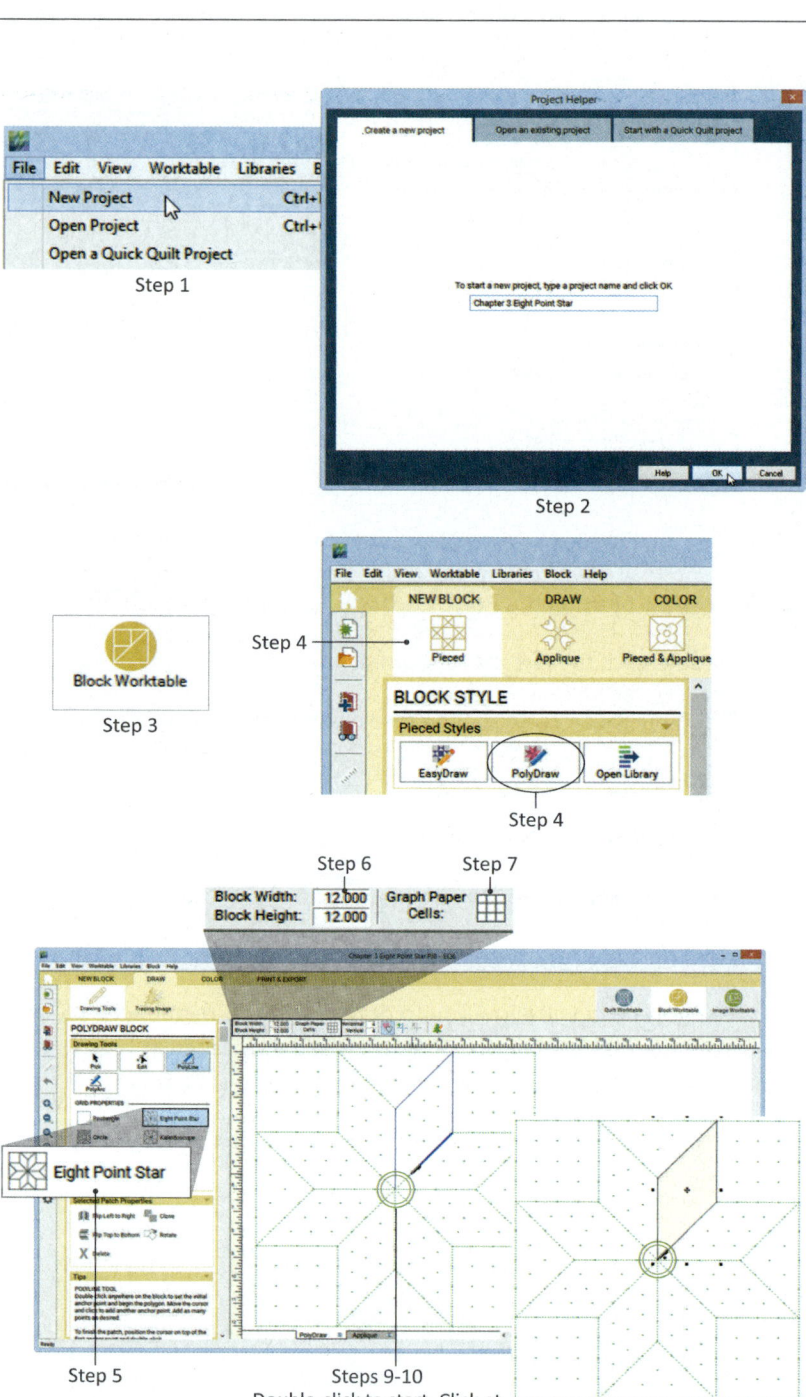

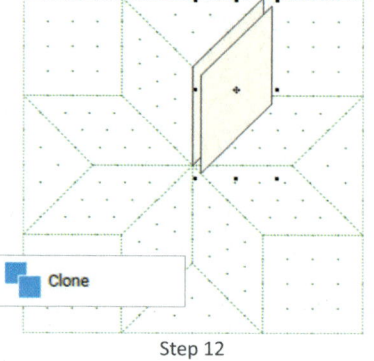

Step 12

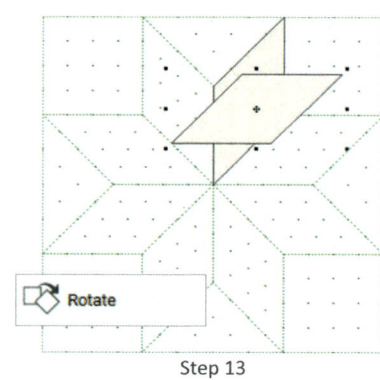

Step 13

Chapter 3: Block Worktable: After the Basics

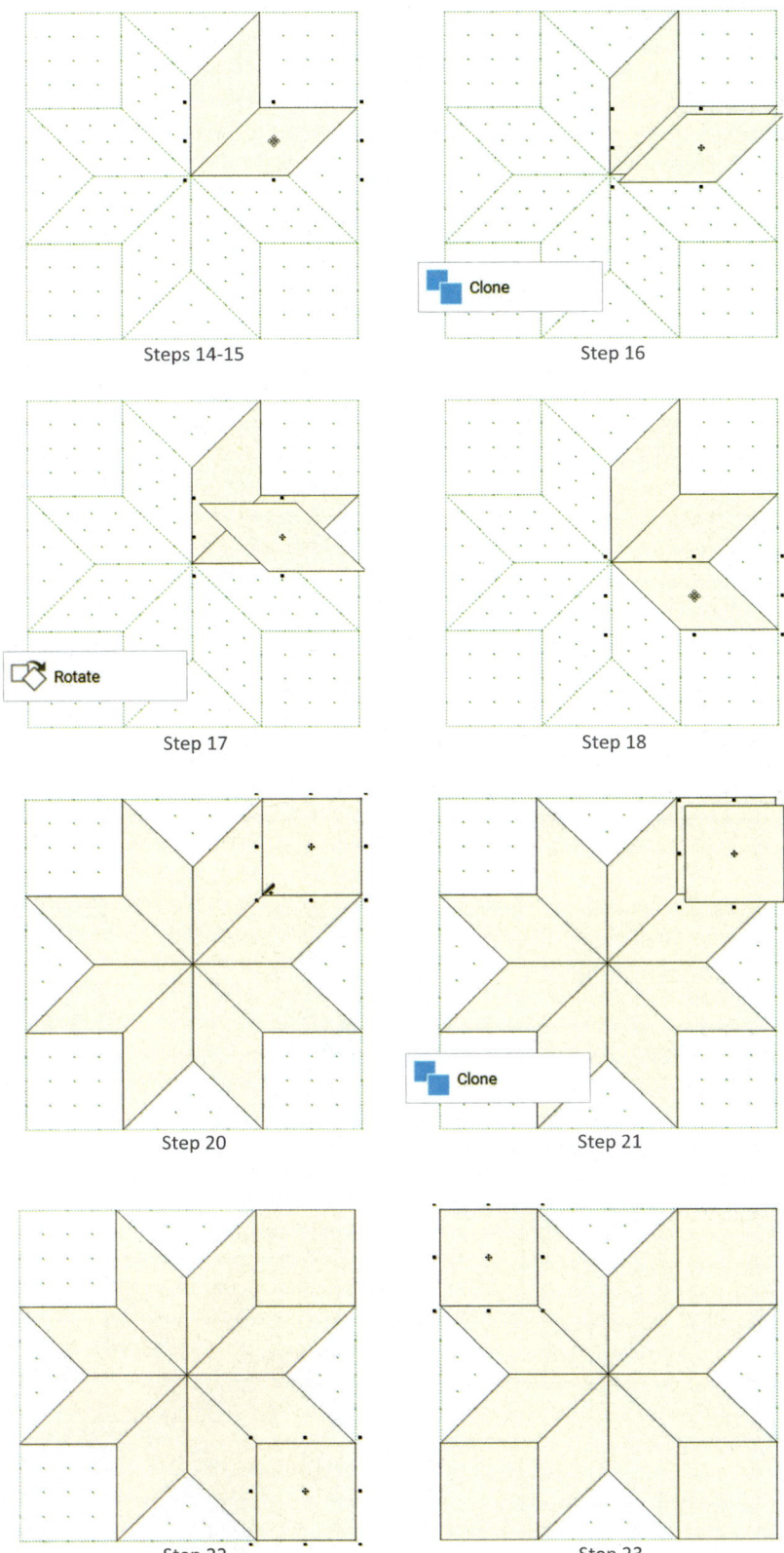

14. Position the cursor over the **four-headed arrow** in the center of the patch. Click, hold and **drag the patch** to move it into the position of the next diamond, clockwise from the original patch.

15. **Release the mouse button** and the patch will snap into position.

16. Click **Clone** in the palette. The newly created clone will be selected.

17. Click **Rotate** in the palette.

18. **Move the patch** to the position of the next diamond and **release** to snap the patch into place.

19. Continue to **clone** and **rotate** until all eight points are created.

If the patch does not snap into the correct position, simply move it closer to the correct position and release it again. If you accidentally deselect the patch, use the Pick tool to select it again and continue. Remember that you need to click on the edge of the patch to select it, not in the middle.

Tip: Switch between the Pick tool and a drawing tool by pressing the Spacebar on the keyboard.

20. Now use the same method to draw the square patch in the upper-right corner of the block.

21. While the square patch is selected, click **Clone** in the palette.

22. There is no need to rotate this time so simply **move the patch** to one of the outer squares.

23. Click **Clone** and **move** the third square and repeat to clone and move the final square patch.

To complete the block, we need to draw four triangles.

24. **Draw the triangle** at the top-center of the block.

25. While the triangle patch is selected, click **Clone** in the palette.

26. Click **Rotate** in the palette. The patch will be rotated but not enough.

27. Click **Rotate** again.

With the special grids, other than Rectangular, the amount of rotation depends on the underlying grid. EQ knows the appropriate amount to rotate, but you may need to click the Rotate button more than once.

28. Position the cursor over the **four-headed arrow** and move the triangle into position and release the mouse to snap it into position.

29. Click **Clone**.

30. Click **Rotate** twice.

31. **Move** the triangle into position.

32. Repeat the steps to create the final triangle and move it into position.

Your block is complete!

33. Click the **COLOR** tab and color the block as desired.

34. Click **Add to Project Sketchbook** to save the block and its coloring.

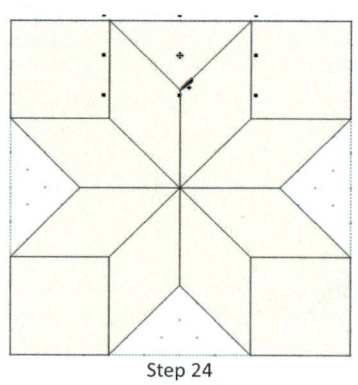
Step 24

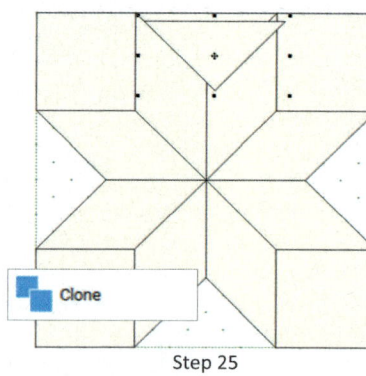
Step 25

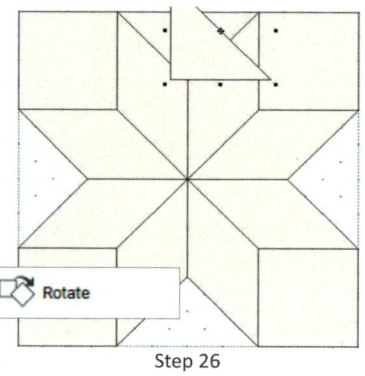
Step 26

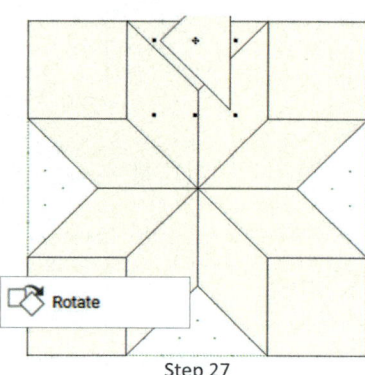
Step 27

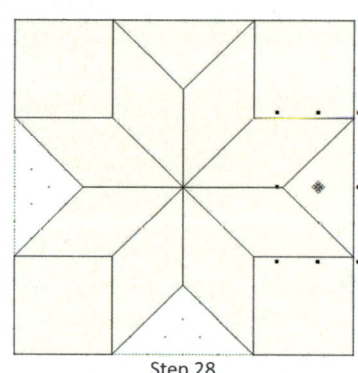
Step 28

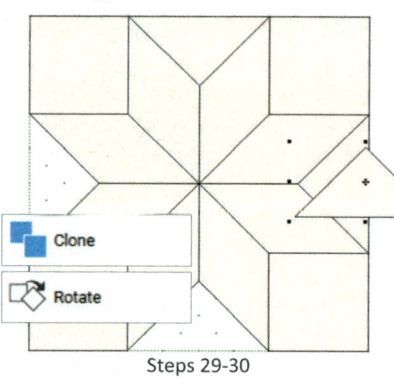
Steps 29-30

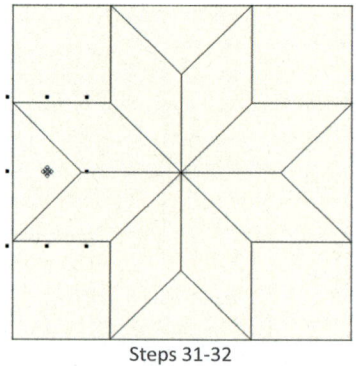
Steps 31-32

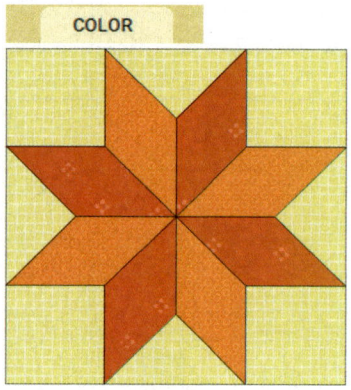
Step 33

Step 34

Chapter 3: Block Worktable: After the Basics

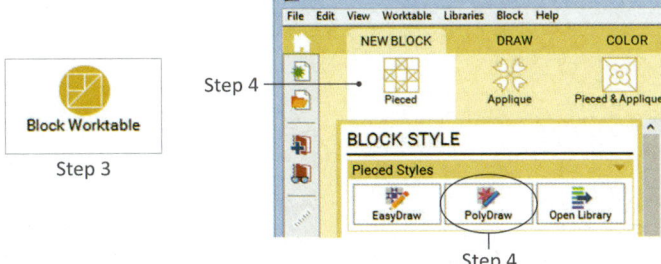

Step 1

Step 2

Step 3

Step 4

LESSON 3: DRAWING ARCS WITH THE POLYARC TOOL

The PolyArc tool is used with the Circle Grid and the Arc Grid. When the segment path is an arc, the drawing will automatically snap to the arc. If there is no underlying arc in the drawing path, then this tool draws a straight line. Let's try it.

1. Click **File > New Project**, or click on the New Project button on the Main Toolbar.

2. Type **Chapter 3 Blocks with Arcs** on the Create a new project tab, and click **OK**.

3. Click **Block Worktable** on the ribbon.

4. Click **NEW BLOCK > Pieced > PolyDraw**.

5. Click **Arc** under GRID PROPERTIES.

6. Type **4** in the palette for the number of **Rings and Spokes**.

7. Set the block size in the precision bar to **6 for Width** and **6 for Height**. This will make each ring measure 1.5 inches on the rulers.

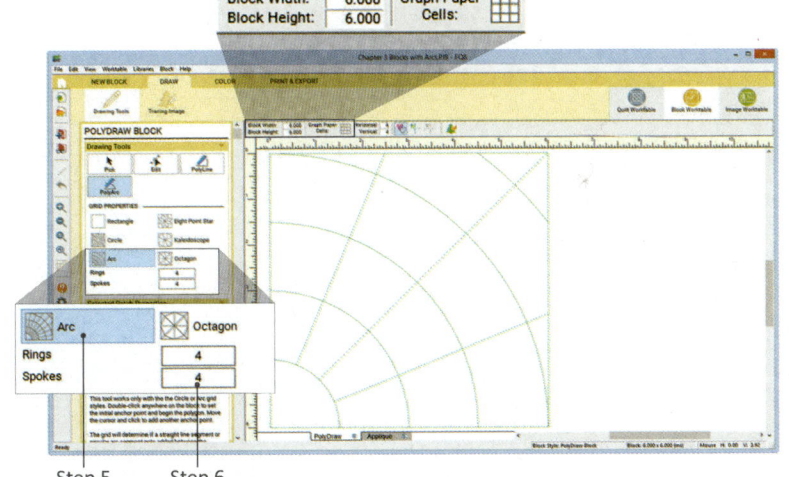

Step 5 Step 6

When typing numbers in the palette or Precision bar, press the keyboard's Enter key to update the worktable with the new setting.

8. Make sure the **Graph Paper** is turned **OFF** in the precision bar.

9. Click the **PolyArc** tool.

10. Position the cursor at the lower-left corner of the block and **double-click** to start the drawing.

11. **Move the cursor** up the left side of the block to the first ring and **click** to anchor.

12. Now follow the path of the first ring **clicking at each intersection point** of a spoke to anchor a point. You'll end up clicking 4 times as you travel along the path of the ring.

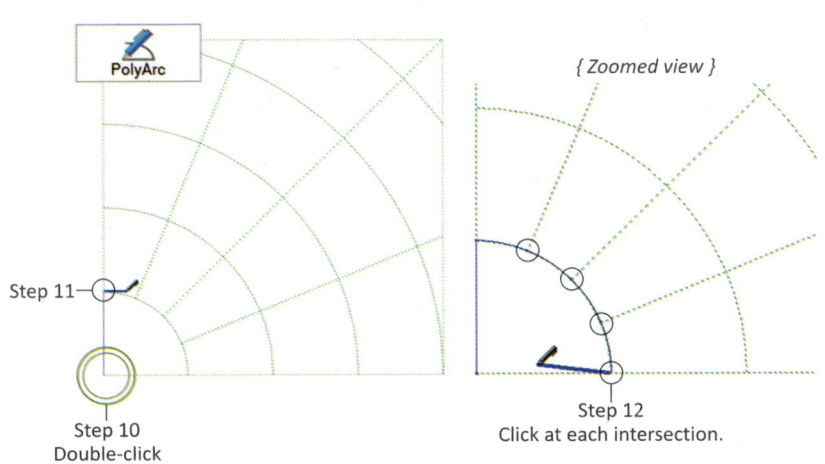

Step 10 Double-click

Step 12 Click at each intersection.

{ Zoomed view }

103

EQ8 Lessons for Beginners

13. Return the cursor to the lower-left corner of the block and **double-click** to complete the patch.

This completes the quarter circle. We'll repeat those steps to create the next patch.

14. **Position the cursor** at the top of the quarter circle patch which is at 4.5 inches on the vertical ruler.

15. **Double-click** to start the drawing.

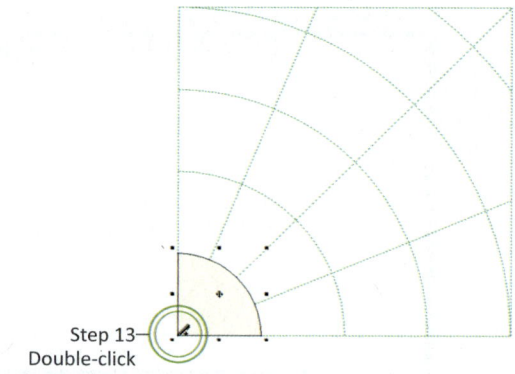

16. **Move the cursor** up the left side of the block to the next ring and **click** to anchor.

17. Follow the path of the second ring **clicking at each spoke** along the path to the bottom of the block.

18. **Position the cursor** at the right side of the quarter circle patch and **click**. This will be 1.5 on the horizontal ruler.

19. Follow the path along the quarter circle patch to return to the original point of the drawing. Make sure to **click on each intersection of a spoke** as you travel that path.

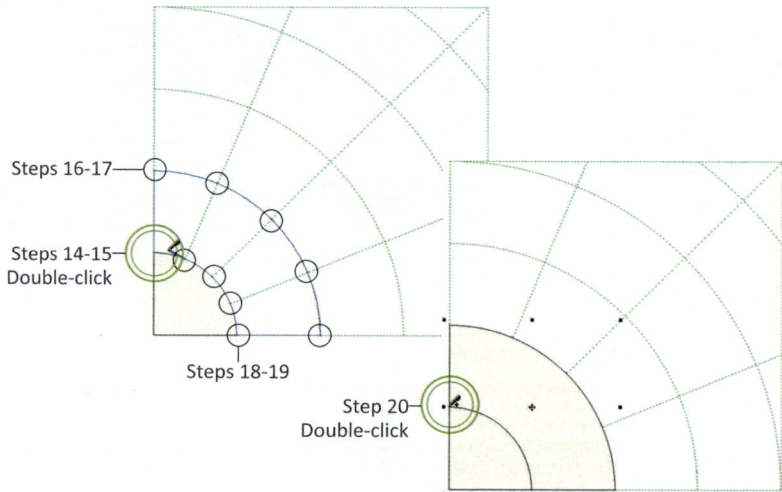

20. **Double-click** to close and finish the patch. It will fill with cream color.

For the third ring, let's partition it into 4 separate wedges defined by the spokes. With Clone and Rotate, it's fast and easy.

21. **Position the cursor** along the left side of the block at 3 inches on the ruler and **double-click** to start the drawing.

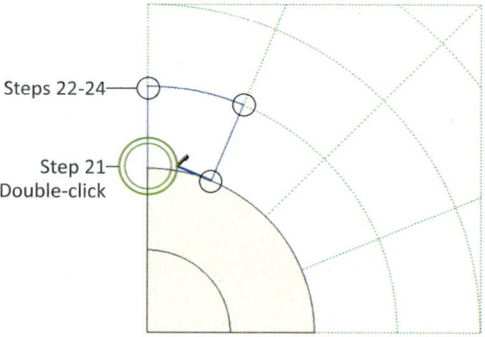

22. **Move the cursor** up the left side of the block to the next ring and **click** to anchor.

23. Follow the path of the ring to the first intersection and **click** to anchor a point.

24. Follow the spoke back down to the second ring and **click** to anchor.

25. Follow along the second ring back to the original point and **double-click** to close the patch.

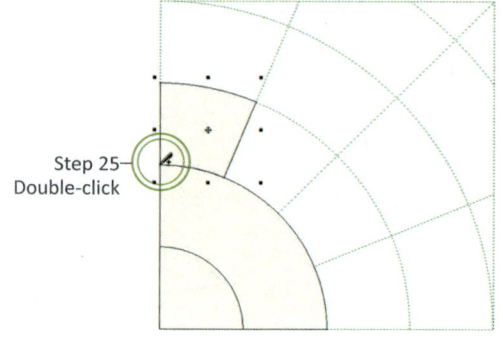

Chapter 3: Block Worktable: After the Basics

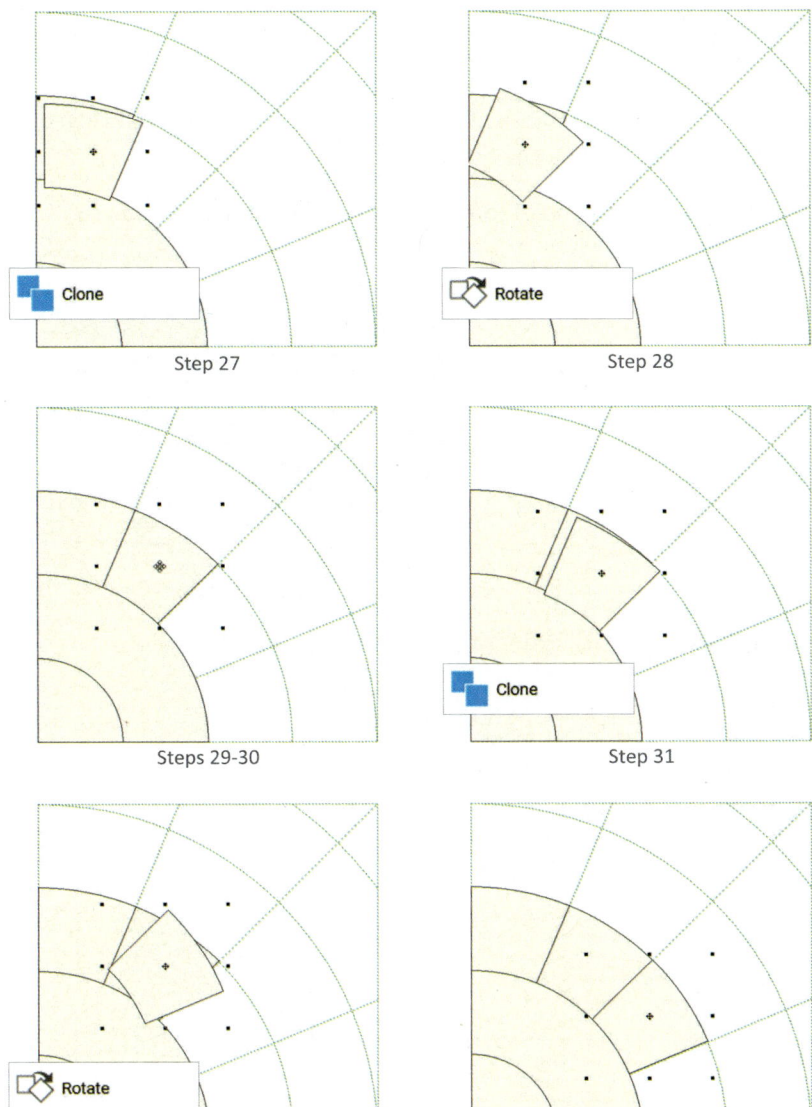

Tip: When using the PolyArc tool, it's a good idea to click on every intersection of a spoke on the ring. When you do this, the arc will be smoother and more accurate.

26. The patch will be selected for you when you finish. If you accidentally click and deselect it, then use the **Pick** tool to select the patch. Remember to click on the outer edge of the patch.

27. Click **Clone** in the palette.

28. Click **Rotate** in the palette.

29. Position the cursor over the **four-headed arrow** in the center of the patch. Click, hold and **drag the patch** to move it into the position of the next wedge, clockwise from the original patch.

30. **Release the mouse button** and the patch will snap into position.

31. Click **Clone** in the palette.

32. Click **Rotate** in the palette.

33. Position the cursor over the **four-headed arrow** and move the patch into the next position.

34. **Repeat the steps** to clone, rotate and move the final patch of this ring into position.

The PolyArc tool automatically bends the lines when the underlying grid is an arc, but you don't have to always follow the arc. It's up to you. Below are three different variations for finishing this block.

35. With the **PolyArc** tool selected, **finish drawing your block** using one of the examples as a guide.

Your block is complete!

36. Click the **COLOR** tab and color the block as desired.

37. Click **Add to Project Sketchbook** to save the block and its coloring.

Variation Examples

Step 37

EQ8 Lessons for Beginners

LESSON 4: DRAWING BASICS FOR APPLIQUE BLOCKS

Let's explore the Applique tools for drawing applique blocks. When you draw applique patches, the important element to remember is that the patch must be closed so that EQ can fill the patch with fabric. Some of the tools let you pull out closed patches, but some draw single segments so you need to connect the segments and close the patches.

Let's take a look at some of the tools. Since we're just exploring, **we do not need to save a project for this lesson**. You can continue to work in whichever project you currently have open.

1. Click **Block Worktable** on the ribbon.

2. Click **NEW BLOCK > Applique > Block** in the palette.

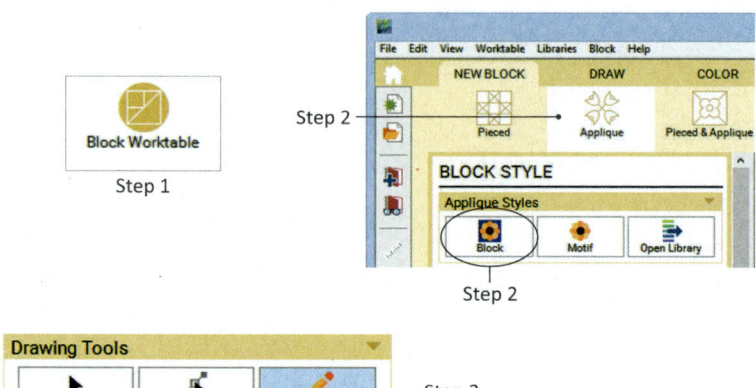

The Applique drawing tools appear in the palette. There will be two tabs along the bottom of the block. One says PolyDraw. Since we want to draw an applique block, we will stay on the Applique tab.

3. Click the **Draw** tool. Notice the five sub-tools that appear. Each has a pencil icon on it and the selected tool will have a blue background. Float the mouse cursor over each sub-tool to read a tooltip about it.

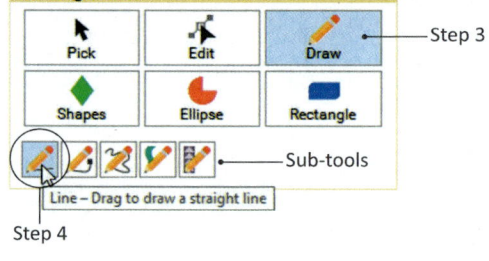

4. Click the **Line** sub-tool.

5. Position the cursor over the block and press, hold and **drag to draw a straight line**.

6. **Draw two more lines** in any direction.

Notice that there is no snapping when you start or stop the line. Snapping is turned off by default for applique drawing to give you the most flexibility when drawing.

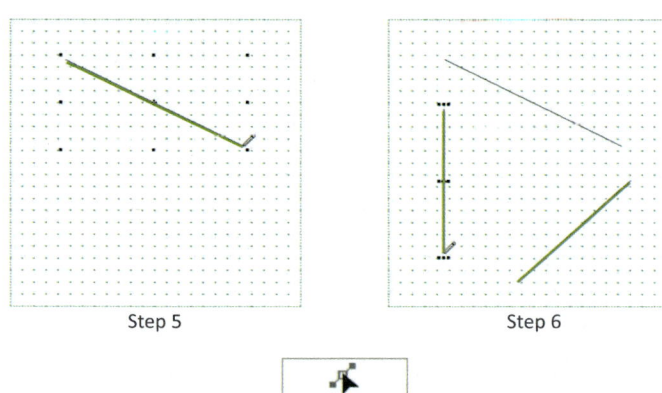

7. Click the **Edit** tool.

The Edit tool will let you move either end of the line. You can add nodes to the line using the button in the palette or by double-clicking directly on the line. Double-clicking will also remove a node.

8. Practice moving the ends of the lines and adding nodes and removing nodes.

9. Click the **Pick** tool and click on each segment and press the **Delete** button in the palette to remove all the lines.

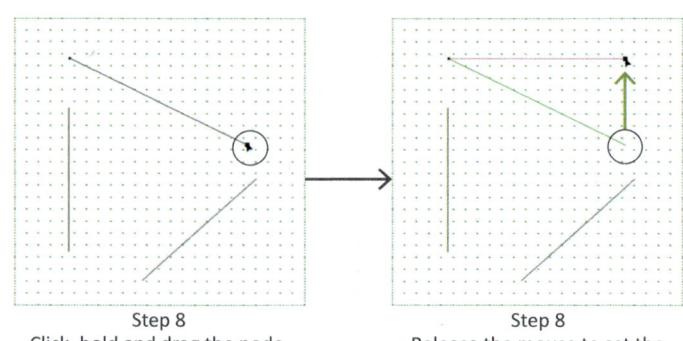

Step 8
Click, hold and drag the node.

Step 8
Release the mouse to set the new position for the node.

106

Chapter 3: Block Worktable: After the Basics

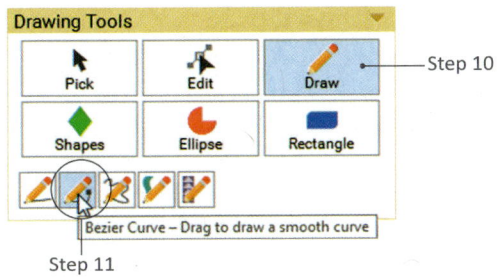

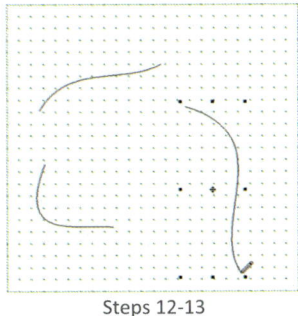

Step 10

Step 11

Steps 12-13
Draw several curves.

Step 14

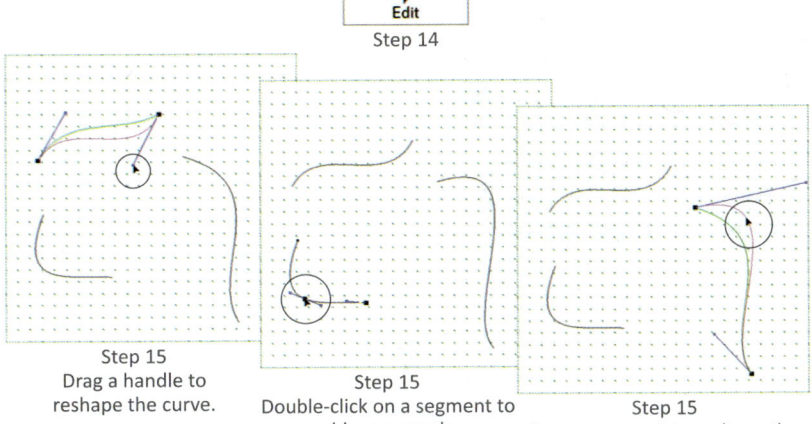

Step 15
Drag a handle to reshape the curve.

Step 15
Double-click on a segment to add a new node.

Step 15
Drag a segment to reshape the curve.

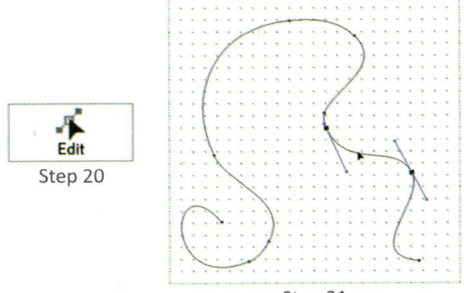

Step 17

Step 18

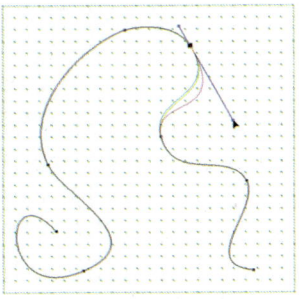

Step 19
Draw a long curvy line.

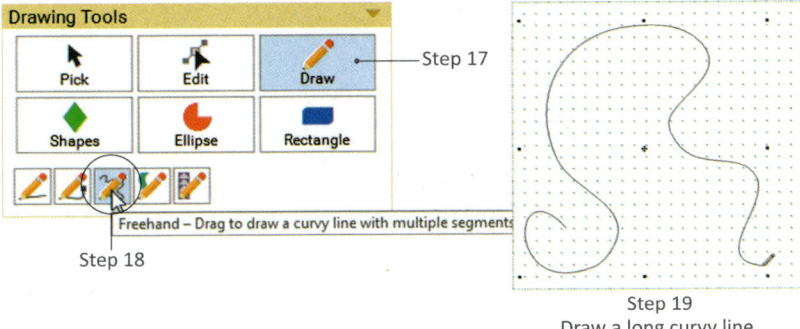

Step 20

Step 21
Notice all of the connected curves between the nodes.

Step 22
Reshape the curves.

10. Click the **Draw** tool.

11. Click the **Bezier Curve** sub-tool.

12. Position the cursor over the block and press, hold and **drag to draw a single curved segment**.

13. **Draw two more curves** in any direction.

14. Click the **Edit** tool.

The Edit tool will let you move either end of the curve, plus you can adjust the curve by moving the handles for each node. You can also adjust the curve by dragging the curve itself. When you edit the curve this way, the handles will move automatically. You can add and remove nodes using the palette or by double-clicking directly on the curve.

15. Practice moving the ends of curves. Try moving the handles to see how it changes the curve. Try adjusting the curve by dragging the curve itself. Practice adding and removing nodes.

16. Click the **Pick** tool and click on each curve and press the **Delete** button in the palette to remove all the curves.

17. Click the **Draw** tool.

18. Click the **Freehand** sub-tool.

19. Position the cursor over the block and press, hold and **drag to draw a long curvy line** across the block.

20. Click the **Edit** tool.

21. Click the line to see several curves all connected to one another.

22. Practice moving the nodes and handles, and adding and removing nodes.

When you click on a single node, the palette gives several options for changing the way the handles can move. The Smooth option works well for even curves. The Corner option lets each handle move independently creating sharp corners. Click the **Read More** button at the bottom of the palette to learn more about these node properties.

23. Click the **Pick** tool and delete all the segments on the worktable.

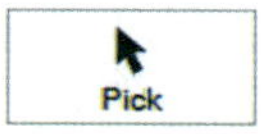

Step 23

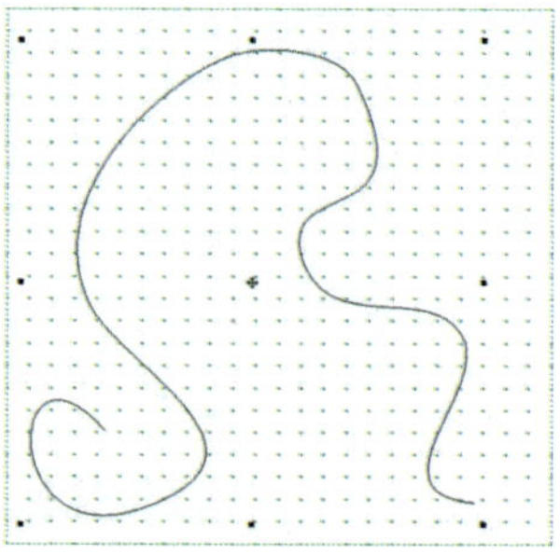

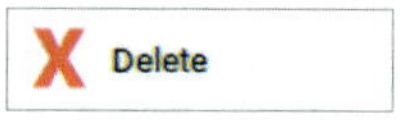

Step 23
Select the drawing, then click the Delete button.

These three tools draw open curves. It's up to you to connect these curves to create a closed patch that can be filled with fabric.

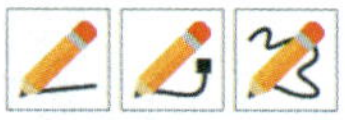

The rest of the applique drawing tools will draw closed curves for you. You may find using the pre-defined shapes is an easier way to draw applique. We'll look at a few of them.

24. Click the **Shapes** tool. Several different pre-drawn shapes appear in the palette.
25. **Float the mouse cursor** over several of these sub-tools to read their names.
26. **Select a shape** and practice dragging to create the shape on the worktable. When you release the mouse, the patch will automatically be filled with a cream color to indicated that it is closed.

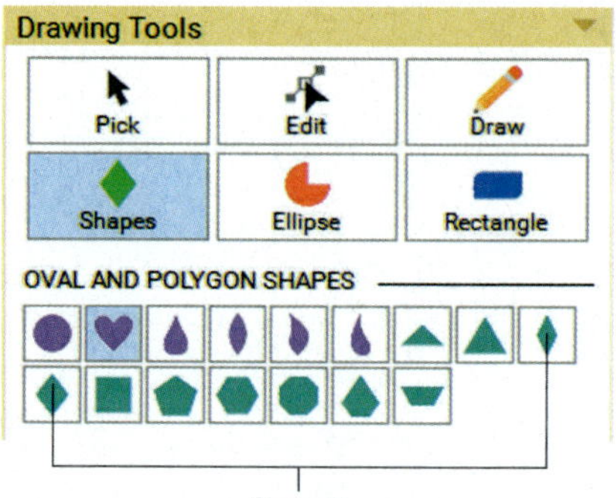

Step 24

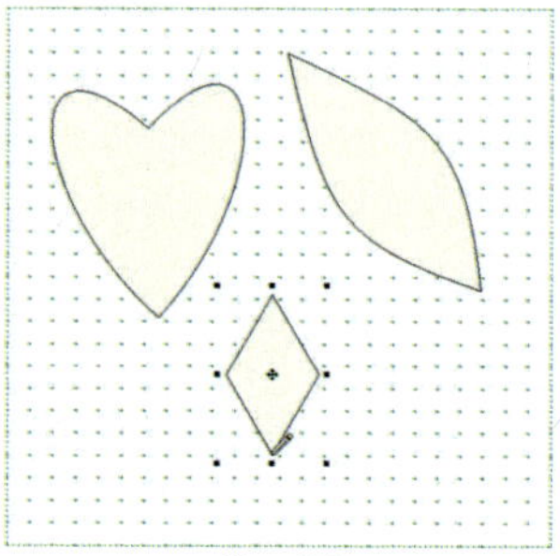
Step 26

27. Click away from patches in the block to deselect the patch.
28. Click the **Pick** tool.

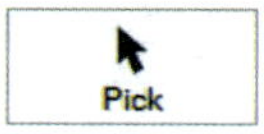

Step 28

29. **Click on the patch** to select the shape. If the patch is not showing the solid cream fill (has an outline only), then you must click on the edge of the patch to select the shape.

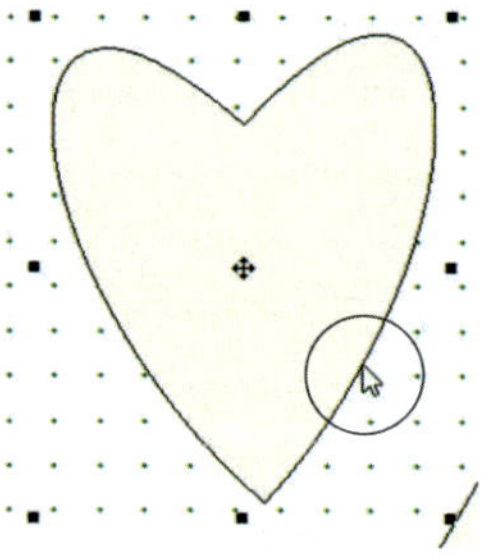
Step 29
Click on the patch (inside the shape or on the edge) to select it.

30. **Drag any corner node** to resize the patch. You can also select from various buttons in the palette to flip, clone, rotate and resize.

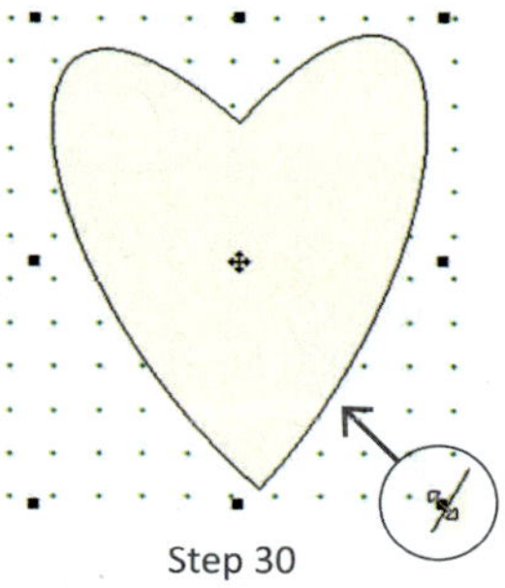
Step 30
Click, hold and drag a corner to resize the patch.

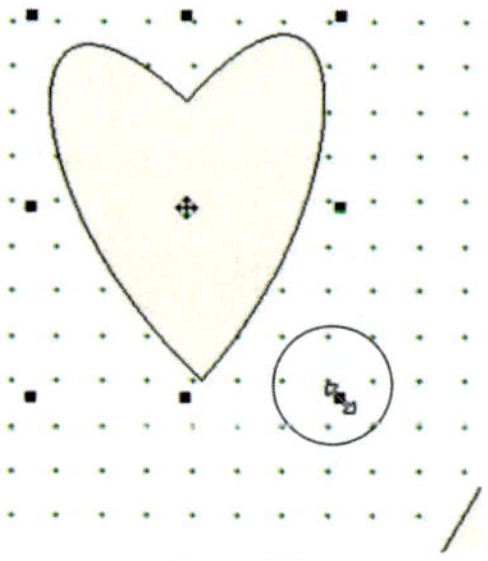
Step 30
The heart is now smaller.

31. Click the **Edit** tool. Again, click the edge of the patch.

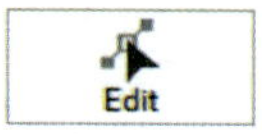

Step 31

32. **Drag a node or a handle** to change the shape of the patch. Don't worry about how the patch looks. Just practice moving handles and nodes to make adjustments to the patch.

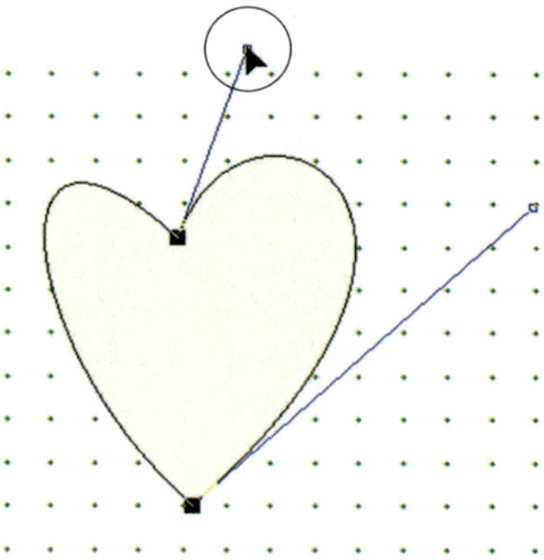
Step 32
Drag a node or handle to reshape the patch.

33. Click away from all patches in the block to deselect.

3

Chapter 3: Block Worktable: After the Basics

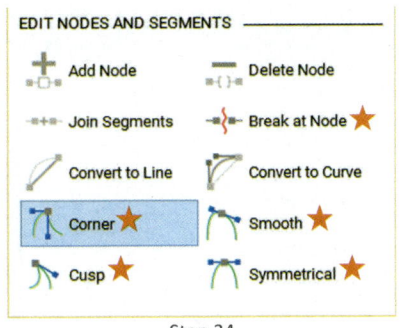

Step 34
When you select a *node* with the Edit tool, these options are enabled.

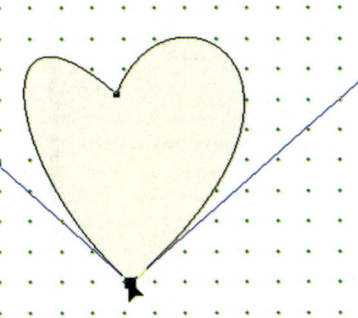

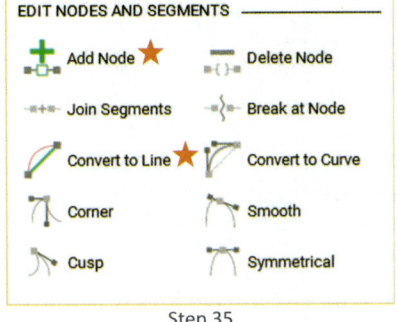

Step 35
When you select a *segment* with the Edit tool, these options are enabled.

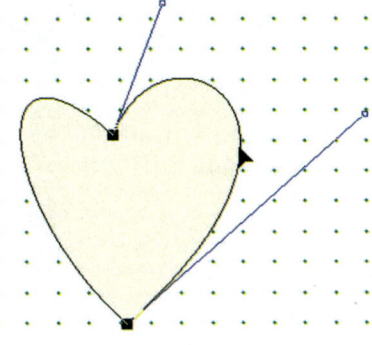

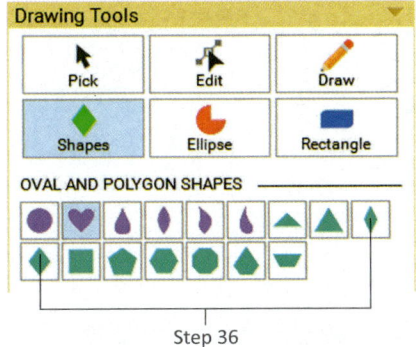

Step 36

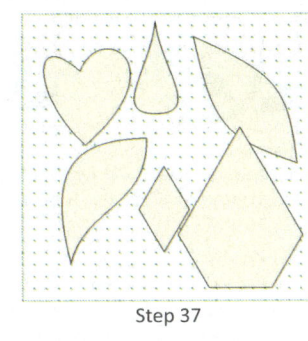

Step 37

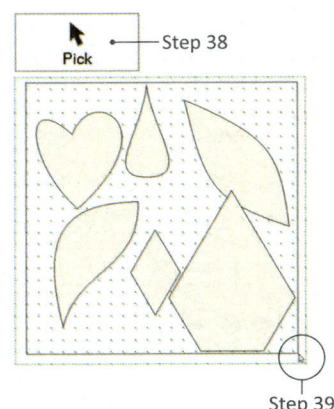

Step 39

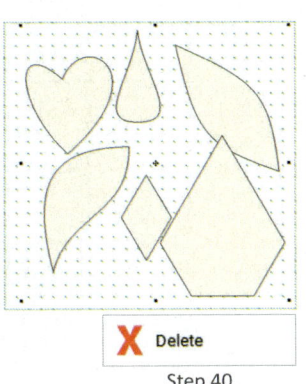

Step 40

34. **Practice clicking directly on a node** and observe the properties that become enabled in the palette. Changing the properties of a node will determine how the handles move.

35. **Practice clicking directly on a segment** between two nodes. Observe the palette. Now the palette will let you Add Node or Convert. You can convert from line to curve or curve to line depending on your selection.

36. Click the **Shapes** tool.

37. Practice pulling out several different shapes on the worktable. Don't worry if they overlap. We are just practicing.

38. Click the **Pick** tool. Instead of clicking each patch individually to delete it, let's select them all to delete at once.

39. **Drag a large box around all the patches**. Make sure the box surrounds all the patches.

40. Click the **Delete** button in the palette.

We didn't use all the applique drawing tools, but we have practiced using several of them. Remember that every tool gives you help in the palette. Click the **Read More** button at the bottom of the palette to open the online help that's written specifically for the currently selected tool.

EQ8 Lessons for Beginners

LESSON 5: APPLIQUE MOTIF VS. APPLIQUE BLOCK

Let's draw a couple of blocks and become familiar with the difference between an applique motif and an applique block.

1. Click **File > New Project**, or click on the New Project button on the Main Toolbar.

2. Type **Chapter 3 Drawing Applique** on the Create a new project tab, and click **OK**.

3. Click **Block Worktable** on the ribbon.

4. Click **NEW BLOCK > Applique > Motif** in the palette.

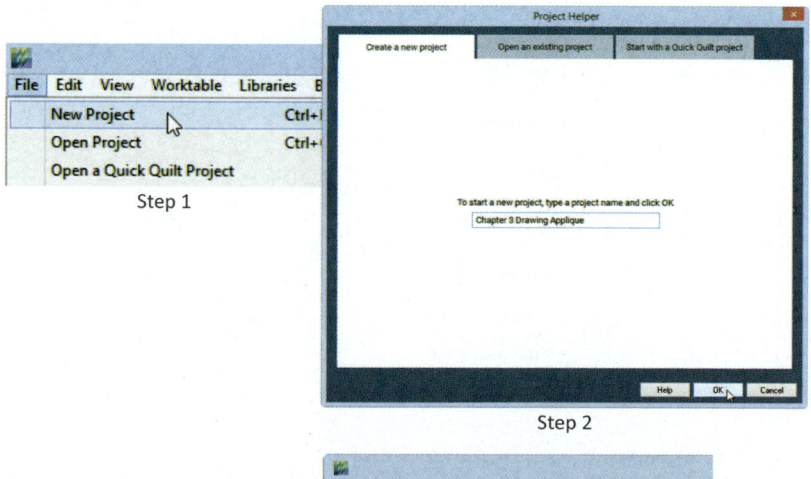
Step 1

Step 2

An applique motif has no background patch. These are designed to be set on Layer 2 of a quilt. Layer 2 allows the motif to be positioned anywhere on the quilt. You can place motifs overlapping several blocks and over borders, if you like.

The dotted grid background you see when drawing a motif is resizeable to help you determine the overall size of the motif. Just like any block in EQ, sizes are never set in stone because you can, of course, resize when on the Quilt Worktable.

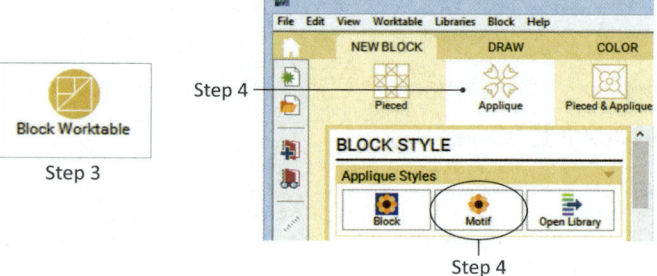
Step 3

Step 4

When you choose *Applique Block*, you'll have a background patch to color.

When you choose *Applique Motif*, there is no background patch.

Step 5

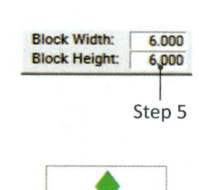
Step 6

5. In the Precision Bar, type **6** for both **Block Width** and **Block Height** and press the keyboard **Enter** key.

6. Click the **Shapes** tool in the palette.

7. Click **PosieMaker** under PATCHMAKER SHAPES.

8. Click the *second* **Auto Shape** button.

9. Make the *Size of center* larger by dragging the slider to any number between **65 and 70**.

10. Click **OK**.

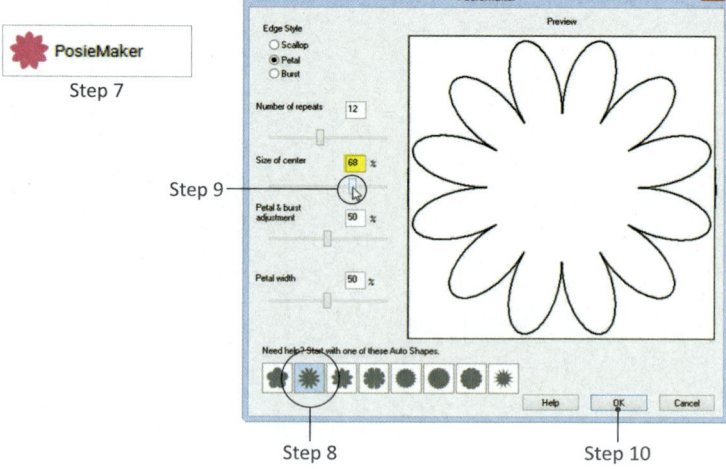
Step 7

Step 8

Step 9

Step 10

110

Chapter 3: Block Worktable: After the Basics

Step 11

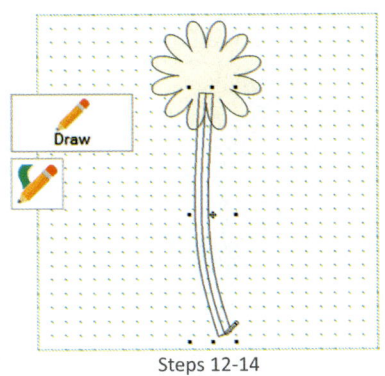
Steps 12-14

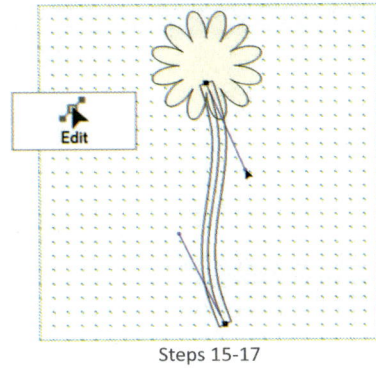
Steps 15-17

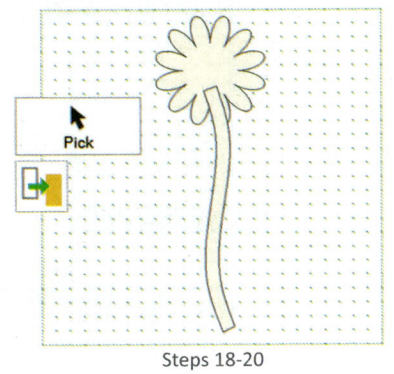
Steps 18-20

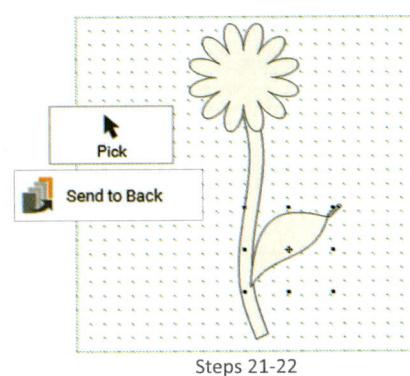
Steps 21-22

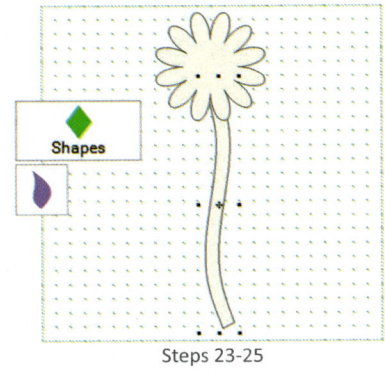
Steps 23-25

Step 26

Steps 27-28

11. Position the cursor over the **four-headed arrow** and **move** the patch to the top center of the block.

12. Click the **Draw** tool in the palette.

13. Click the **Brush Stroke** sub-tool. We'll use this tool to create a stem for the flower.

14. **Drag from the flower head towards the bottom of the block**. Make sure the end of your stem sits on top of the flower head a bit. Release the mouse.

15. Click the **Edit** tool in the palette.

16. Click on the **center line** (spine) of the brush stroke. This will display handles for adjusting the shape.

17. **Move the handles** to create a lazy curve for the stem.

18. Click the **Pick** tool in the palette.

19. Click on the stem to select it.

20. Click **Convert to patch** in the palette. This converts the Brush Stroke into a fillable patch, and fills it with a cream color.

The stem should be underneath the flower head. Let's send it to the back.

21. With the **Pick** tool still selected, click the **stem patch**.

22. Click **Send to Back** in the palette.

23. Click the **Shapes** tool in the palette.

24. Click the **Curvy Leaf** sub-tool.

25. **Draw a curvy leaf** on the right side of the stem starting close to the bottom.

26. **Draw a second curvy leaf** on the left side of the stem starting more in the middle.

27. Click the **Circle** sub-tool.

28. **Draw and position a small circle** in the center of the flower head.

EQ8 Lessons for Beginners

29. Click the **COLOR** tab.

30. Use the **Paintbrush** tool to fill all the patches with fabric.

31. Click **Add to Project Sketchbook**.

32. Click **View Project Sketchbook**.

33. Click **Blocks** and remember to click the **Motifs** tab along the top to view your newly created flower motif.

34. Click **Close**.

What if we wanted to add a background patch to this block? We could draw a background patch, but this block started as a motif so it would still be considered a motif and need to be set on Layer 2 of a quilt. We don't need to redraw the flower. We can copy and paste the design.

35. Click the **DRAW** tab.

36. Click **Edit > Select all**. This will automatically change to the Pick tool and select all the patches on the worktable.

37. Click **Edit > Copy**. This copies the patches to the clipboard.

38. Click **NEW BLOCK > Applique > Block** in the palette.

We now have a PolyDraw tab and an Applique tab along the bottom of the worktable to indicate that this block has a background patch. We'll stay on the Applique tab.

39. Click **Edit > Paste**. The flower design is now on the background patch. Let's turn this design into a wreath.

40. With the entire flower design selected, click **WreathMaker** in the palette.

The WreathMaker tool will repeat the selected patches in a circular pattern giving you the ability to adjust the number and size of the clusters and the size of the center.

Steps 29-30

Step 31 Step 32

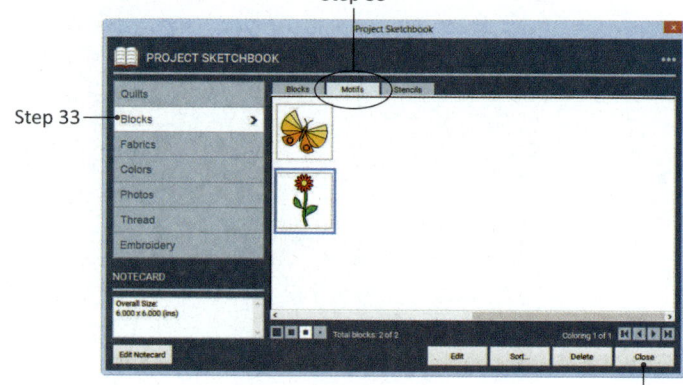
Step 33

Step 34

Step 35

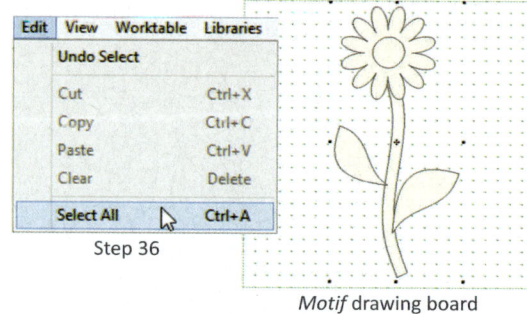
Step 36   Step 37
Motif drawing board

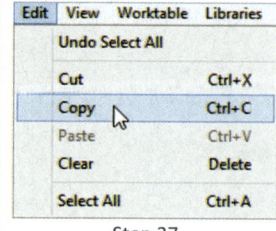

Step 38

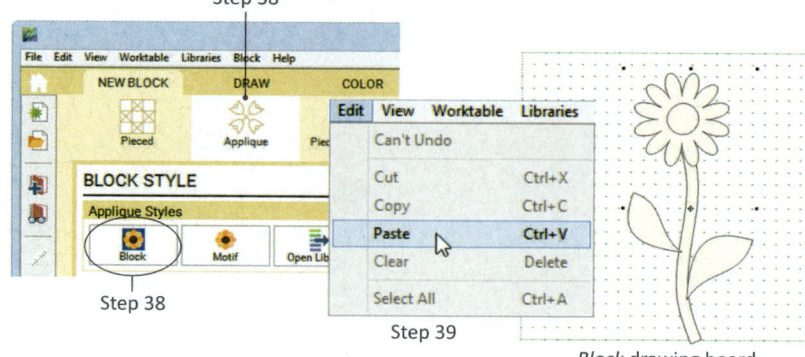
Step 38   Step 39
Block drawing board

Step 40

112

Chapter 3: Block Worktable: After the Basics

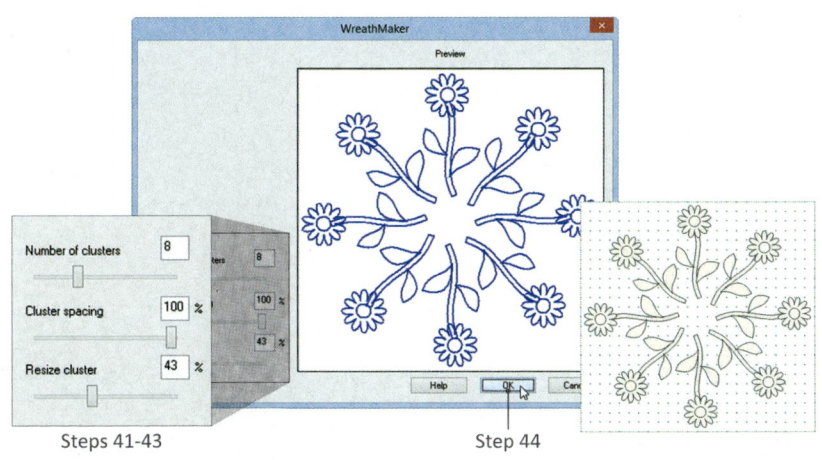

Steps 41-43   Step 44

41. Type **8** for the number of clusters.
42. Set the **Cluster** spacing to **100%**.
43. Use the **Resize** cluster control to adjust the size of the cluster so they don't touch one another.
44. Click **OK**. Voila!

Tip: You can make interesting designs by applying the WreathMaker more than one time. To make the design more random, delete some of the elements between uses of the WreathMaker.

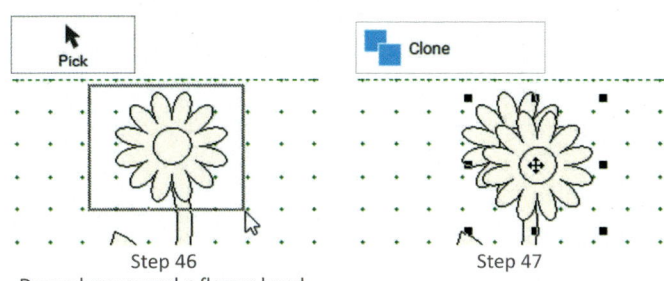

Step 46 Step 47
Drag a box around a flower head.

45. Click outside the block to deselect the patches.
46. With the **Pick** tool selected, drag a marquee box around one of the flower heads to select the flower and its center circle.
47. Click **Clone** in the palette.
48. Click **Center in Block** in the palette.

We can change the size at any time. These patches will be pretty small if the block is only 6 inches. Let's make this block bigger.

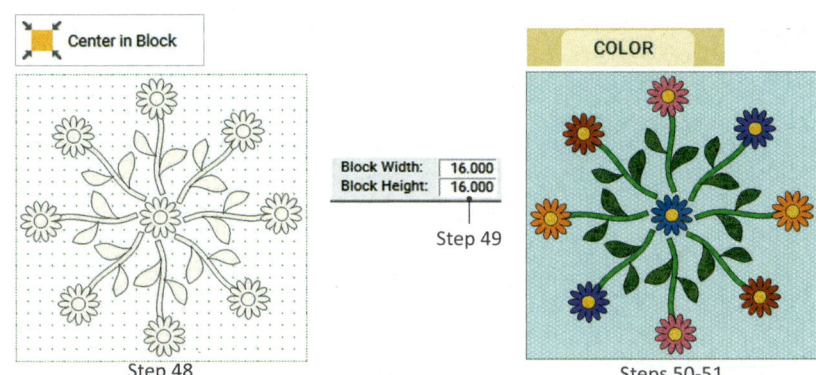

Step 48   Step 49   Steps 50-51

49. In the Precision Bar, type **16** for both **Block Width** and **Block Height** and press the keyboard **Enter** key.
50. Click the **COLOR** tab.
51. Use the **Paintbrush** tool to fill all the patches with fabric.
52. Click **Add to Project Sketchbook**.
53. Click **View Project Sketchbook**.
54. Click **Blocks**. Since this block has a background patch, it appears on the Blocks tab. This block can be set on Layer 1, 2 or 3 of a quilt.
55. Click **Close**.

Step 52   Step 53

Step 54

Step 55

In the steps above, we added a background patch to a motif. The same technique can be used to turn a *block* into a *motif*. Edit the block. Copy all the patches on the Applique tab. Start a new motif and paste the patches.

CHAPTER 4
Important to Know—Yet Just for Fun

This last set of lessons is nothing but fun, fun, fun! Creating blocks without drawing sounds impossible, but it's not. Use EQ8's Serendipity features to create new block drawings by clipping, flipping, merging and more. Learn to use the various search features of the block and fabric libraries. And finally, be sure to read our special notes about EQ's rotary cutting charts. It's a must-read.

Lesson 1: Creating Blocks with Serendipity 116

Lesson 2: Searching for Blocks by Category 119

Lesson 3: Searching for Fabrics by Color 120

Lesson 4: Understanding Rotary Cutting Charts in EQ 121

Lesson 5: Creating Your Own Default Project 124

Homework 125

EQ8 Lessons for Beginners

LESSON 1: CREATING BLOCKS WITH SERENDIPITY

EQ gives you the ability to create new blocks without drawing. It's called Serendipity. Let's look at how easy it is to create new blocks.

1. Click **File > New Project**, or click on the **New Project** button.

2. Type **Chapter 4 Serendipity Blocks** on the **Create a new project tab**, and click **OK**.

3. Click **Block Worktable** on the ribbon.

4. Click the **NEW BLOCK** tab.

5. Click **Create Serendipity** on the ribbon.

The tools found in the palette are the Serendipity options. Take a minute to read the Tips in the palette about each one. Let's open the Library and gather a few blocks to use.

6. Click **Open Library** in the palette.

7. Use the tree on the left to find the library, style and block names below. Click on the **block** to select it, and click **Add to Sketchbook** for each block.

    - 01 Classic Pieced > Nine Patch Stars > Strawberry Smoothie
    - 02 Contemporary Pieced > Frames > Wobbly Frame
    - 02 Contemporary Pieced > Prairie Style > Bulfinch

8. Click **Close**.

9. Click **Tilt Block** in the palette.

This feature lets you tilt any block in the Sketchbook by any degree between 0 and 90. The default is set to 30 degrees. The viewer on the left displays the blocks in the Sketchbook.

10. **Drag the vertical scrollbar** on the viewer to see how each block will look when tilted 30 degrees.

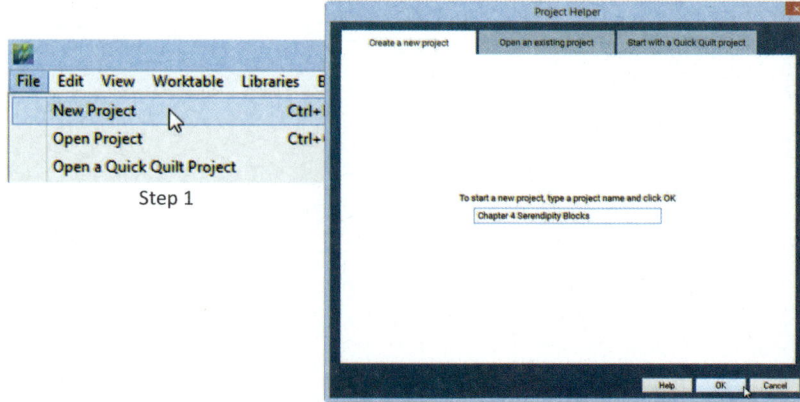
Step 1

Step 2

Step 3

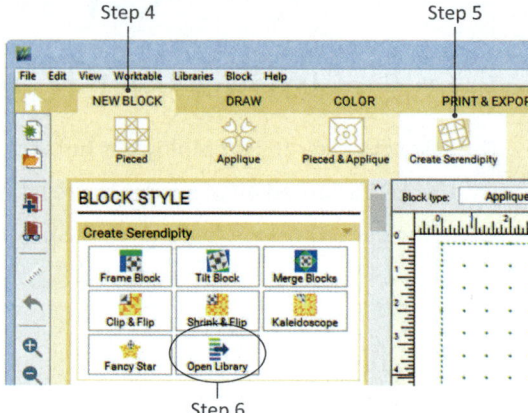
Step 4 Step 5

Step 6

01 Classic Pieced > Nine Patch Stars > Strawberry Smoothie

02 Contemporary Pieced > Frames > Wobbly Frame

02 Contemporary Pieced > Prairie Style > Bulfinch

Step 7

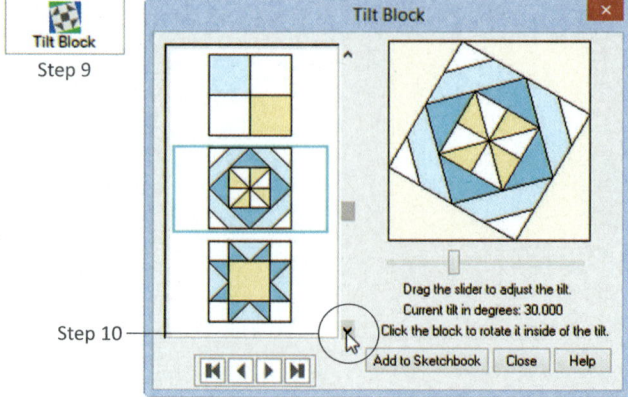
Step 9

Step 10

Chapter 4: Important to Know—Yet Just for Fun

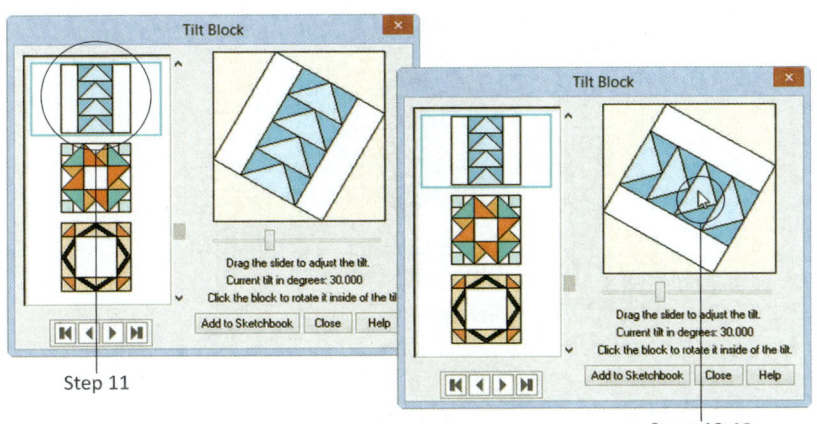
Step 11

Steps 12-13
Click to rotate.

11. Stop when you get to the last default block – the **Flying Geese** block.

12. Now click directly on the **tilted Flying Geese** block. This will rotate the block 90 degrees.

13. Continue to rotate the block back to the original position.

14. Drag the vertical slider to the last block in the Sketchbook which is the last block that we added – **Bulfinch**.

15. To create the new block using this Tilt Block feature, simply click **Add to Sketchbook**.

The newly created block is added to the Sketchbook. It will now be the last block.

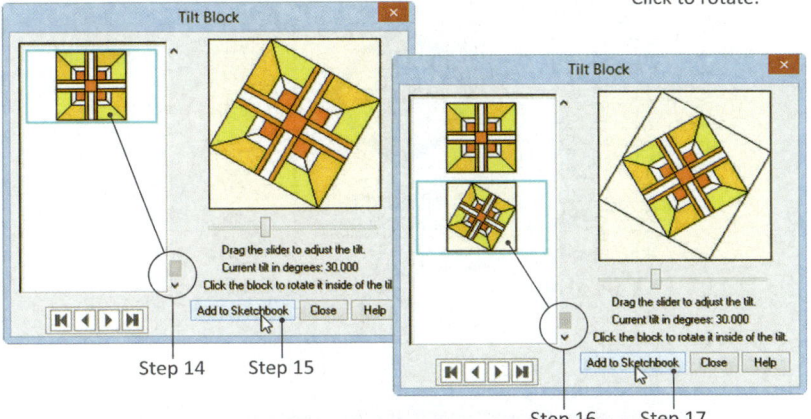
Step 14 Step 15

Step 16 Step 17

16. Continue to drag the scrollbar to see the last block.

17. Click **Add to Sketchbook**. This feature can be used repeatedly to create a twisted effect.

Use the slider under the block to adjust the angle. If you're having trouble stopping the slider at the exact number you want, click directly on the slider to the right or left of the control to make fine adjustments to the number.

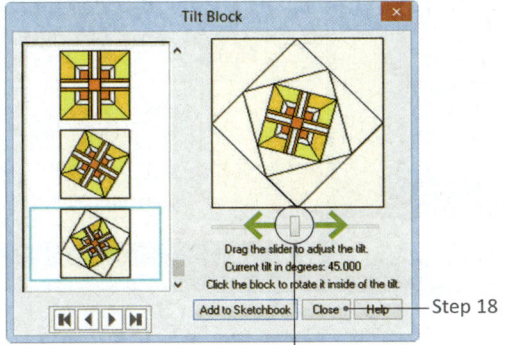
Step 18

Adjust the slider to change the angle of the tilt.

18. Click **Close**.

19. Click **Merge Blocks** in the palette.

This Serendipity feature lets you merge two blocks into one. EQ evaluates all the blocks in the Sketchbook and puts the appropriate ones for the background block in the viewer on the left. These blocks need to be **drawn with the EasyDraw tools** and have **at least one parallelogram that covers a sizeable amount** of the block. *Not every Sketchbook block will appear in the viewer on the left.*

The viewer on the right shows *all* the blocks in the Sketchbook. Any block can be merged into an appropriate background block.

Step 19

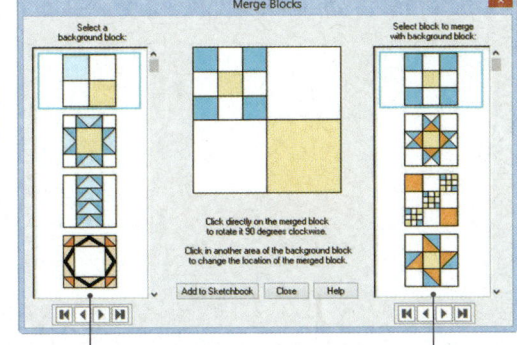

This column displays possible background blocks from the Sketchbook. These blocks must meet specific requirements.

This column displays all blocks currently in your Sketchbook. Any block (excluding motifs or stencils) can be merged with a background block.

117

20. Scroll to find the **Wobbly Frame** block in the viewer on the left and click directly on it to select it. It will appear in the center of the box.

21. Scroll to find the **Strawberry Smoothie** block in the viewer on the right.

22. Click directly on the block to select it. This will merge the Strawberry Smoothie block into the center of the Wobbly Frame block. (Now you have a Wobbly Strawberry Smoothie! Sounds delicious!)

23. Click **Add to Sketchbook**.

24. Scroll down in the viewer on the right to place the Bulfinch block into the Wobbly Frame.

25. Click **Add to Sketchbook**.

26. Click **Close**.

27. Click **View Project Sketchbook** and click **Blocks**. Scroll to the end of the blocks to see the three blocks we added from the Library and the four newly created blocks using Serendipity.

28. Click **Close**.

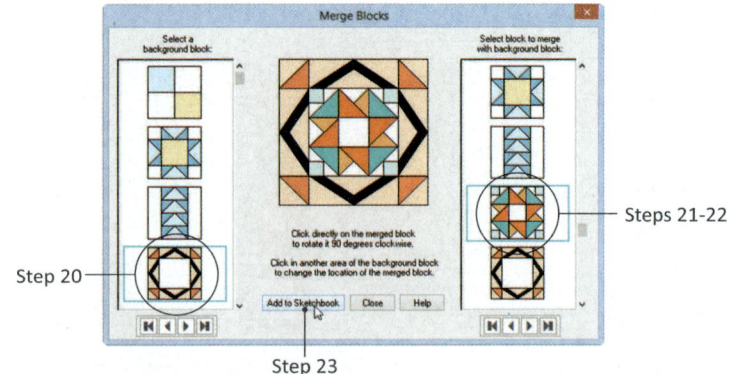

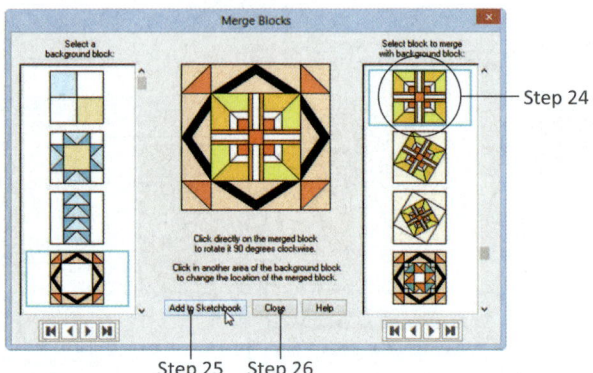

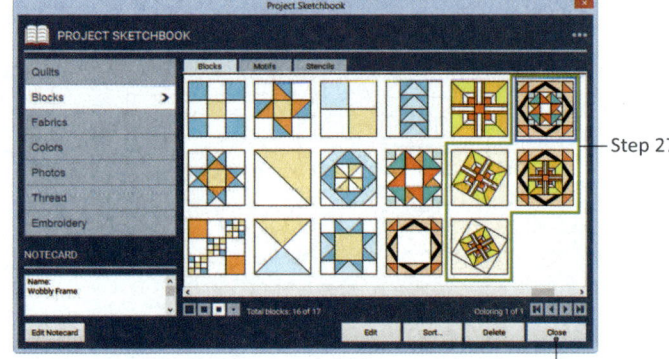

*Tips: Remember that you can find help on using Serendipity by clicking the Help button in each dialog box or the **Read More** button in the palette.*

The Contemporary Pieced Block Library style titled Frames has over 50 blocks that work great as background blocks with Serendipity's Merge Blocks.

Chapter 4: Important to Know—Yet Just for Fun

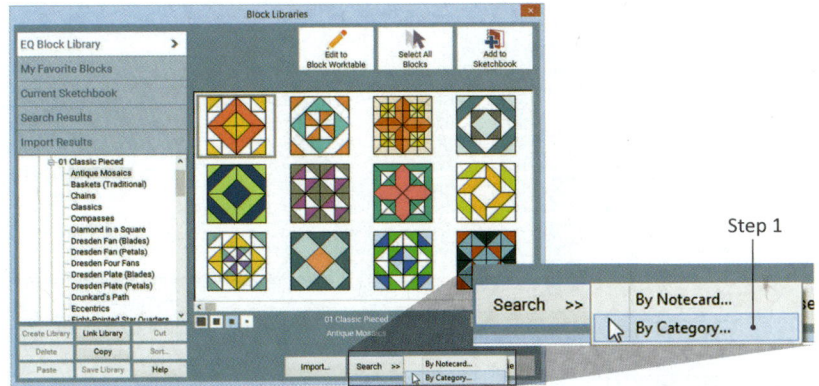

Step 1

Search categories are: Difficulty & Piecing Info, Holiday, Events, Pieced, and Applique.

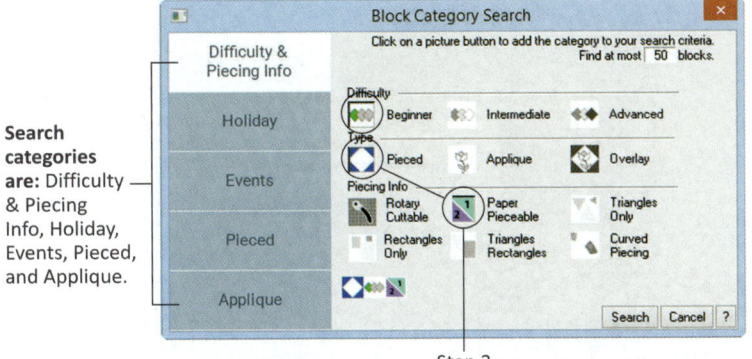

Step 2

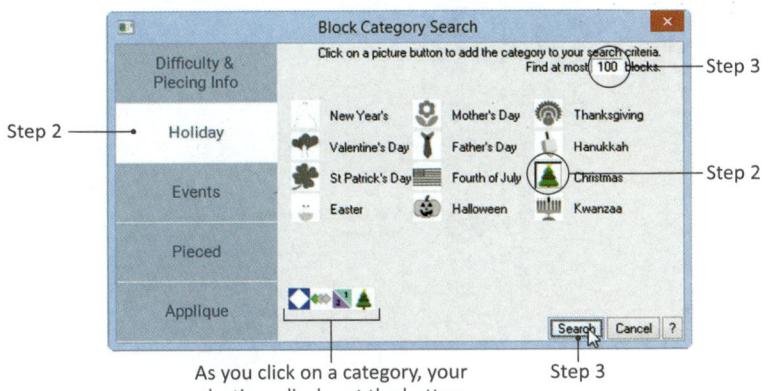

Step 2

Step 3

Step 3

As you click on a category, your selections display at the bottom.

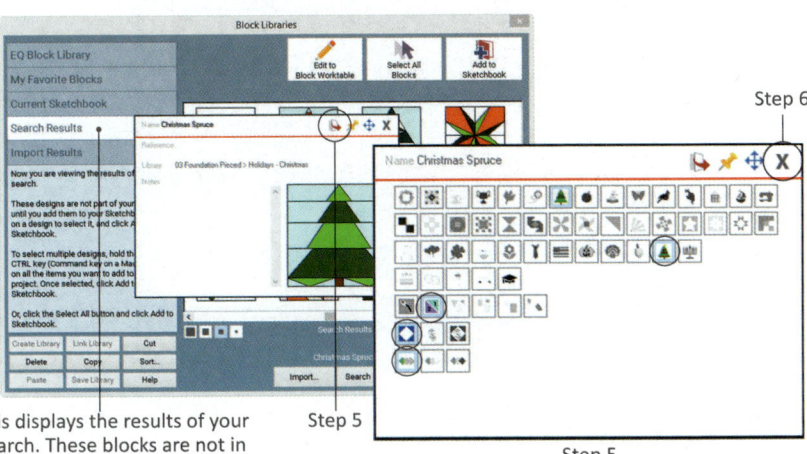

Step 6

Step 5

This displays the results of your search. These blocks are not in your project until you add them to your Sketchbook.

Step 5
This block is marked with the categories we selected in step 2.

LESSON 2: SEARCHING FOR BLOCKS BY CATEGORY

The EQ Block Library has over 6,000 blocks. Besides searching for a block by name, you can search by category.

1. Click **Libraries > Block Library > Search > By Category**.

There are five main categories that appear on the left. Each category has several options for searching. When you select an option, it will display the icon, in color, at the bottom of the dialog box. You can select several options at once from any of the categories.

2. Click on **each category** to observe the options in each. Click to select the following options:

   - **Difficulty & Piecing Info**: Beginner, Pieced, Paper-Pieceable
   - **Holiday**: Christmas

If you accidentally click the wrong icon or you want to change your search selections, click the icon again to remove it from the list.

3. In the upper-right, change the maximum number of blocks to **100**, then click the **Search** button.

4. A message will display indicating how many blocks were found. Click **OK**.

The results will appear. Notice the library button changes to Search Results.

5. Click the **Notecard** button, and then click the **Flip** button in the upper-right of the Notecard. This will show how this block is marked. There may be more icons marked than we had selected.

6. Click **Close** on the Notecard.

7. Click **Search > By Category** and make new search selections of your own choosing. Click **Search** to see the results.

8. Add any blocks to your project using the **Add to Sketchbook** button.

119

EQ8 Lessons for Beginners

LESSON 3: SEARCHING FOR FABRICS BY COLOR

Many times when you're designing, you'll want to find a family of fabrics that are a similar color. EQ can help.

1. Click **Libraries** on the main menu > **Fabric Library**.

2. Browse through the fabrics and **click on any fabric** that you want to use for the search.

3. Click **Search > By Color**. The Search by Color dialog box will display giving options for searching. The fabric you had selected in the library will be the current search color.

4. **Put a check** next to all the libraries you want to search. This list will show EQ8 and any other libraries you may have linked to your program.

5. Enter the **number of fabrics** you want from the search. The default is 50 and the allowable numbers are 1 to 999.

If you would like to change the search color, click the down arrow next to the color chip. Scroll to see all the available colors. Click on a color to change the search to the newly selected color.

6. Click the **Search** button.

7. A message will display indicating how many fabrics were found. Click **OK**.

The results will appear. Notice the library button changes to Search Results.

8. Add any fabrics that you want to your project by clicking the **Add to Sketchbook** button.

Step 3
Step 2

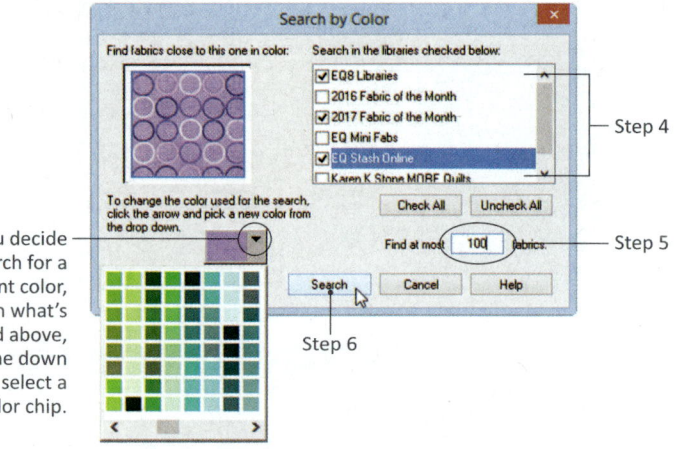
Step 4
Step 5
Step 6

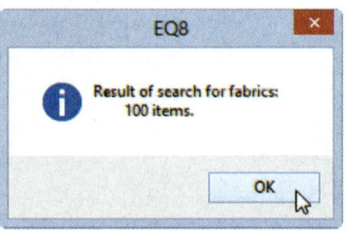
Step 7

Step 8

This displays the results of your search. These fabrics are not in your project until you add them to your Sketchbook.

120

Chapter 4: Important to Know—Yet Just for Fun

LESSON 4: UNDERSTANDING ROTARY CUTTING CHARTS IN EQ

Using a rotary cutter is essential to quilting today. It's important to understand a few of the special aspects of EQ's Rotary Cutting Charts before you use them to achieve success and avoid frustration.

One Block at a Time

EQ gives rotary cutting charts for blocks. If you're printing from the Quilt Worktable, you'll need to select the block first, and then print the rotary cutting chart for that block. **EQ does not print a chart for a whole quilt.**

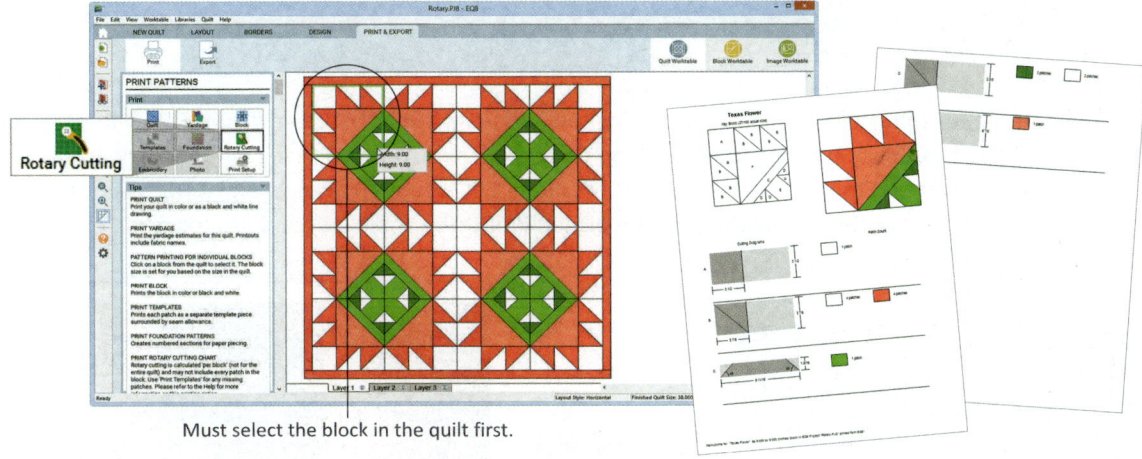

Must select the block in the quilt first.

Not All Patches are Rotary Cuttable

EQ does not give results for all shapes. Kite shapes are one example. These shapes will be lettered in the Key Block but not listed in the chart. This is not a mistake. EQ intends for you to use templates for any patches not included in the chart. Depending on the number of patches that may be missing, selecting a different pattern type, like templates or foundation patterns, may be a better alternative.

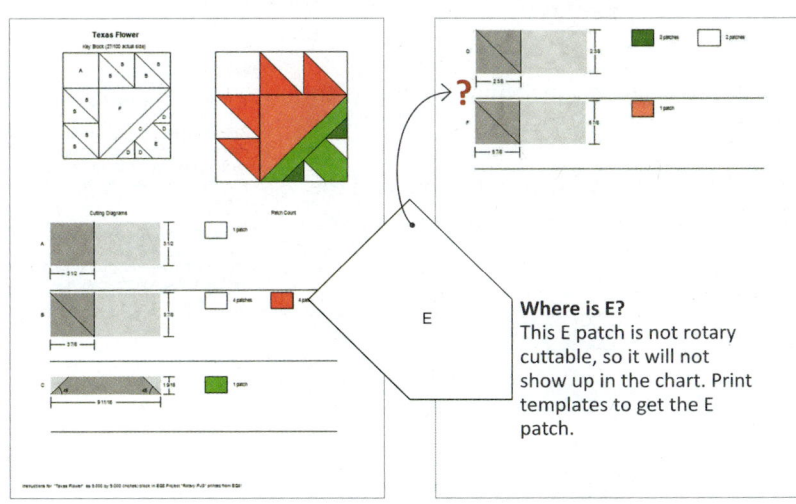

Where is E?
This E patch is not rotary cuttable, so it will not show up in the chart. Print templates to get the E patch.

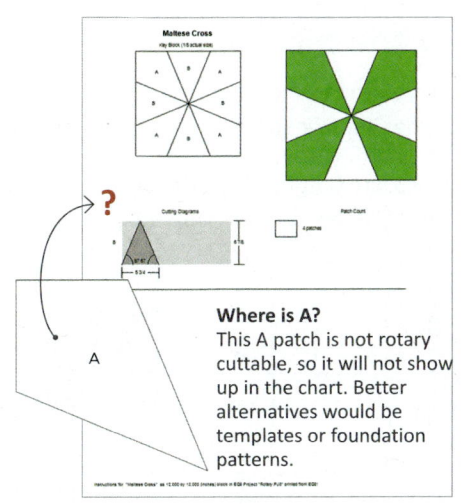

Where is A?
This A patch is not rotary cuttable, so it will not show up in the chart. Better alternatives would be templates or foundation patterns.

121

Rotary Cutting Requires Rounding

Rotary cutting dimensions are nearly always approximations. For example, the 7/8 inch (.875) that quilters conventionally add for half-square triangles is really .85355 inches, rounded off to the nearest 1/8 inch so that we can read it on the ruler. Experienced quilters, in fact, cut a little "shy" in this case, since .85355 is a little less than .875.

Because rounding is inevitable, this means that several small inaccuracies can add up to something significant. For example, this block has 7 patches across by 2 patches down. If you wanted a 10 inch block, this would mean that each rectangle has a finished size of 1.428" by 5" so we would need to cut 1.928" by 5-1/2" (includes 1/4" seam allowance) and 1.928 is not to be found on the ruler. EQ will round to 1-7/8" by 5-1/2". By the time we pieced 7 of these small inaccuracies together, our finished block is 9-5/8" by 10". **That's 3/8" too narrow!**

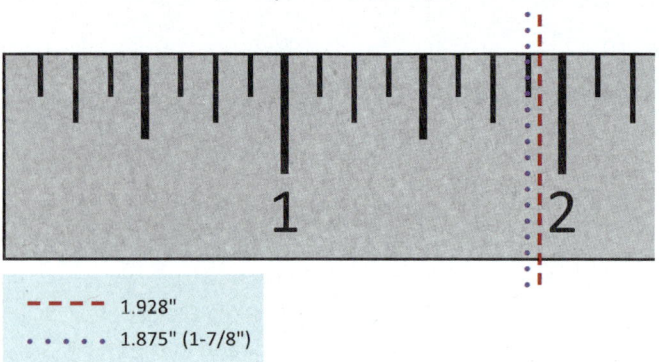

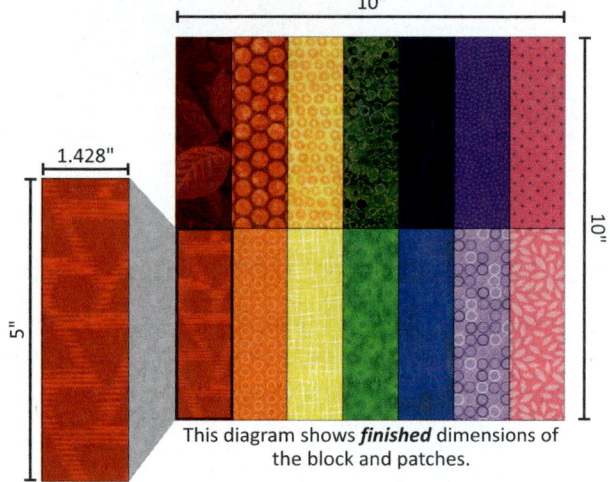

This diagram shows *finished* dimensions of the block and patches.

Getting the Most Accurate Charts

EQ will give you the exact measurement of the patches so that you can decide if you want to use the Rotary Cutting Chart or some other pattern printing method.

In the Print Rotary Cutting Chart dialog box, choose No Rounding. Preview the results. Compare the sizes with the rounded values. This will give you the information you need in order for you to make a judgment on using the chart.

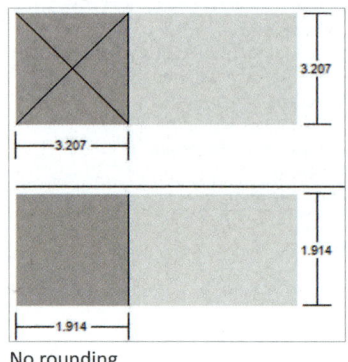

No rounding

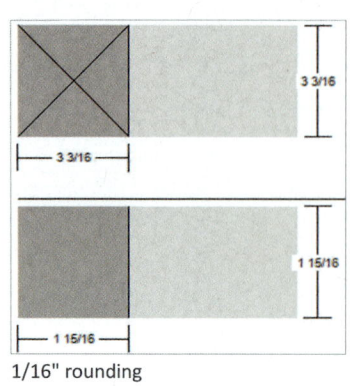

1/16" rounding

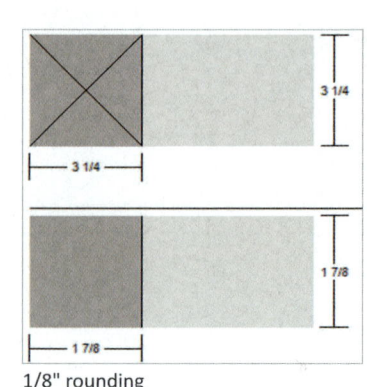

1/8" rounding

Chapter 4: Important to Know—Yet Just for Fun

Templates May Be Used as a Check

EQ8 templates are always accurate. If you are uncertain about rotary cutting dimensions in some cases, print the templates as a check. The actual (unrounded) dimensions for rotary cutting may be measured from the dotted (seam allowance) lines on the templates. First extend the dotted lines until they cross. Then measure the resulting total length and height.

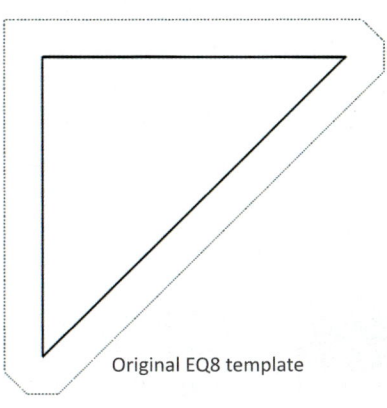
Original EQ8 template

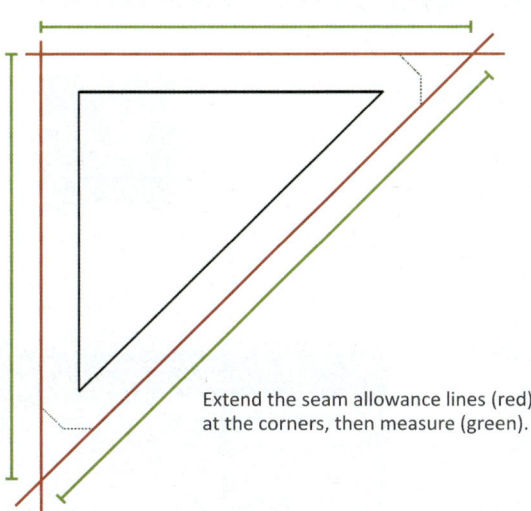
Extend the seam allowance lines (red) at the corners, then measure (green).

Remember Design and Size Go Hand-in-Hand

Visualize a grid of squares over the design of the block to help you determine the best size to make a block. For example, a Nine Patch style block works well at 3, 6, 9, 12 and so on for the overall size.

In the sample block on page 122, with 7 across, 10 inches is not a good size choice. If we choose 10.5 inches for the size of the block and turned off all rounding, the Rotary Cutting Chart tells us to cut the strips 2.0" by 5.75". When we turn on rounding, we get the same sizes! So by changing the overall block size, we've eliminated all the rounding.

This Nine Patch block has a grid of 3 x 3. You will get nice rotary cutting dimensions if you print the block at a size that is a multiple of 3. For example: 3, 6, 9, or 12 inches.

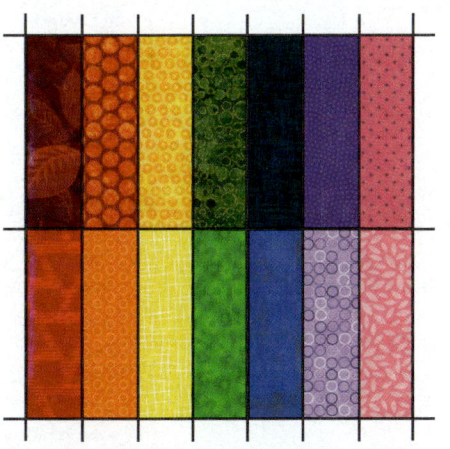
This example has a horizontal grid of 7. You know that you want the finished block to be about 10", but that would not give you nice dimensions. If the finished block size is flexible, you would get nicer dimensions if you printed the rotary cutting for a 10.5" block instead.

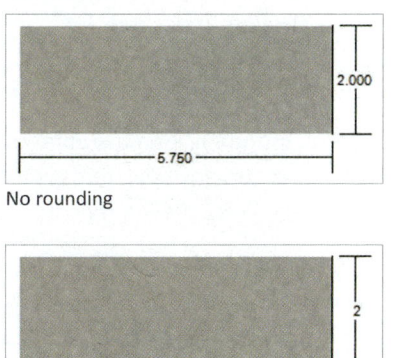
No rounding

1/8" and 1/16" rounding

LESSON 5: CREATING YOUR OWN DEFAULT PROJECT

Follow the instructions below to change your default project. The next time you open EQ8, or start a new project, you will be starting with the Sketchbook items YOU selected, instead of what was pre-loaded in EQ8.

WARNING: Make sure you are in a new, clean project file, as you don't want to lose any of your in-progress designs.

Delete the Default Content

1. **Open EQ8**. If you already have EQ8 open, close it by choosing File > Exit, then re-open. It's very important that you start with a blank project.

2. Click **View Project Sketchbook**.

3. Click the **Blocks** section. You'll see the pre-loaded blocks.

4. Click the **3-dot Options** button in the upper-right of the Sketchbook window.

5. Choose **Clear all unused blocks**.

6. Click **Yes** to the prompt. The Blocks section should be empty.

7. Repeat steps 4-6 for the **Motifs** and **Stencils** tabs in the Blocks section, and also for **Fabrics** and **Threads**, if desired.

8. **Close** the Sketchbook.

9. (Optional) Open the libraries and add any new items you'd like. Close the library.

10. When you have your project just as you would like, click **File > Save Palette as Default**. Click OK to the prompt. The next time you start a new project, you will see *your* default palettes, whether completely empty, or with your own content.

To revert back to the default settings, see the instructions on page 7.

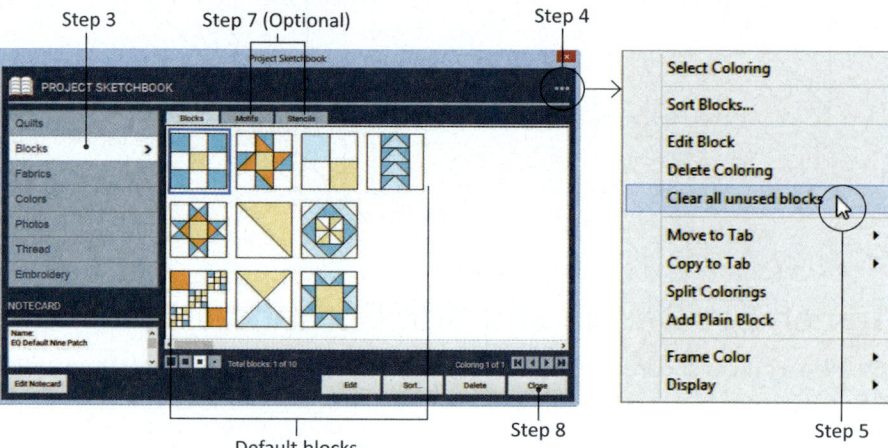

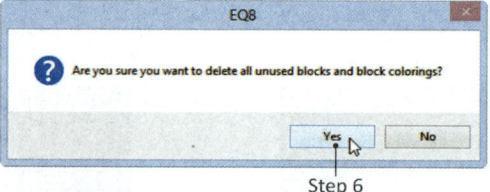

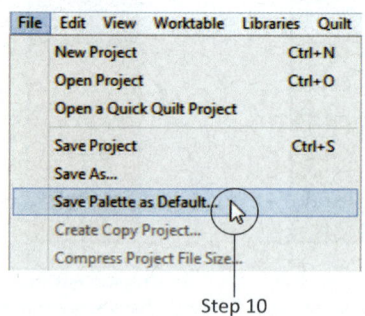

Note: You can also save your default project with newly sorted content. For example, in the Colors section of the Sketchbook, you might want to put black and white swatches at the beginning of the Color palette. Sort the colors so black and white are first in the list. When you choose File > Save Palette as Default, the black and white will always be at the beginning of all new projects.

Chapter 4: Important to Know—Yet Just for Fun

HOMEWORK!

What's a lesson book without homework? First of all, congratulations for finishing this lesson book. We hope you feel confident about creating your own designs. Just like anything in life, practice makes perfect. So if you'd like more practice, we've given you a few sample quilts below and then a short recipe on how to create the quilts. Test your skills by starting new quilts, setting up the layout and borders, then filling them with blocks. The overall size can be whatever you want. It's more about practicing the steps. Feel free to make the colorings your own. Have fun. (And don't let the dog eat your homework!)

Recipe for this Quilt
- **On-point layout:** 3 x 3
- **Library blocks:** Goose Frame 2
- **Borders:** 4 Long Horizontal
- **Tip:** Use CTRL+click *twice* to set the block. (Command+click on a Mac.)

Recipe for this Quilt
- **Horizontal layout:** 8 x 8
- **Library blocks:** Basket with Handles
- **Borders:** 1 Long Horizontal
- **Tip:** Use the Spraycan tool to color blocks, and the Symmetry tool to create the rotation.

Recipe for this Quilt
- **Horizontal layout:** 4 x 4
- **Library blocks:** Blue Spruce, Spruce, Sixteen Patch
- **Borders:** 1 Blocks border with 4 blocks per side
- **Tip:** Block width is half of the block height.

Recipe for this Quilt
- **Horizontal layout:** 1 x 1
- **Library blocks:** Star of Bethlehem, Connecticut Star, Prairie Star 2, Blazing Star 2
- **Borders:** 1 Spaced Squares

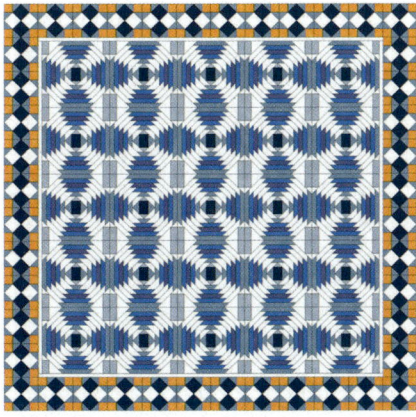

Recipe for this Quilt
- **Horizontal layout:** 5 x 5
- **Library blocks:** Pineapple with Rectangles, Four Patch Art Square
- **Borders:** 1 Long Horizontal, 1 Blocks border
- **Tip:** Use CTRL+click to set the blocks in the quilt and border. (Command+click on a Mac.)

Recipe for this Quilt
- **Horizontal layout:** 5 x 6 with sashing
- **Library blocks:** Valentine Heart
- **Borders:** 2 Long Vertical

INDEX

Symbols

01 Classic Pieced *21*
02 Contemporary Pieced *21*
08 Overlaid *49*
75 pixels per inch *56*
*.BMP *69*
*.GIF *69*
*.JPG *69*
*.PNG *69*
*.TIF *69*

A

Add to
   Project Sketchbook *16, 36, 61, 91*
   Sketchbook as Fabric *60, 64*
   Sketchbook as Photo *89, 91*
Adjusting borders *11*
Adjust the number of colorings per block *17*
Adjust tool *79, 80, 81, 83, 88, 91, 94*
Applique block *106, 110*
Applique motif *106, 110*
Applique pattern printing *51*
Applique tab *49, 106*
Applique text *88, 90*
Applique tools *44, 106*
Apply Crop *59, 64, 93*
Apply Effects *73*
Apply Fabric Scale *64*
Apply Fabric Straighten *58*
Arc in EasyDraw *42*
Arc in PolyDraw *103*
Asymmetrical blocks *23*

B

Bezier Curve sub-tool *107*
Big & Little Points Out border *87*
Block Library *20, 119*
Block tools *12*
Block width and height *110, 113*
Block Worktable *33, 54, 96, 100, 110*
BORDERS tab *11, 77*
Border styles *11, 77, 87*
Brush Stroke sub-tool *111*

C

Center Horizontally *91*
Center in Block *44, 113*
Center Vertically *91*
Circle sub-tool *111*
Clear all unused blocks *124*
Clone *100, 102, 105*
Color Balance *71*
Coloring arrows *17*
Command key (Mac) *77, 78, 83*
Contact EQ *31*
Convert to patch *111*
Copyright statement *31*
Create a new project tab *76*
Create Library *46, 67*
Create Quilt from Block *85*
Create Serendipity *116*
Creating a Custom Block Library *46*
Creating a Custom Fabric Library *67*
Creating Your Own Default Project *124*
Crop button *59, 64*
Crop tool *93*
CTRL+C *83*
CTRL+click *78*
CTRL key *77*
CTRL+V *83*
Curvy Leaf sub-tool *111*
Custom library *46, 48, 67*
Custom quilt *81, 82, 85*

D

Default border style *11*
Default project *12, 124*
Delete border *20*
Delete button when drawing *38, 99, 106, 107, 109*
Detach button *60*
Drag the node *98*
Draw arcs *42, 43, 103*
Drawing basic pieced blocks *33*
Draw tool for applique *106*

E

EasyDraw *33, 34*
EasyDraw + Applique *49*
EasyDraw rule *36*
Editing a quilt *24, 76*
Editing blocks *48*
Editing photos *70, 71, 92*
Edit notecard *17, 40, 45, 65*
Edit quilt name *24*
Edit tool *48, 98, 106*
Eight Point Star grid *100*
Embellished Alphabet *49*
Erase Block tool *83*
Erase quilt *94*
Esc key *97*
Exit *32*

Export to Facebook *30*
Eyedropper tool *22, 77*
Eye icon *49, 80*

F

Fabric images *69*
Fabric Library *69, 120*
Fabric pattern repeat *59*
Fabric preview window *14, 60*
Fabric scale *64*
Fabric scans *56*
Fabric straighten *58*
Fabric tools *12, 14*
Facebook sharing *30*
File formats *69*
Fit in Window button *56, 58, 63, 64*
Flip Block tool *79*
Flip notecard button *119*
Flip the arc *42*
Foundation patterns *26*
Freehand sub-tool *107*

G

Graph paper *34, 41, 48, 100*
Grid, Eight Point Star *100*
Grid lines for custom quilt *82*
Grid, PolyDraw *96, 100, 103*
Grid properties, PolyDraw *96, 100, 103*
Grid snap increments for custom quilt *82*
Grid tool for pieced blocks *41*

H

Handles, editing curves *111*
Help button *25*
Hide/show quilt patch lines *79*
Home button *31*
Home screen *10, 31, 33, 55*
Horizontal Layout *10*
Hue/Saturation/Lightness *72*

I

Image Info *56, 63*
Image Worktable *55, 74*
Import, Fabric Library *69*
Import Image tool *55, 62*
Importing a Fabric from the Internet *62*
Import Results *20*
Intersection point when drawing *103*

Index

K
Key block *29*
Kite shapes *121*

L
Layer 1 *78*
Layer 2 *79*
Layer 3 *80*
Layers, Quilt *76*
Layout Library *76*
Layouts by Size *76*
Layout styles *10*
Lessons on website *31*
Line sub-tool *106*
Line tool, EasyDraw *36, 39, 42*
Log Cabin-Like *21*

M
Map to fabrics *79*
Marquee box *63*
Memory quilts *94*
Merge Blocks with Serendipity *117*
Mirror patterns *26, 29*
Modify library style *46, 67, 68*
Motif *44, 110*
Motifs tab *78, 112*
Move the foundation sections *28*
Moving templates *27*
Multiple Borders *19*
My Favorite Blocks *20, 46*
My Favorite Fabrics *67, 68*

N
Naming a block *37*
Naming the project *16, 37, 57*
New Project *76, 85*
No blocks to display *46*
Node *35*
Node properties *107*
No rounding in rotary cutting *53*
Notecard *17, 40, 45, 57, 65, 119*

O
Open an existing project *19, 24*
Open Library *20, 77, 92, 116*
Outline drawing when printing *51*
Oval and polygon shapes *45*

P
Paintbrush tool *14, 22, 36, 78, 88*
Paper piecing patterns *26*
Partition and stagger *48*
PatchMaker shapes *44, 110*
Patch outlines *79*
Pattern repeat, fabric *59*
Patterns
    Antique Mosaics *21*
    Basket with Handles *125*
    Blazing Star 2 *125*
    Blue Spruce *125*
    Bulfinch *116*
    Compasses *48*
    Connecticut Star *125*
    Diamond in the Square *77*
    Drunkard's Path *42*
    Eight Point Star (PolyDraw) *49*
    EQ Default Ohio Star *52*
    Fan Rails *21*
    Flying Geese *117*
    Four Patch *65*
    Four Patch Art Square *125*
    Goose Frame 2 *125*
    Mariner's Star *48*
    Mosaic, No. 2(2) *13, 15, 26, 28*
    Nine Patch *41*
    Nine Patch Chain *85*
    Pineapple with Rectangles *125*
    Prairie Star 2 *125*
    Sixteen Patch *125*
    Spruce *125*
    Square in a Square *37*
    Star of Bethlehem *125*
    Strawberry Smoothie *116*
    Valentine Heart *125*
    Variable Star *13, 15, 28*
    Wobbly Frame *116*
Photo Layout *73, 89*
Photo Library *70*
Photo of fabric *63*
Pick tool *38, 99, 101, 106, 107, 108*
PolyArc tool *99, 103*
PolyDraw *33, 96, 100*
PolyDraw + Applique block *49*
PolyDraw grid *96, 100, 103*
PolyLine tool *96, 100*
PosieMaker *44, 110*
Post to my Facebook Page *30*
Precision Bar *34, 110, 113*
Pre-designed quilt labels *90*
Printable fabric *87*
Print block name *27*
Printing a block *50*
Printing a quilt *24*
Printing Foundation patterns *26, 27*
Printing photos *73*
Printing style for blocks *51*
Printing Templates *28*
Printing yardage estimates *25*
Print Quilt dialog *24*
Project Sketchbook *17*

Q
Quilt borders *11, 77, 87*
Quilting stencil *51*
Quilt label *87, 90*
Quilt layers *76*
Quilt layout styles *10, 76, 81, 85, 87*
Quilt Worktable *10, 81*

R
Randomize tool *79*
Read More button *107*
Rectangular grid *99*
Remove nodes *98*
Resize blocks *82, 94*
Resize in Photo Layout *89, 91*
Resize motif patch *44*
Resize photo *73*
Resize WreathMaker cluster *113*
Restore default settings *7, 33, 55*
Ring, PolyDraw grid *104*
Rings and Spokes *103*
Rotary Cutting *52, 121*
Rotate Fabric tool *58*
Rotate patches in drawing *100, 102, 105*
Rotating Templates *29*
Rounding in rotary cutting *52, 122*
Rulers *63*
Rules of EasyDraw *34*

S
Saturation *72*
Save As *16*
Save Library *47, 68, 69*
Save Palette as Default *124*
Scale fabric *56, 64*
Scanning fabric *56*
Screen resolution *56*
Search Block by Category *86, 119*
Search Fabric by Color *120*
Search Results *20, 119, 120*
Select All Fabrics button *70*
Serendipity *116*
Set Block *12*
Set Photo tool *92*
Set Text tool *88, 90*
Setting blocks in the quilt *13*
Shapes tool *44, 108, 109, 111*
Sharing to Facebook *30*
SHIFT key *88, 97*

Show grid on custom quilts *81*
Showing fabrics in printouts *52*
Size of the pattern *29*
Sketchbook
    Add as Fabric *60, 64*
    Add as Photo *89, 91*
    Add to Project *16, 36, 61, 91*
    View Project *17, 24, 32, 45, 57*
Snapping in custom quilts *81, 96*
Snap points *34, 35*
Snap to grid points *35*
Snap to lines and arcs of drawing *35*
Snap to nodes of drawing *35*
Spacebar *42*
Special Effects *72*
Speed keys *13*
Spine of drawing *111*
Spoke, PolyDraw grid *104*
Spraycan tool *14*
Spray Thread *80*
Starting a new quilt *10*
Start with a Quick Quilt project *90, 92*
Stencils tab *80*
Straighten *58*
Swap Color tool *15, 78, 90*
Symmetry tool *22*

T

Templates *123*
Text Tools *88*
Thread properties *80*
Tiling large patterns *27*
Tilt Block with Serendipity *116*
Tip of the Day *31*
Title bar *37*
T-Shirt quilt *92*

U

Undo button *36, 50*
Untitled project *16, 37*

V

Videos on website *31*
View Actual Size button *56*
View Project Sketchbook *17, 24, 32, 45, 57*

W

WreathMaker tool *112*

Z

Zip files *69*
Zoom in print preview *25, 53*